C000137068

Point and Figure Charting:

The Complete Guide

by
Dr. Carroll Aby, Jr.

TRADERS PRESS, INC.®
I N C O R P O R A T E D
PO BOX 6206
GREENVILLE, SC 29606

*Books and Gifts
for Investors and Traders*

©Copyright 1996 by Dr. Carroll Aby, Jr.

All rights reserved. No part of this work may be reproduced or transmitted in any form or by any means, electronic or mechanical, including photocopying and recording, or by any information storage or retrieval system without the prior written permission of the copyright owner unless such copying is expressly permitted by federal copyright law.

ISBN 0-934380-30-9

Published by **TRADERS PRESS, INC.**

The material contained herein is not to be taken as advice to buy or to sell specific securities. The information presented is based on sources we believe to be reliable and has been carefully checked for completeness and accuracy but cannot be guaranteed.

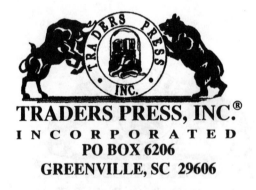

TRADERS PRESS, INC.®
I N C O R P O R A T E D
PO BOX 6206
GREENVILLE, SC 29606

Books and Gifts
for Investors and Traders

800-927-8222
Fax 864-298-0221
Tradersprs@aol.com

Biographical Sketch
for
Dr. Carroll D. Aby, Jr.

Dr. Carroll D. Aby, Jr. is Professor of Finance at Northwestern State University in Natchitoches, Louisiana. He has previously served as a professor at the University of Southern Mississippi, Mississippi State University, The University of Tennessee, and in the North Carolina system at Western Carolina University. Previous positions include the N.B. Morrison Professor of Applied Management at Northwestern, Professor of Finance and Head, Department of Economics and Finance at Western Carolina, Hardy M. Graham Distinguished Professor of Finance and School of Business Research Professor at the University of Tennessee at Martin, and J.D. Sims Professor and Dean of the School of Business at William Carey College.

Dr. Aby has authored numerous books and articles in the areas of Investments, Security Analysis and Portfolio Management, Personal Financial Management, Personal Financial Planning, and related areas. As a former financial consultant and investment broker, Dr. Aby's experience also embraces such firms as Merrill Lynch, PaineWebber and A.G. Edwards and Sons, Inc. He received professional investment training in New York and St. Louis.

Dr. Aby brings approximately 20 years of academic background and classroom teaching experience to his classroom and research and writing activities. His consulting practices involve investments, financial planning, business valuations, and financial and economic valuations involving wrongful death and personal injury.

Dr. Aby holds the B.S. degree in Business and Finance from Louisiana State University, the M.S. degree in Finance from the University of Southern Mississippi and the Ph.D. degree in Finance and Investments from Louisiana State University. In addition to other scholarly contributions, Dr. Aby has previously served as a financial and investments columnist. One column was carried in the *Coast Business Journal*, while another column circulated in a series of papers across Central and North Louisiana. He has made numerous professional presentations at the national and regional levels.

Dr. Carroll Aby, Jr.

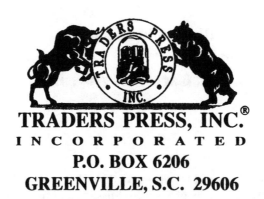

TRADERS PRESS, INC.®
INCORPORATED
P.O. BOX 6206
GREENVILLE, S.C. 29606

Books and Gifts
for Investors and Traders

Publishers of:

Commodity Spreads: A Historical Chart Perspective (Dobson)
The Trading Rule That Can Make You Rich* (Dobson)
Viewpoints of a Commodity Trader (Longstreet)
Commodities: A Chart Anthology (Dobson)
Profitable Grain Trading (Ainsworth)
A Complete Guide to Trading Profits (Paris)
Traders Guide to Technical Analysis (Hardy)
The Professional Commodity Trader (Kroll)
Jesse Livermore: Speculator-King (Sarnoff)
Understanding Fibonacci Numbers (Dobson)
Wall Street Ventures & Adventures through Forty Years (Wyckoff)
Winning Market Systems (Appel)
How to Trade in Stocks (Livermore)
Stock Market Trading Systems (Appel & Hitschler)
Study Helps in Point and Figure Technique (Wheelan)
Commodity Spreads: Analysis, Selection and Trading Techniques (Smith)
Comparison of Twelve Technical Trading Systems (Lukac, Brorsen, & Irwin)
Day Trading with Short Term Price Patterns and Opening Range Breakout (Crabel)
Understanding Bollinger Bands (Dobson)
Chart Reading for Professional Traders (Jenkins)
Geometry of Stock Market Profits (Jenkins)

Please write or call for our current catalog describing these and many other books and gifts of interest to investors and traders.

1-800-927-8222   FAX 864-298-0221
Tradersprs@aol.com

INTRODUCTION TO SECOND EDITION
of
The Complete Guide to Point & Figure Charting
by Carroll Aby

For some traders, like myself, Point and Figure charting used to be a guilty secret. It was such an old, and apparently outdated method, that few traders admitted to using it. Thankfully Point and Figure charting has undergone a renaissance in the past few years.

As one of the oldest methods of market technical analysis it was largely abandoned when computers made it easier to graphically display complex indicators. For many years the search for ever more complex indicators seemed to offer an answer to the elusive questions of market timing and prediction. Point and Figure was pushed behind the door.

Point and Figure survived this time in isolated pockets - notably on the trading floor. Floor traders continued to chart price action on the back of their trading cards using Point and Figure. A few older technicians clung stubbornly to the system.

The rise of technical analysis software designed for the wider trading public using desktop PCs often included Point and Figure as one of the charting options. Intrigued by this apparent technical analysis relic, a few of the new generation of traders made an effort to understand the method. They found it an extremely effective market tool.

The power of the PC allowed new Point and Figure combinations to be explored quickly and easily. These traders found Point and Figure gave an interesting context to the market. The philosophy of its construction isolated and emphasized the price action that propelled the market to new highs, or lows, and those points which stopped the market in its tracks. By revealing this context, Point and Figure tantalized the trader with a hint of more effective ways of combining the new computer driven analysis with this old tool.

Intrigued, traders tracked down the out-of-print and difficult to get Point and Figure classics. They rediscovered the lessons of a previous generation of traders and applied them to todays markets. Carroll Aby has taken this an important step further. The first edition of *The Complete Guide to Point & Figure Charting* built on classic Point and Figure approaches, modifying, developing and applying them to a variety of modern markets. Here was a book that stretched Point and Figure by making full use of the computational ability of the desktop PC. Traders using Point and Figure discovered a treasure trove of new ideas. The second edition builds on the strengths of the first, expanding the envelope by developing new applications of Point and Figure charting and new analysis of the dynamic patterns created by the disarmingly simple columns of X's and O's.

For some traders, like myself, Point and Figure charting is the first analytical tool used and the last. It provides the context for market analysis, highlighting developing opportunities. When the opportunity has been analyzed with the assistance of other indicators, Point and Figure is also the last analytical tool used before taking a position. It is the initiating and the confirming indicator for entering a position.

It is also offers particularly useful ways of delineating likely price targets. And as with any useful market tool, Point and Figure indicates the way to the exit. Carroll Aby explores and develops some very interesting Point and Figure refinements which enhance well timed exits.

The first edition of The *Complete Guide to Point & Figure Charting* offered a guided tour of modern possibilities. This edition explores more fully some of the nooks and crannies glimpsed in the first tour and also takes the trader into new territory. It adds further fine tuning to the way I use Point and Figure. What you bring back to your trading screen from this tour is your choice - but what a range to select from.

Daryl Guppy
--professional private trader

To The Memory of Carroll D. Aby, Sr.
My Best Friend and Role Model For Life

&

To Esther Lea Aby
Who Believed In And Fought For Me During
The Tough Times

They Taught Me That There Is No Greater
Love Than That of Christian Parents

ACKNOWLEDGEMENTS

As in any large undertaking, many people deserve special thanks for their contributions. The preparation of this manuscript was made possible by the tireless efforts of a dedicated group, many of whom extended themselves beyond the call of duty in their commitments.

I am particularly indebted to Kerri Veuleman, Angela Williams, Annie James, and Karen Benefield, my outstanding research assistants who placed the manuscript in final form. Their willingness to expend extra effort was both refreshing and appreciated. Special gratitude and a heartfelt thanks go to my good friend Hurshell Knox, a computer guru who developed some of the original graphs in earlier printings. Most of the individually prepared computer graphics and illustrations throughout the book can be attributed to Kerri and Angela, who made the completion of this book possible through their combined efforts. Others at the Northwestern State University were also most supportive of this project. Special thanks are extended to Dr. Barry Smiley, Dr. Claude Simpson, Dr. Edward Graham and President Robert Alost. Finally, Dr. John F. McCreary, Dean of the School of Business at Western Carolina University, deserves special kudos for his advice, computer assistance, and overall contributions.

I would be remiss without acknowledging A.W. Cohen and Earl Blumenthal for their overall contributions, both to this book and to the discipline of point and figure charting. Many of us have learned from these gentlemen over the years and have reaped the benefits of their pioneering past. The point and figure approach is a much better tool from their advancement of the field.

From a professional and personal standpoint, I cannot imagine finer, more supportive people than the staff at Chartcraft/Investors Intelligence, Inc. My friendship with Michael Burke and John Gray spans many years. However, Mike and John literally facilitated the completion of this manuscript with their countless graphs, written contributions, encouragement, and advice. Mike certainly is entitled to his reputation as one of Wall Street's finest scholars and students of the market. Somehow, words of thanks seem inadequate.

Margaret Hudson, Allan Dobson and Theresa Pulyer of Traders Press performed yeomen duties in bringing this version of the manuscript to fruition. Their tireless efforts in editing and refining were invaluable. Finally, my close friend Ed Dobson, President of Traders Press, served as a catalyst in this production. His friendship and support have greatly enhanced my career and been a boost to me personally. Thanks for everything, Ed.

Last, and certainly not least, I have received unequivocal support from my family. Thanks to my beautiful wife, Carol Ann, whose behind-the-scenes commitment to my career and to our family stands alone as a testimony of unflagging devotion. Regretfully, I sometimes forget to recognize the important roles that my children, Trey and Jennifer Lea ("Jaybird"), have played in my life. Like Carol Ann, their love transcends the highest of peaks and deepest of valleys. When times are darkest, Jaybird is always the ray of hope that we all need so desperately. Her positive outlook, cheerfulness and radiant smile represent the solution to so many problems. Also, thanks to our "second daughter," Rhonda Bobo Aby, and to the growth stocks in our lives -- T.J. Aby and Justin Trevor ("Big Dude") Aby. God bless you all.

TRADERS PRESS, INC.®
I N C O R P O R A T E D
P.O. BOX 6206
GREENVILLE, S.C. 29606

BOOKS AND GIFTS FOR
TRADERS AND INVESTORS

TRADERS PRESS, INC. stocks hundreds of titles of interest to investors and traders in stocks, options, and futures. In addition, we carry a full line of gift items for investors. Please contact us, and we will gladly forward you our current *"TRADER'S CATALOG"* by return mail.

800-927-8222   Fax 864-298-0221
Tradersprs@aol.com

PREFACE

As we enter the last decade of the 20th century, indecision and turbulence prevail in the financial markets. Investors seem preoccupied with escalating political and economic instabilities. Meanwhile, attempts to identify major price swings in the stock market dominate investment strategies. Perhaps more than ever before, people seem unable or unwilling to venture into investment decisions. Growing numbers of individuals depend on others for acceptable investment returns. To accommodate increasing expectations for better investment performance, timing strategies in the equity markets must play a larger role.

This material represents a compendium of technical investment analysis for entrepreneurial investors. The book includes a unique blend of pragmatic investment management concepts and real-world applications. The approaches developed herein appeal to individual investors because the manuscript offers readability and conceptual understanding. Academic jargon and mathematical emphasis are excluded for the sake of pragmatism. Broad-based treatment of investment management principles in diverse settings functions as a surrogate to mathematical and theoretical "overkill."

Although sequential reading represents the more conventional approach, the book's structure allows readers to single out specific areas of interest for immediate study. Despite the continuity and flow of the book, readers will find that individual sections can still offer their autonomy and ability to stand alone.

The book differs from competitors in several ways. The author draws upon many years of practical experience in asset evaluation, selection, and allocation techniques. The emphasis centers on taking complex subject matter and reducing it into a workable presentation for readers. Concepts that have heretofore been regarded as esoteric by some will be made quite lucid by supporting illustrations. Chart configurations, relative strength, and other frequently misunderstood techniques help identify supply and demand imbalances and pinpoint issues primed for price moves in either direction.

In summary, this book offers a total perspective on personal portfolio management. The author will continually espouse the view that undervalued and overvalued assets offer uncommon profit opportunities. Our coverage is in sharp contrast to the more arcane academic view relating to market efficiency. Academicians subscribe to the idea that all markets are efficient and that returns may be increased only by the assumption of additional risk. Their view states that all known information about securities is embodied in the current market price. Securities adjust instantaneously to new information disseminated about different firms. In other words, academicians propose that undervalued and overvalued assets do not exist. Therefore, it is virtually impossible to earn superior returns or outperform the market.

CHAPTER 1

UNDERSTANDING TECHNICAL ANALYSIS

INTRODUCTION

As we enter the 1990's and approach the 21st century, the stock market remains an enigma to most investors. They find that logical reactions to economic events and news developments are frequently unsuccessful. Rational courses of action encounter frustration and futility. Brokerage firm customers fail to understand why "buy" and "sell" recommendations are often poorly timed. The average investor picks up today's issue of *The Wall Street Journal* and notices that a firm's earnings are sharply higher. He (she) buys the stock only to be victimized by a price decline shortly after the transaction. And the beat goes on.

We can apparently conclude that decisions based on obvious judgments are obviously wrong. It may be argued that prognostication and forecasting are more of an art as opposed to a science. We cannot rebut this contention. However, developing such a talent depends strongly on how we analyze and react to different investment situations. This book introduces appropriate methods for making careful deliberations and logical, timely decisions. Hopefully, you can significantly improve profits while reducing poor decisions and investment losses with the insights provided herein.

Before examining more advanced analytical techniques, a framework for technical analysis should be developed. Technical analysis helps monitor investor sentiment and behavior. As a result, the flow of investment dollars into and out of the stock market may be gauged to evaluate market activities. The suspense of and damage from major turning points can be minimized by understanding technical analysis and its role as an integral part of investment strategy. Let's examine the theoretical underpinnings of technical analysis.[1]

CROWD PSYCHOLOGY

For most people, there is a tendency to be influenced by the opinions and judgments of others. Human nature dictates that we seek approval from our peers. Thus people develop similar thought and behavioral patterns. Whether or not individuals achieve success, their reasoning and actions are at least similar. Majority opinions therefore constitute the mainstream point of view. Unfortunately, the investment process does not accommodate the majority. Financial success appears to be reserved for the creative minority; in other words, those who dare to be different seem to receive the rewards.

Supporting viewpoints are well documented. Goethe once remarked, "I find more and more that it is well to be on the side of the minority, since it is always the more intelligent." Let's analyze Goethe's position as it relates to the stock market. In July 1982, the U.S. economy was in the midst of a deep recession with no relief in sight. The popular view suggested that the stock market offered little if any potential over the near-term. Wall Street oracles spoke of the gloom and doom ahead. However, the greatest bull market in our history originated in a sea of pessimism. More than five years later, in the fall of 1987, the uptrend was still intact. Investment sages began to predict levels of 3000, 3600, and even 4000 for the Dow Jones Industrial Average. The masses unanimously agreed that the market was headed higher and continued to offer attractive rewards. Stocks responded with unprecedented declines more severe than those of 1929. Price slides of bear market proportions occurred during strong economic conditions and a wave of investor optimism. Common stock prices moved in exactly the opposite direction anticipated by public opinion.

The anecdotal moral of these unexpected market reversals becomes clear. Investors must learn to form their own judgments and think for themselves. In turn, the market has two obviously well-defined extremes -- greed and fear. When the vast majority of investors are overly optimistic, they invest heavily and exhibit greedy tendencies. Conversely, when investors are confronted by deep-seated fears, they become panicky and sell stocks on a broad scale. Excessive optimism (greed) is synonymous with market tops, while too much pessimism (fear) warns of an approaching market bottom. Such states of extreme emotion must be recognized by informed investors as opportunities for profits. However, individual investors need some timing-oriented tools for detecting the presence of extreme investor sentiment in either direction. Clearly, informed investors must go contrary to the thinking of the stock market majority.[2] The foundation for these timing devices rests in the discipline of technical analysis.

Although the 1987 market slide seemed shocking to investment neophytes, the realities are that little has changed in the stock market. On September 3, 1946, a drastic market decline was initiated. The Securities and Exchange Commission concurrently polled registered investment advisors and knowledgeable brokers throughout the United States. Only 4.1 percent of the financial gurus were correctly bearish. In other words, 95.9 percent of the experts failed to recognize an impending market top. Wall Street's finest were incorrectly bullish. They were wrong when it paid to be right -- at the key junctures or turning points in the market.[3]

Opinions of experts assume added significance because they influence the thoughts and actions of many investors. Therefore, individual judgments may be impaired or dissuaded by the opinions of "uninformed experts." Caution must be exercised when unanimity of thought occurs, even if "recognized authorities" are involved.[4] Peter Wyckoff argues that ". . . if everyone were truly intelligent, no one would sell too cheaply or pay too much, and the result would be that wide price swings would not occur."[5]

Investors must clearly avoid subscribing to consensus viewpoints and majority opinions for stock market profits.[6] Investment returns depend on one's ability to make independent decisions while escaping the influence of ill-timed investment advice, public opinions, and generally accepted theories. In effect, investors need to be "contrarians." They should contest the popular view and make investment decisions on the basis of realities rather than emotions.[7] To reiterate, proper investment action requires a timing orientation, which in turn depends on identifying and understanding market cycles. Correctly timed investment decisions must correspond favorably to strategic points in market cycles.

MARKET CYCLES

Since its inception, the stock market has been characterized by recurring cycles. Economic events, earnings reports, political developments, recessions, depressions, prosperity, inflation, stagflation, changes in corporate management or policy, war, and peace may all be tied to the elucidation of cycles. However, a cycle will continue undaunted until it has run its course. Obvious or surface explanations fail to suffice and do not, in any way, disrupt the continuation of the cycle.[8]

In Wall Street parlance, most market cycles consist of a bottoming phase or period of accumulation where informed investors began to buy stocks. The next stage manifests a bull market advance. This is followed by a topping out process or period of distribution where knowledgeable participants begin to liquidate long positions and consider puts and/or short selling. The cycle finishes in a bear market with accelerating downside price action.

Economists refer to the stock market as a **barometer** because its movements typically precede changes in the economy by several months. Stock prices usually anticipate changes in earnings and economic developments and move in advance of fundamental information. Let's assume that we begin a cycle with the economy in the throes of a recession. Few investors understand that a recession offers optimum investment opportunities. During depressed economic environments, interest rates decline. Informed investors become dissatisfied with returns from fixed-income investments and look toward stocks as an alternative. Low interest rates serve as an incentive to speculate in margin accounts. Meanwhile, the average investor's outlook diminishes due to declining earnings reports and worsening economic news. However, one must remember that bull markets originate from the depths of pessimism, despair, and disbelief.

It is at this point that technical analysis and its emphasis on individual thought must continually be utilized. Charts and other technical tools implicitly remind us that the stock market buys expected future earnings. For example, investors bought Chrysler at $3 when all pronouncements concerning the company were bleak at best. However, informed buyers did not purchase Chrysler because of its existing dilemma but rather their belief that the firm's profit picture would be restored in the future. Recessions remind us to buy expected future earnings.

During the midst of a recession, stocks display their first strong, sustainable upmove. After the market has undergone a sizable advance, economic fundamentals begin to improve. Corporate earnings rise and company projections have an optimistic tone. Investors become confident and believe the stock market should undergo further advances to reflect a more positive economic state. Near market tops, investors reach a state of euphoria. They fail to understand why firms' post record earnings figures are often followed by declining stock prices. Investment and economic fundamentals alone will not enable investors to maximize returns. Research departments from investment firms often provide buy recommendations on companies with big earnings announcements. Brokers recommend these companies to clients because the fundamentals ensure "an easy sale." Since the market moves in advance of the economy, earnings per share figures increase as the stock prices begin to decline. The stock market later enters a bottoming phase while economic conditions deteriorate. The cycle stands ready to be repeated and begins another succession of similar events, news items, and investor activities that will last for another four to four-and-one half years.

History Repeats Itself

Technical analysis continues to be a successful investment strategy because of its emphasis on charts, supply and demand, and individual, contrary thinking. These points are reinforced throughout the book. Technicians further subscribe to the view that investors will continue to make the same mistakes in the future that they have made in the past. They believe that an uninformed majority will repeatedly fail in their efforts to recognize key junctures or critical turning points in the market. Remember, unexpected stock price turns stem from extremes in

Figure 1-1

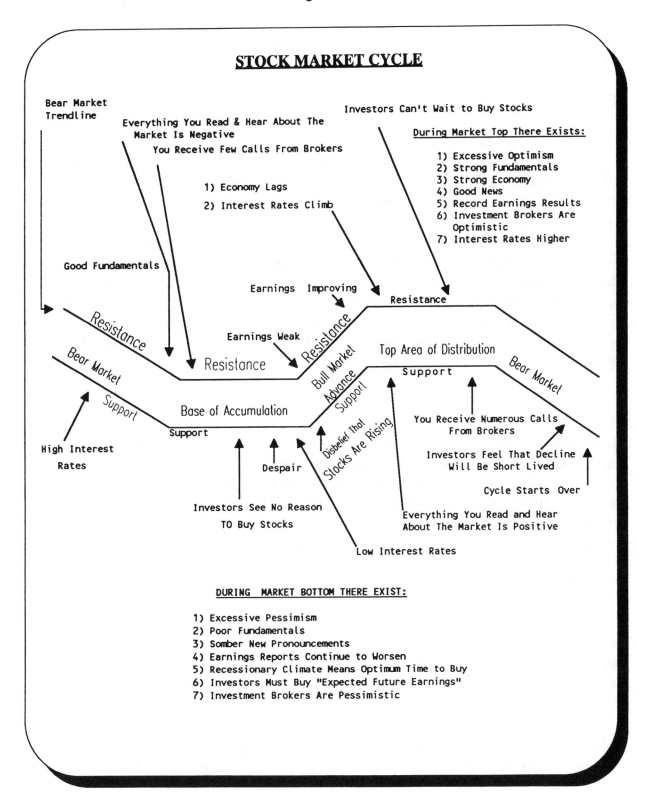

STOCK MARKET CYCLE

Bear Market Trendline

Everything You Read & Hear About The Market Is Negative

You Receive Few Calls From Brokers

1) Economy Lags
2) Interest Rates Climb

Investors Can't Wait to Buy Stocks

During Market Top There Exists:

1) Excessive Optimism
2) Strong Fundamentals
3) Strong Economy
4) Good News
5) Record Earnings Results
6) Investment Brokers Are Optimistic
7) Interest Rates Higher

Good Fundamentals

Earnings Improving

Resistance

Earnings Weak

Resistance

Resistance

Bear Market

Bull Market Advance

Top Area of Distribution

Resistance

Support

Support

Support

Base of Accumulation

Bear Market

High Interest Rates

Support

Disbelief That Stocks Are Rising

You Receive Numerous Calls From Brokers

Despair

Investors Feel That Decline Will Be Short Lived

Investors See No Reason TO Buy Stocks

Everything You Read and Hear About The Market Is Positive

Cycle Starts Over

Low Interest Rates

DURING MARKET BOTTOM THERE EXIST:

1) Excessive Pessimism
2) Poor Fundamentals
3) Somber New Pronouncements
4) Earnings Reports Continue to Worsen
5) Recessionary Climate Means Optimum Time to Buy
6) Investors Must Buy "Expected Future Earnings"
7) Investment Brokers Are Pessimistic

13

investor behavior, a progressive state which most individuals can never anticipate despite their roles in the sequence of events. Those who fail to remember their past mistakes are destined to err again. Patrick Henry once remarked, "I have but one lamp by which my feet are guided, and that is the lamp of experience. I know of no way of judging the future but by the past. "[9]

The Importance of Market Timing

If we are to buy low and sell high, recognition of market bottoms and tops becomes essential. Ideally, the most attractive stocks to own are those which are rising in a bull market within an advancing industry group. If the individual stock, the aggregate market, and the industry group of which the stock is a member are all moving upward, chances for positive investment performance are good. Conversely, one should liquidate and/or sell short a declining stock in a deteriorating industry group during a bear market decline. In other words, investors need to be as concerned about the timing and direction of the stock market (and industry group) as they are individual stocks. It accomplishes nothing for an investor to be right about a particular stock but wrong in his (her) forecast of the general market trend. Strong market moves mean most stocks are moving in the same direction. Therefore, chances for making money in individual issues improve considerably. A cardinal rule remains that you should never go against the trend of the aggregate market.

SUMMARY

The foundation for technical analysis rests closely with charts, individual judgments, questioning viewpoints, challenging decisions, crowd psychology, and stock market cycles. The decade of the 1990's and beyond will continue to be greeted by turbulent markets and wide price swings. In the early 1960's, four or five million shares represented an active trading session. In the 1980's, daily trading volume soared to 200 and 300 million shares. The return to the market of affluent individual investors, expanding institutional participation, and increasing numbers of foreign investors should contribute to larger price gyrations and more pronounced trends in either direction. More than at any time in our history, investors need to develop a system for making investment decisions.

We are now ready to develop a pragmatic approach to technical analysis of price trends. In contrast to esoteric valuation methods espoused by some advisors and authors, you will find that this approach makes for easy reading.

P & F charts represent a clear-cut, objective system for evaluating both the market and individual stocks. The subjectivity inherent in other techniques, such as vertical bar charts, disappears. Price movements above a previous top(s) furnish a buy signal, while falling prices

14

that penetrate an earlier bottom(s) designate a sell signal. Buy and sell signals, low poles, high poles, and triple tops and bottoms either appear on the charts, or they do not. Little is left to the imagination, so problems of interpretation are minimized.

Furthermore, supply, demand, money flows, and investor activities depicted by technical analysis underlie market strengths and weaknesses. Of interest is the ease of detecting points where buy and sell strategies should be implemented. By providing coverage of proven technical approaches, the efficacy of investment strategies should be quickly upgraded while improving your overall market acumen. All charts and technical indicator information are supplied by Chartcraft, Inc. of New Rochelle, NY. And away we go!

ENDNOTES

[1]For an excellent treatment of technical analysis, see Robert D. Edwards and John Magee, Technical Analysis of Stock Trends (Boston: John Magee, Inc., 1966).

[2]For more on the concept of contrary thinking, see Humphrey B. Neill, The Art of Contrary Thinking (Caldwell, Idaho: The Caxton Printers, Ltd., 1963).

[3]Cited by Garfield A. Drew, New Methods for Profit in the Stock Market (Wells, Vermont: Fraser Publishing Company, 1966), 179.

[4]Harry D. Schultz, Bear Markets: How To Survive and Make Money in Them (Englewood Cliffs, N.J.: Prentice-Hall, Inc., 1966), 173.

[5]Peter Wyckoff, The Psychology of Stock Market Timing (Englewood Cliffs, N.J.: Prentice Hall, Inc., 1966), 123.

[6]J.E. Granville, A Strategy of Daily Stock Market Timing for Maximum Profit (Englewood Cliffs, N.J.: Prentice-Hall, 1966), 162.

[7]H.B. Neill, Tape Reading and Market Tactics (Wells, Vermont: Fraser Publishing Company, 1960).

[8]For a treatment of this thesis, see Harry D. Schultz, Bear Markets: How To Survive and Make Money In Them (Englewood Cliffs, N.J.: Prentice-Hall, Inc., 1966).

[9]From Patrick Henry's speech given in the Virginia House of Delegates, March 23, 1775.

CHAPTER 2

AN INTRODUCTION TO POINT AND FIGURE CHARTING

Point and figure (P & F) charts are recognized as the oldest form of graphically following the market. In contrast to vertical bar graphs, P & F charts consist of alternating columns of X's and O's. However, point and figure charts similarly assist in the timing of investment decisions. They also lend the added dimension of accurately forecasting future prices. By enabling investors to project price movements, these graphs help determine "when to sell" as readily as they identify timely purchase opportunities. Most seasoned investment professionals argue that knowing when to sell is more important than learning when to buy.

THE UNDERLYING THEORY OF POINT AND FIGURE CHARTS

Point and figure charts have proven to be exceptional decision-making tools, particularly with their emphasis on timing. Alternating columns of X's and O's reflect the interplay of supply and demand.[1] As lateral or sideways price movements continue with additional columns of X's and O's, an overall state of equilibrium exists between supply and demand. Buy and sell signals from P & F chart patterns confirm the dissolution of equilibrium conditions and the initial phases of supply and demand imbalances. Bullish chart patterns evolve when demand for a security exceeds supply and a sustained upside price move occurs. On the other hand, bearish chart patterns stem from an excess of supply over demand, and a well-defined downmove results.

Point and figure charts thus provide a timing mechanism in the selection of individual stocks. Their emphasis on when to buy and sell makes these charts invaluable to technical analysts who manage portfolios. Investors who stress timing-oriented decisions are considered to be technicians. Conversely, those who seek to identify undervalued and overvalued securities in terms of earnings, dividends, sales, and growth rates are considered to be fundamentalists. They compare market prices to intrinsic values. Fundamentalists make decisions for expanded time horizons and are more concerned with long-term positive or negative recommendations as opposed to when decisions should be made. In effect, investment strategists may typically be classified according to either shorter-term orientations (technicians) or longer-term objectives (fundamentalists). However, contrary to the popular viewpoint, these two schools of thought are not mutually exclusive and in fact can be used to complement each other.

The Influence of Charles Dow

Around the year 1900, Charles Dow formulated some basic investment principles collectively known as the Dow Theory. The most recognized aspect of Dow's work is the concept of "confirmation." Dow argued that if the industrial average made either a new high or low for the current price move, the rails (now the transportations) must confirm this new directional signal with a corresponding new high or low. The confirmation served notice to market followers that a bull or bear market price trend existed.

However, another dimension to Dow's work leads to the basic principle of reading and evaluating charts. Dow reasoned that bullish trends displayed higher tops and higher bottoms. Similarly, bearish price moves were characterized by lower tops and lower bottoms. When charting emerged as a discipline, budding technical analysts used Dow's thoughts about the general market to analyze bullish and bearish chart patterns on individual stocks. Dow's premise of higher or lower tops and bottoms remains firmly entrenched as the underlying thesis of chart interpretation.

CONSTRUCTING POINT AND FIGURE CHARTS

Point and figure charts provide graphic evidence of the ongoing struggle between supply and demand with alternating columns of upside and downside price movements. Remember, columns of X's depict price advances, while columns of O's reflect price declines. The significance of portraying this contest between supply and demand lies in projecting the extent and direction of future price movements.

Point and figure charts are plotted on an arithmetic scale with each square below $5 having a value of $.25. Squares between $5 and $20 are valued at $.50 each, while squares between $20 and $100 represent $1. On higher-priced securities from $100 up, each square is valued at $2. The **Chartcraft approach**[2] using the three-square reversal method of point and figure charting is incorporated throughout the book. Three-square reversal charts furnish a better view for intermediate and long-term investment strategies. Further, the three-square reversal approach eliminates many false and misleading price movements. Conversely, traders tend to utilize one-square reversal charts, which are highly sensitive to short-term price changes and require more recordings. One-square P & F charts are harder to interpret and can lead to more meaningless price moves. However, one-square charts always have at least two recordings in each column.

Table 2-1

CONSTRUCTING A POINT AND FIGURE CHART

(1) DATE	(2) DAILY HIGH (DH)	(3) DAILY LOW (DL)	(4) PREVAILING TREND	(5) CHECK 1st READING	(6) CONTIN. JUSTIFIED ? ? ?	(7) CHECK 2nd READING ?	(8) REVERSAL OR DISCON. JUSTIFIED ?	(9) POSTED CHART RECORDING
4/15	34 1/4	33 1/8	UP	DH	Yes	DL - No	No	X (34)
4/16	35 3/4	34	UP	DH	Yes	DL - No	No	X (35)
4/17	36 7/8	35 1/4	UP	DH	Yes	DL - No	No	X (36)
4/18	37 3/8	36 1/2	UP	DH	Yes	DL - No	No	X (37)
4/19	37 1/2	34 7/8	UP	DH	No	DL - Yes	No	------
4/22	35 5/8	33 3/4	UP	DH	No	DL - Yes	Yes	O (36)
								O (35)
								O (34)
4/23	34 1/4	32 7/8	DOWN	DL	Yes	DH - No	No	O (33)
4/24	33	32	DOWN	DL	Yes	DH - No	No	O (32)
4/25	33	31 1/8	DOWN	DL	No	DH - Yes	No	------
4/26	34 1/8	32 7/8	DOWN	DL	No	DH - Yes	No	------
4/29	33 5/8	32	DOWN	DL	No	DH - Yes	No	------
4/30	34	32 3/8	DOWN	DL	No	DH - Yes	No	------
5/1	35 1/8	33 5/8	DOWN	DL	No	DH - Yes	Yes	X (33)
								X (34)
5/2	35 5/8	34	UP	DH	No	DL - Yes	No	X (35)
5/3	34 1/2	73	UP	DH	No	DL - Yes	No	------
5/6	34 1/8	33 3/4	UP	DH	No	DL - Yes	No	------
5/7	35	34 3/8	UP	DH	No	DL - Yes	No	------
5/8	35 1/8	34 5/8	UP	DH	No	DL - Yes	No	------
5/9	34 1/2	33	UP	DH	No	DL - Yes	No	------
5/10	35	33 1/2	UP	DH	No	DL - Yes	No	------
5/13	36 1/8	33 3/4	UP	DH	No	DL - No	No	X (36)
5/14	37 3/8	36	UP	DH	Yes	DL - No	No	X (37)
5/15	37 1/2	35	UP	DH	No	DL - Yes	No	------
5/16	37	35	UP	DH	No	DL - Yes	No	------
5/17	36 1/2	35 1/8	UP	DH	No	DL - Yes	No	------
5/20	37	35	UP	DH	No	DL - Yes	No	------
5/21	36 1/8	34	UP	DH	No	DL - Yes	Yes	O (36)
								O (35)
								O (34)
5/22	34 3/4	32 7/8	DOWN	DL	Yes	DH - No	No	O (33)
5/23	34	33 3/8	DOWN	DL	No	DH - Yes	No	------
5/24	35 1/8	33 7/8	DOWN	DL	No	DH - Yes	No	------
5/27	36	34 1/2	DOWN	DL	No	DH - Yes	Yes	X (34)
								X (35)
								X (36)
5/28	36 1/2	35 7/8	UP	DH	No	DL - No	No	------
5/29	36 3/4	36 1/8	UP	DH	No	DL - No	No	------
5/30	37 1/4	37	UP	DH	Yes	DL - No	No	X (37)
5/31	37 7/8	37 1/4	UP	DH	Yes	DL - No	No	------
6/1	38 3/8	37 1/2	UP	DH	Yes	DL - No	No	6 (38)
6/2	39 5/8	38	UP	DH	Yes	DL - No	No	X (39)

18

An Actual Example

Let's review Table 2-1 for an understanding of actual chart construction. Hypothetical dates and prices appear in columns (1), (2), and (3). Notice that point and figure charts utilize daily highs and lows and disregard closing prices. Daily highs and lows are also employed for OTC stocks, but only the bid price is considered. However, ignoring closing price information can prove to be a mistake. We will address this issue shortly. Column 4 indicates the prevailing price trend in the stock. If the chart currently is in a column of X's, an uptrend exists. Charts in a column of O's suggest a current downmove. A basic premise of point and figure charting is to assume a continuation of the existing price trend.[3] On the 4/18 market date in Table 2-1, we are in a column of X's with the price trending upward. Column 5 gives the price that chartists would read first when scanning daily prices. For example, we have a column of X's with a price of $36 recorded on 4/17. Chartists will check (or read) the daily high to see if another X can be recorded. Since the daily high (DH) on 4/18 reached $37\frac{3}{8}$, an additional X can be added to the column at 37. Column 6 indicates that the price continuation can be justified.

Column 6 also lets us know whether another recording can be made in the present column. If another recording results, one need not check for a second reading in Column 7. Note that on 4/18, Column 7 reads "DL-No", saying no need exists to check the daily low (DL) as the second reading.[4] The first reading or price checked (daily high or DH) justified a continuation of the existing column. Since the trend continues, no reversal column originates in the opposite direction.

To reiterate, plotting intraday high and low prices presupposes a continuation of the prevailing trend. If the trend does not continue, check for a discontinuation or price reversal. In a column of Xs, one should look at the intraday high to see if an X can be added. If not, look at the intraday low to determine whether a reversal should be recorded. Movements of one, two, or three squares -- whichever reversal rule is being followed -- may constitute a price swing in the opposite direction. In a column of O's, look to see if one or more O's can be added. If not, check the intraday high to evaluate whether sufficient price change merits a reversal in trend (i.e., one, two, three, five squares, etc.).

Column 8 designates whether a price reversal ensues. To illustrate, let's review prices for 4/19. A daily high of $37\frac{1}{2}$ does not justify another X at $38. Column 6 reveals that the uptrend does not move higher, so Column 7 reads "DL-Yes". Since the 1st reading does not yield another recording, we must examine the daily low price or second reading option. The price did not decline the necessary three squares to 34 on an intraday low basis, so a reversal column likewise did not result. Therefore, no recording transpires.

However, let's assume the stock closed at the daily low price of $34\frac{7}{8}$. For those who choose to ignore closing prices, a potential timing error may result. With the final price near a level which would yield a three-square downside reversal (@ 34), the stock suggests near-term price weakness which may extend into the next few sessions. Chartists who neglect the closing price still see the stock's price at 37. Continued selling pressure on the stock during the next few days will be observed late from failure to consider depressed closing prices from late-session selloffs. Subsequent transactions may therefore be undertaken too late and translate into diminished profits.

Column 9 helps keep track of recordings posted in either continuing or reversing price trends. Notice that an X is posted on 4/18 at the 37 level and continues the price move to the upside. However, on 4/19, we could not justify another X to continue the uptrend nor another O for a price reversal and another column of O's. However, on 4/22, our suspicions from examining the closing price on 4/19 were confirmed. The daily high (DH) only reached $35\frac{5}{8}$ and failed to continue the uptrend, but the daily low (DL) reached $33\frac{3}{4}$. Since the last recording was an X at 37, a daily low of 34 represents a three-square downside price reversal in a column of O's. Notice that column 9 has O's recorded in the 36, 35, and 34 price squares. Thus a new column is formed.

Time is recorded by many P & F chartists. A number 1 through 12 may be recorded in place of X's and O's to illustrate the first price recording in a particular month. For example, Figure 2-1 has a 5 recorded in a column of X's at 35 because it represents the first recording in the month of May. If the first recording in a given month is a three-square reversal, the numerical entry appears in the third square. Some technicians use the numbers 1 through 9 for January through September and the letters A, B, and C to represent October, November, and December. Double digit entries (i.e., 10, 11, and 12) to record beginning monthly prices in the last quarter of the year are therefore avoided.

An Illustration of P & F Charts

We are now ready to take the data from Table 2-1 and construct one-square and three-square reversal charts in Figures 2-1 and 2-2 respectively. The principal difference in the one-square chart stems from establishing another column any time the price of the stock changes by one square in the opposite direction. One-square reversal charts are more sensitive and occupy extra space because they require additional recordings. The three-square chart in Figure 2-2 is more compact. Another column is not formed unless a price reversal of at least three squares takes place. Only more meaningful price shifts appear on the chart.

Figure 2-1
A ONE-SQUARE REVERSAL P & F CHART

```
40
                        X
                        B(6)
           X      X X X
           XO     XOXOX
35         XO5 X XO OX
           XOXOXOX  OX
            0X0 O    O
            O
30
```

Figure 2-2
A THREE-SQUARE REVERSAL P & F CHART

```
40
                X
                B(6)
          X X X
          XOXOX
35        XO5OX
          4OXOX
           OXO
            O
30
```

SOME REMINDERS ABOUT PRICE SCALES

Charts with stocks priced under $5 and valued at 3 point per unit are known as $\frac{3}{4}$ point charts because three-square reversals (i.e., 3 x $\frac{1}{4}$ = $\frac{3}{4}$) equal three-fourths of a point. Similarly, stocks that sell at prices from $5 to $20 are called $1\frac{1}{2}$ point charts because three square reversals require a $1\frac{1}{2}$ point price move in the opposite direction. Three-point reversal charts apply to stocks priced from $20 to $100 because each unit of measurement amounts to $1. Charts need $3 or points for a reversal swing. Higher priced issues of $100 or more are valued at $2 per square. Thus issues with 3-digit prices are said to be on 6-point charts because three-square reversals demand 6 points. P & F charts give no consideration to fractions on stocks selling for $20 or more. For example, you are evaluating a chart in a column of X's with the most recent recording at 28. The daily high for the session is $29\frac{7}{8}$. You record an X at 29 because of the 3-point chart. Conversely, a downtrend stock carries to $36\frac{1}{8}$. The lowest O recorded is 37.

A situation requiring some clarification stems from a chart with recordings on two different scales such as above and below $20. If a stock appears in a column of X's at 22, it will need a three-square reversal move to $19\frac{1}{2}$ (i.e., 21, 20, $19\frac{1}{2}$) to justify another column of recordings (O's) in the opposite direction. Another example might involve a stock in a column of X's that move to 105, with the highest recording in the 104 square. A three-square reversal will carry to 99 (i.e., 102, 100, 99).

SUMMARY

Point & Figure charts represent the oldest form of graphically following the stock market. As with other areas of technical analysis, P & F charting has received much of its influence from the pioneering efforts of Charles Dow. Although recognized primarily for his work in the area of bull and bear market confirmation, Dow first emphasized the importance of trend characteristics. He argued that bull markets consisted of higher tops and higher bottoms, while bear markets were composed of lower tops and lower bottoms.

A three-square reversal method of P & F charting is utilized throughout the book. However, different reversal rules such as one-square and five-square can be utilized. Larger reversal rules such as the three-square are less sensitive than one-square charts, which are more appropriate for traders.

ENDNOTES

[1]A.W. Cohen, <u>How To Use the Three-Point Reversal Method of Point and Figure Stock Market Trading</u>, 9th ed. (New Rochelle, NY: Chartcraft, Inc., 1987).

[2]Michael L. Burke, <u>The All New Guide to the Three-Point Reversal Method of Point and Figure Construction and Formations</u> (New Rochelle, NY: Chartcraft, Inc., 1990).

[3]Earl Blumenthal, <u>Chart For Profit Point and Figure Trading</u> (Larchmont, NY: Investors Intelligence, 1975).

[4]Ibid.

SECTION 1

The first section of the book acquaints the reader with the traditional wisdom of point and figure charts. We will explore basic chart patterns, trendlines, and forecasting techniques to determine price targets. Material in the introductory section is generally recognized as a part of the conventional body of knowledge drawn upon my most chartists.

In later sections, however, we will introduce some new chart configurations and technical tools designed to improve the entire discipline of point and figure charting. The new approaches seek to correct existing criticisms that false breakouts and late buy and sell signals impede the use of P & F analysis.

CHAPTER 3

BASIC POINT AND FIGURE CHART PATTERNS

An inherent advantage of point and figure charts is its systematic approach to decision making. In reviewing traditional chart patterns, we explain how "buy" and "sell" signals develop. In later chapters, however, we describe patterns which improve buy and sell decisions. Criticism of P & F charting in its conventional form may be merited. However, some revision of traditional thinking plus some new configurations enhance P & F charting as an investment strategy. These new approaches can assist in selecting stocks, bonds, commodities, futures, and options.

ELEMENTARY CONFIGURATIONS

Figure 3-1 includes the **double top and double bottom continuation patterns**, which appear during the course of bull and bear markets respectively.[1] Throughout coverage of chart patterns, the reading sequence includes the bullish pattern first followed by its bearish counterpart. Double top illustrations (A&B) contain only three columns with the last upmove penetrating the previous top. The double bottom illustrations (C&D) also have three columns with downside penetrations occurring in column three at 28 and 25 respectively. Both double top and double bottom continuation patterns occur during well-defined bull and bear markets and signal that the trend will continue. "B" and "S" recordings disclose "buy" and "sell" points for illustration purposes.

Movement above a previous top suggests a "buy" signal at 76 and 44 (A&B) respectively. The logic of buy and sell signals is straightforward. Technicians view the highest X in either a single or series of rising columns as a potential trouble spot for future price advances and term it a **resistance level**. Any move which exceeds a top or series of tops can be called an **upside breakout (buy signal)** because it penetrates previous resistance areas where selling is anticipated. Conversely, chartists perceive the lowest O in a down column or series of declining columns as **a support level**. Moves which penetrate a bottom or series of bottoms can be called a **downside breakout (sell signal)** because they violate previous support areas where buying should logically take place.

Figure 3-2 discloses the **double top and double bottom reversal patterns**, respectively. Double top reversal patterns (A,B,&C) consist of four columns with a buy signal received as the price advances exceed the previous tops at 25, 49, and 60, respectively. A buy signal marks a juncture or major turning point in the trend of the stock. The first column reveals a marked decline in price and may be identified by an extended column of O's. Downtrends are later reversed by the buy signal in the fourth column. The double top typically occurs among volatile stocks with high beta factors.

FIGURE 3-1
DOUBLE TOP AND DOUBLE BOTTOM CONTINUATION PATTERNS

Double Top Continuation Patterns

(A)

			B
75	X	O	X
	X	O	X
	X	O	X
	X	O	X
	X	O	X
70	X	O	X
		O	

(B)

			B
45			
	X		X
	X	O	X
	X	O	X
	X	O	X
40		O	X
		O	

Double Bottom Continuation Patterns

(C)

		X	
	O	X	O
	O	X	O
	O	X	O
30	O	X	O
	O		O
			S

(D)

		X	
		X	O
30		X	O
	O	X	O
	O	X	O
	O	X	O
	O		O
25			S

FIGURE 3-2

DOUBLE TOP AND DOUBLE BOTTOM REVERSAL PATTERNS

The Double Top Reversal Pattern

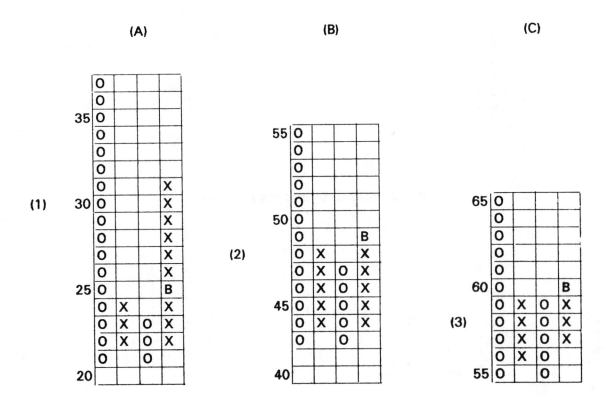

FIGURE 3-2

DOUBLE TOP AND DOUBLE BOTTOM REVERSAL PATTERNS
Continued

The Double Bottom Reversal Pattern

(D) (E) (F)

(1)

60				
	X		X	
	X	O	X	O
	X	O	X	O
	X	O		O
55	X			S
	X			O
	X			O
	X			O
	X			O
50	X			
	X			
	X			
	X			
	X			
45	X			
	X			
	X			
	X			
	X			
	X			

(2)

45				
	X		X	
	X	O	X	O
	X	O	X	O
	X	O	X	O
40	X	O	X	O
	X	O		O
	X			S
	X			
	X			
35	X			
	X			
	X			
30				

(3)

	X		X	
	X	O	X	O
	X	O	X	O
	X	O		O
30	X			S
	X			
	X			
	X			
	X			
25	X			

Less volatile stocks tend to need extra time to bottom and usually build wider base patterns before price reversals.

The double bottom reversal patterns (D, E, & F) include four columns with sell signals occurring in the fourth column as previous bottoms are penetrated at 55, 38, and 30. As with its bullish counterpart, the double bottom reversal pattern marks a change in the stock's trend; in this case, a shift from bullish to bearish develops. In the first column, an extended column of X's unveils a sharp price run-up. A swift downside price reversal in the fourth column exceeds the previous bottom. Volatile stocks also display double bottom formations.

Figure 3-3 illustrates the **bullish signal formation** (A, B, C, & D) and the **bearish signal formation** (E, F, & G). As in the case with double tops and bottoms, bullish and bearish signal formations consume four chart columns. The chief distinction lies in the bottom area of the pattern. Bullish signal patterns exhibit higher or rising bottoms combined with a buy signal in column four. The bullish signal formation displays both ascending tops and bottoms and reverses the downtrend with an upside breakout.

Similarly, the bearish signal formation has descending tops combined with lower bottoms furnishing a sell signal in column four. The previous uptrend is reversed by the sell signal. Bullish signal patterns display higher tops and bottoms. Lower tops and bottoms fit the classic Dow definition of bearish price trends. The principal difference in the illustrations from Figure 3-3 lies in the degree of ascent in the rising bottoms (bullish signal formation) or degree of descent in the declining tops (bearish signal formation). In many cases, steeper levels of ascent or descent may warn that more volatile price moves will emerge from the pattern.

THE ALL-IMPORTANT TRIPLE TOP

Figure 3-4 illustrates the **triple top reversal formation** which consists of six alternating columns and indicates a distinct change in trend from bearish to bullish. In other words, triple top reversals identify a key juncture in the stock. Illustrations A, B, C, and D provide variations of the triple top reversal. Notice in A that the bottoms are "level"; in other words, each occurs at $25. A buy signal surfaces when the price advance in the last column moves above the tops (@ 29) in the two previous columns of X's to 30. In B, the bottoms are level with rising tops at 63 and 64. A buy signal appears at 65 when the final column of X's penetrates both previous tops.

In C, level bottoms are accompanied by tops at different levels (25 and 23) with a buy signal at 26 where both previous tops are exceeded. Part D differs in that descending or lower bottoms develop within the lateral price movement. The descending bottom is followed by an immediate price advance and buy signal at 48. According to Blumenthal, triple tops with

Figure 3-3

BULLISH AND BEARISH SIGNAL FORMATIONS

The Bullish Signal Formation

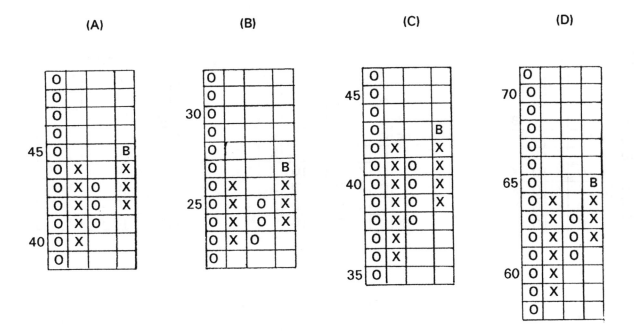

The Bearish Signal Formation

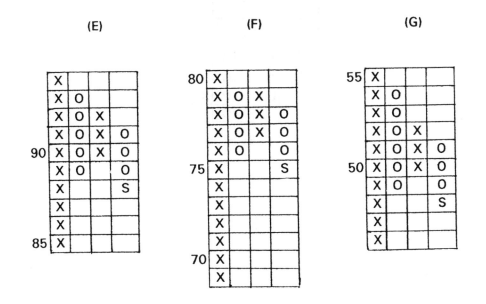

Figure 3-4

TRIPLE TOP REVERSAL FORMATION

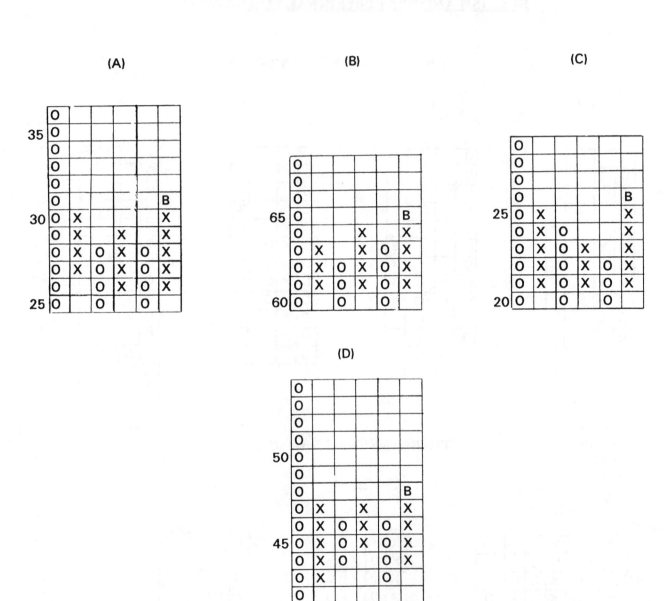

lower bottoms often are not as strong as similar formations with level or rising bottoms. Furthermore, triple tops and bottoms are usually completed within six to twelve weeks when they involve volatile stocks. The faster patterns are completed, typically the more explosive the move in either direction. Low-beta issues usually require more time to build a triple top reversal pattern and to complete price moves.[2]

Figure 3-5 illustrates the **triple top continuation formation** which contains five columns. The continuation triple top occurs within a sustained bullish trend and suggests that the upmove will carry to higher price levels. In contrast, the reversal triple top marks a turning point and occurs at the bottom of a downmove prior to a price advance. Buy signals in the triple top continuation materialize when the upmove in the third column of X's (i.e., the fifth column overall) exceeds the two previous tops by one square. Successive tops may be level, rising, or lower. However, a buy signal develops when both tops are breached. Although bottoms are usually level, a descending bottom may occur as shown in D. To reiterate, the principal significance lies in the reduced potential of triple top patterns with descending bottoms relative to those with level bottoms. The strongest price moves following upside breakouts come from triple top patterns with rising bottoms.

The **triple bottom continuation pattern** appears in Figure 3-6 and projects lower prices in the downtrend. As in its triple top counterpart, the triple bottom continuation contains five columns and represents a pause or brief interruption in the overall trend (downtrend in this case). Tops may be level as in A, B, and C, or ascending as in D. Rising tops in a triple bottom hint of a potentially less forceful price move after the breakout occurs. Conversely, triple bottom patterns with level tops typically have stronger moves with the most potent price action reserved for those patterns with declining tops.

Figure 3-7 illustrates the **triple bottom reversal formation** which includes six alternating columns. This reversal confirms the directional change in the stock from bullish to bearish. As in the corresponding triple top reversal configuration, the triple bottom reversal suggests a critical turning point in the stock. Different illustrations occur in A, B, C, and D of Figure 3-7. In A, there are three level tops at 45. Two bottoms follow at the $41 level with a sell signal appearing at 40 as the price moves below the two previous bottoms. In example B, level tops at 58 are accompanied by descending bottoms at 54 and 53 respectively. A sell signal comes into play at 52 with both previous bottoms exceeded.

In 3-7(C) tops are level at 76 with bottoms at different prices (71 and 72). A sell signal appears at 70 where both previous bottoms are penetrated. Example D differs because the tops are not level. Tops may rise to provide marginally higher peaks, but the ultimate confirmation stems from price moves below previous bottoms. High beta-factor stocks usually complete triple bottom patterns more quickly than do low-beta issues.

Figure 3-5

TRIPLE TOP CONTINUATION PATTERN

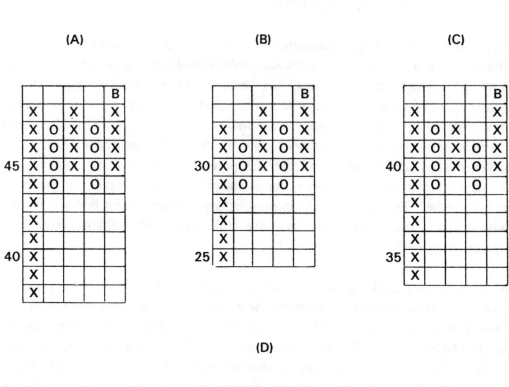

Figure 3-6

TRIPLE BOTTOM CONTINUATION PATTERN

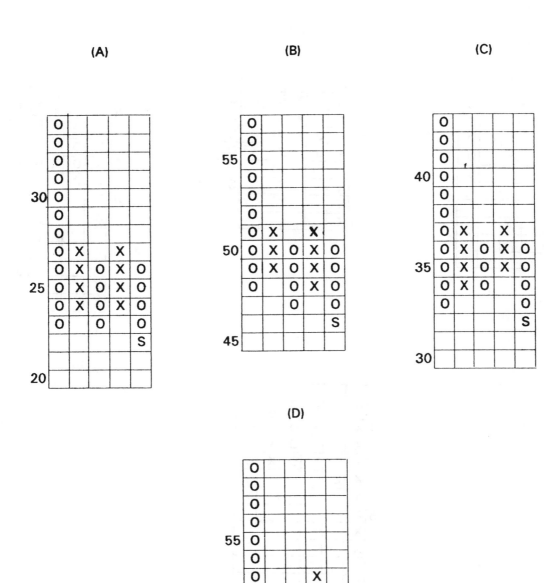

(A) (B) (C)

(D)

Figure 3-7

TRIPLE BOTTOM REVERSAL FORMATION

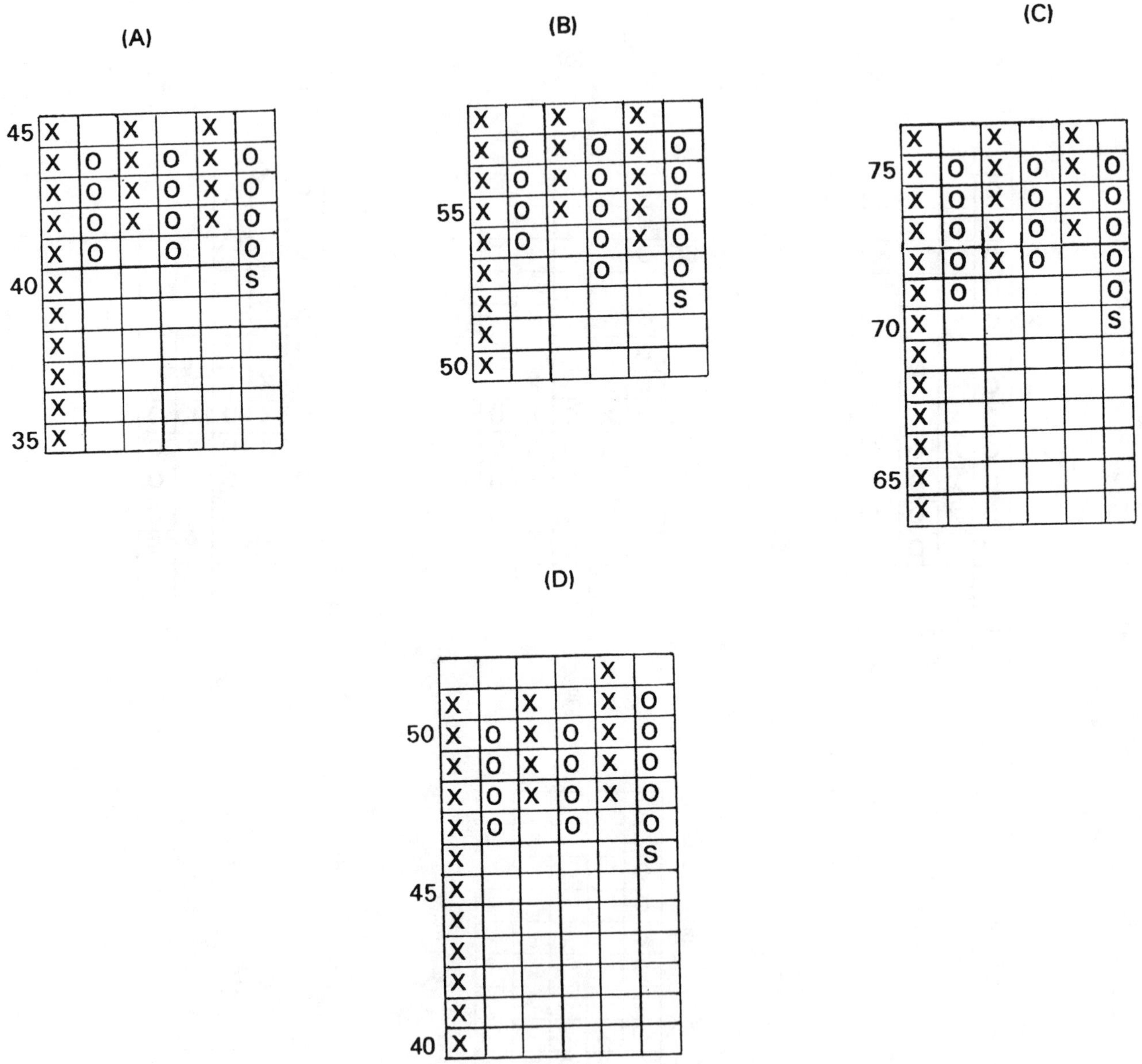

(A)

45	X		X		X	
	X	O	X	O	X	O
	X	O	X	O	X	O
	X	O	X	O	X	O
	X	O		O		O
40	X					S
	X					
	X					
	X					
	X					
35	X					

(B)

	X		X		X	
	X	O	X	O	X	O
	X	O	X	O	X	O
55	X	O	X	O	X	O
	X	O		O	X	O
	X			O		O
	X					S
	X					
50	X					

(C)

	X		X		X	
75	X	O	X	O	X	O
	X	O	X	O	X	O
	X	O	X	O	X	O
	X	O	X	O		O
	X	O				O
70	X					S
	X					
	X					
	X					
	X					
65	X					
	X					

(D)

					X	
	X		X		X	O
50	X	O	X	O	X	O
	X	O	X	O	X	O
	X	O	X	O	X	O
	X	O		O		O
	X					S
45	X					
	X					
	X					
	X					
	X					
40	X					

36

SUMMARY

Most P & F chart configurations are modifications of basic patterns such as double tops, triple tops, bullish and bearish signal formations, and continuation and reversal patterns. Support and resistance levels represent potential areas of buying and selling, respectively, and play a pivotal role in chart analysis. Buy and sell signals result from penetrations of previous tops and bottoms. Movements above or below previous tops and bottoms are also called breakouts because they eliminate past areas of resistance or support.

ENDNOTES

[1]Many of the basic point and figure chart patterns were developed by Chartcraft, Inc. of New Rochelle, NY. Two men who are largely responsible for enhancing the discipline of technical analysis are Michael L. Burke and the late A.W. Cohen. These men were also instrumental in bringing this book to fruition. For more reading on point and figure charting, see A.W. Cohen, How To Use The Three-Point Reversal Method of Point and Figure Stock Market Trading, 9th ed. (New Rochelle, NY: Chartcraft, Inc., 1987), 6 - 42. Also, see Michael L. Burke, The All New Guide to the Three-Point Reversal Method of Point & Figure Construction and Formations (New Rochelle, NY: Chartcraft, Inc., 1990).

[2]Another contributor to the discipline of point and figure charting was the late Earl Blumenthal, who made initial refinements to the work of A.W. Cohen. Michael Burke represents the latest and most innovative author in the field of point and figure charting. See Earl Blumenthal, Chart For Profit Point & Figure Trading (Larchmont, NY: 1975), 41-42.

CHAPTER 4

SOME MORE SOPHISTICATED PATTERNS

The chart patterns identified to this point cover many of the basic tenets of P & F charts. It is appropriate to introduce some slightly more sophisticated formations at this point. These advanced patterns represent variations of earlier treatments and are necessary to make the transition into later chapters. Improvements introduced in later chapters refute some of the traditional ideas of P & F analysis.

ADVANCED PATTERNS

The **bullish and bearish catapult formations** are illustrated in Figure 4-1. Figures A, B, and C display bullish patterns. A key to interpreting the bullish catapult pattern lies in identifying it as a modified triple top formation. The upside price breakout is followed by a pullback to old resistance levels before the primary advance. Once the pullback is completed, another upmove yields a second buy signal.

In A, the first buy signal from a triple top occurs at 44, followed by a pullback to 41 and a second upside breakout at 45. According to Cohen,[1] two conditions characterize the bullish and bearish catapult patterns. First, the column containing the original breakout (up or down) typically does not have more than seven recordings. In other words, a sizable price increase (decrease) does not evolve from the original breakout. Sustained price movements usually surface following a gradual breakout and partial pullback. Traders may purchase (or sell or sell short) the stock at cheaper (or higher) levels by waiting for the pullback. Secondly, the pullback column does not contain enough recordings to furnish a sell (buy) signal. Price pullbacks are not necessarily confined to slower-moving stocks. However, these price dips can be related more closely to historical tendencies to repeat patterns. In other words, many companies engage in pullbacks before launching major price moves. History also repeats itself with individual stocks.

A key concept emerges from the catapult formations. Upside and downside price breakouts from triple tops, bottoms, and base patterns are followed by a pullback about 50 percent of the time. Investors should evaluate individual companies on long-term charts to detect whether

Figure 4-1

BULLISH AND BEARISH CATAPULT FORMATIONS

The Bullish Catapult Formation

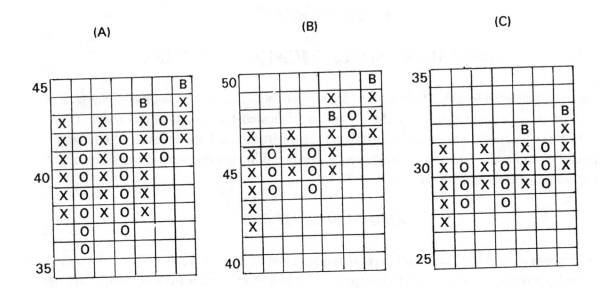

The Bearish Catapult Formation

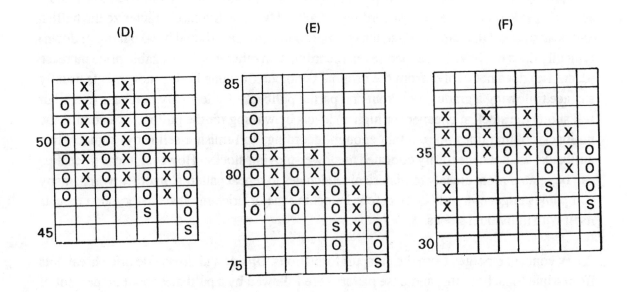

Figure 4-2

<u>BULLISH AND BEARISH SYMMETRICAL TRIANGLES</u>

The Bullish Symmetrical Triangle

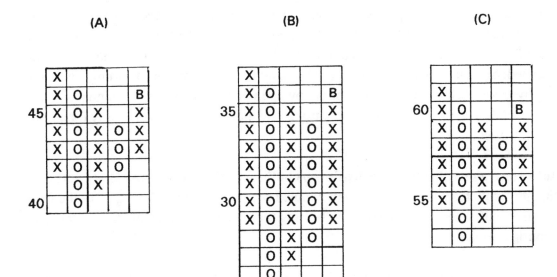

The Bearish Symmetrical Triangle

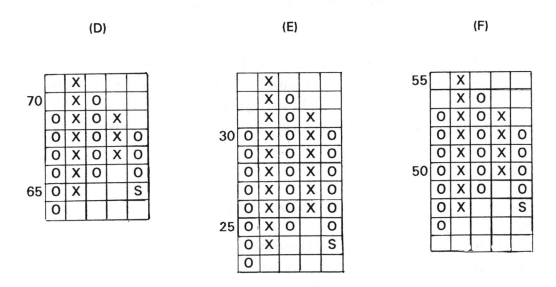

their stocks normally demonstrate pullbacks after major price breakouts. In D, E, and F, triple bottom sell signals are each followed by brief pullbacks prior to the price decline.

Bullish and bearish symmetrical triangles appear in Figure 4-2. Both patterns show a combination of lower tops and higher bottoms as the five-column formation moves toward a common point or apex. Technicians argue that these patterns build compression.
Pressure builds as the stock approaches a point where a definitive move takes place in one direction or the other. Bullish signals in A, B, and C occur when the most recent top is penetrated by one square. All tops do not have to be breached - only the previous top must be exceeded. Similarly, bearish patterns in D, E, and F form when the recordings of O's in column five move below the previous bottom by one square. Any buy or sell signal disrupts the pattern of descending tops and rising bottoms and indicates the stock is ready for a price move in the direction of the breakout.

Figure 4-3 provides a glimpse of the **triple top continuation pattern with higher bottoms.** Continuation patterns with higher bottoms coupled with an upside breakout give us the Dow definition of bullishness. Patterns with both rising tops and bottoms remain the most potent chart configurations.

Figure 4-4 reviews the **triple top reversal pattern with higher bottoms.** Reversal patterns simply indicate a key juncture in the stock's price, and a new trend emerges. The reversing price action contrasts with continuation patterns in Figure 4-3. Continuation patterns indicate a renewal of the previous trend after a pause or consolidation in price. A distinguishing feature concerns the rising bottoms in conjunction with higher tops and upside price breakouts.

Patterns that are diametrically opposed to Figure 4-3 and 4-4 appear in Figures 4-5 and 4-6 where **the triple bottom reversal patterns and the triple bottom continuation patterns with lower tops** are illustrated. In both cases, the two previous bottoms are penetrated by one square in conjunction with descending tops. Lower tops and bottoms emerge with the sell signal. Again, the most potent of all downside patterns result when lower tops are involved.

SOME FINAL MODIFICATIONS

Figure 4-7 contains illustrations of bullish and bearish **broadening formations.**[2] A, B, and C, include simple, five-column bullish patterns. By definition, bullish broadening formations contain five distinct points: (1) a top, (2) a bottom, (3) a higher top, (4) a lower bottom, and (5) another top which moves above both of the two earlier tops. The bearish formation similarly contains five key points -- (1) a bottom, (2) a top, (3) a lower bottom, (4) a higher

Figure 4-3

TRIPLE TOP CONTINUATION PATTERN WITH HIGHER BOTTOMS

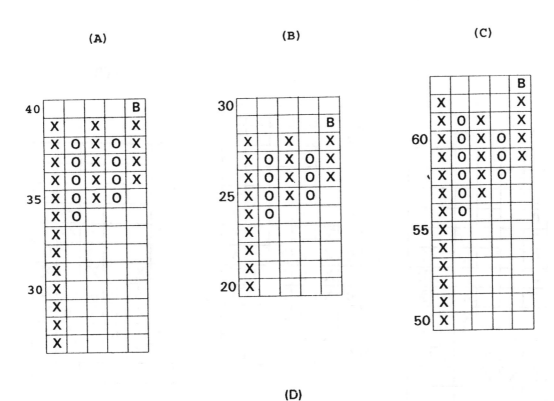

(A)   (B)   (C)

(D)

Figure 4-4

TRIPLE TOP REVERSAL PATTERN WITH HIGHER BOTTOMS

(A)   (B)   (C)

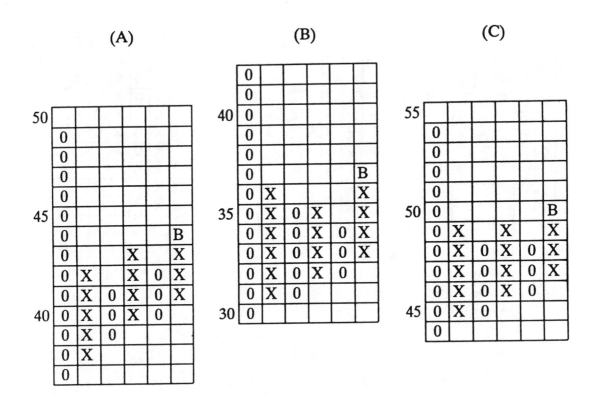

Figure 4-5

TRIPLE TOP REVERSAL PATTERN WITH LOWER BOTTOMS

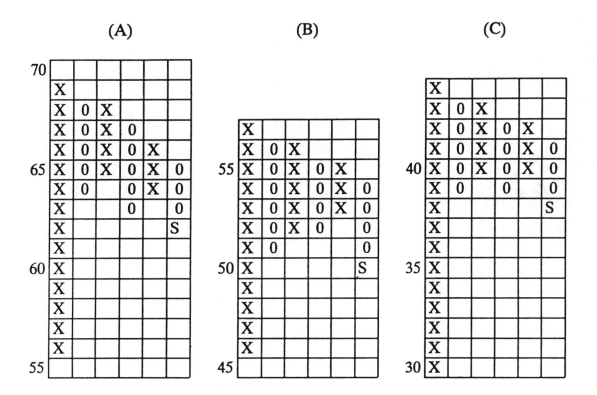

Figure 4-6

TRIPLE TOP CONTUATION PATTERN WITH LOWER TOPS

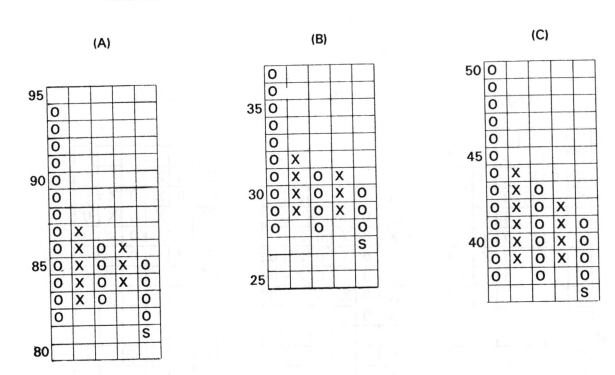

Figure 4-7

BROADENING FORMATIONS

(A)

(B)

(C)

The Bearish Patterns

(D)

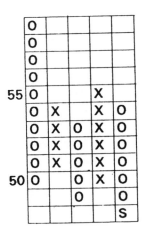

(E)

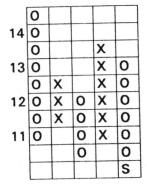

(F)

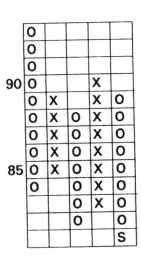

47

Figure 4-7 (continued)

BROADENING FORMATIONS

Stronger Bullish (G) Bearish (H) Formations

(G)

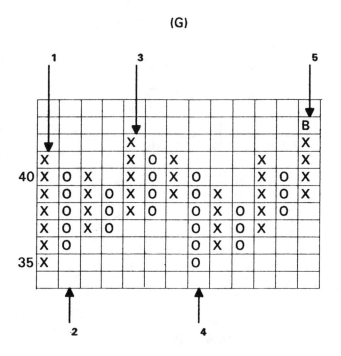

(H)

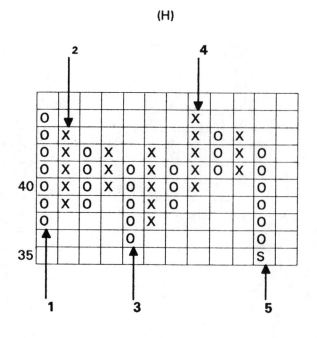

48

top, and (5) another bottom which moves below both the two previous bottoms. Illustrations of the bearish broadening patterns appear in D, E, and F.

Complex bullish and bearish broadening illustrations are more involved. Examples G & H denote each of the five key points cited above. The principal difference between more intricate formations in G and H and basic patterns in A - F lies in the complexity of the formation. Patterns G and H require extra columns, additional sideways price movement, and more time to form. Larger patterns typically suggest a more protracted price move after a buy or sell signal. However, such formations are harder to identify but warn chartists not to dismiss the possibility of their occurrence.

Many technicians regard comparable bar chart patterns as an indication of a possible reversal because of their "choppy" appearance. In other words, stocks seem to move sideways while struggling to make new highs or lows. Broadening formations project uncertainty because chartists remain in a quandary about the future direction of the price move until the breakout. However, in point and figure analysis, most chartists regard broadening patterns as a price consolidation which presages a volatile continuation of the current trend. Breakouts in either direction signal potentially explosive price action.

Another modification of the triple top and bottom patterns may be linked to **the spread triple top formation** and **the spread triple bottom pattern** illustrated in Figure 4-8. The primary difference in the spread formations concerns three level tops which do not occur successively. No predefined sequence exists as with orthodox triple tops or bottoms. In A, three different level tops occur at 31, with a price breakout in the last column at 32. In B, a breakout occurs at 53 with the penetration of two previous level tops that have formed over time. Spread triple tops and bottoms are essentially base patterns which may take several years to complete. As stated earlier, higher beta-factor stocks usually form faster and produce exciting price moves. Conservative, lower beta-factor issues require more time to complete the pattern and generally yield gradual price moves.

The same points may also be made about C and D. In C, three level bottoms appear at 60. The last column provides a sell signal on the downmove to 59. A sell signal likewise results at 42 in D. An important point with spread triple tops and bottoms should be interjected. These formations consume more columns in their sideways price action. The lengthy consolidation move implies greater price potential in either direction once the breakout occurs. However, downside price moves are faster and usually more volatile.

Figure 4-9 includes three examples of **bullish base patterns** which ultimately produce buy signals. Breakouts originate at 22 and $15\frac{1}{2}$ in A and B respectively. In C, one buy signal

Figure 4-8

SPREAD TRIPLE TOP AND BOTTOM FORMATIONS

The Spread Triple Top Formation

(A)

```
                               B
   X              X            X
30 X O            X O          X
   X O            X O X    X   X
   X O X     X    X O X O X O X
   X O X O X O X O X O X O X
   X O X O X O X O   O   O
25 X        O      O
   X
```

(B)

```
                               B
   X              X            X
   X O            X O X    X   X
50 X O            X O X O X O X
   X O X     X    X O X O X O X
   X O X O X O X O   O   O
   X O X O X O X
   X O X O   O
45 X O
   X
```

The Spread Triple Bottom Formation

(C)

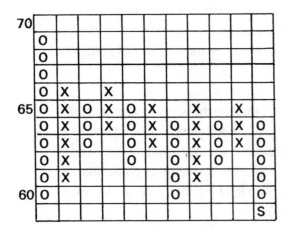

```
70
   O
   O
   O
   O X     X
65 O X O X O X    X    X
   O X O X O X O X O X O
   O X O   O X O X O X O
   O X     O   O X O    O
   O X         O X      O
60 O           O        O
                        S
```

(D)

```
   O
   O
   O
50 O
   O X
   O X O X     X
   O X O X O X O X    X    X
   O X O X O X O X O X O X O
45 O X O     O   O X O X O X O
   O X         O X O   O    O
   O           O           O
                           S
```

50

Figure 4-9

BULLISH BASE PATTERNS

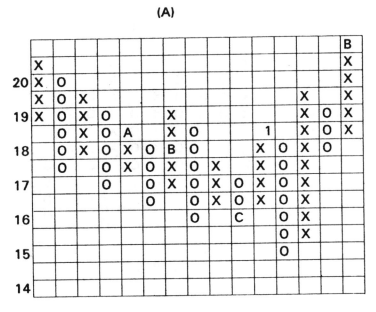

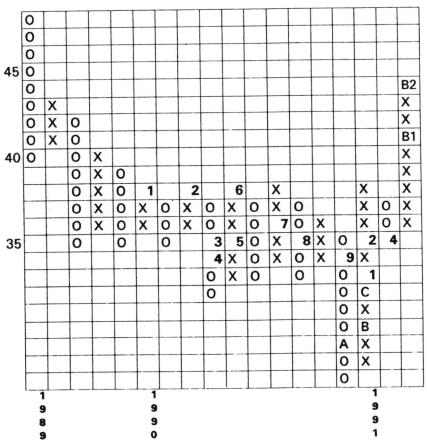

Figure 4-10

BEARISH BASE PATTERNS

(A)

	1	2	3	4	5	6	7	8	9	10	11	12
			X		X		X					
		X	O	X	O	X	O	X				
20		X	O	X	O	X	O	X	O	X		
	X		X	O	X	O	X	O	X	O	X	O
19	X	O	X	O	X	O			O	X	O	X	O
	X	O	X	O	X				O	X	O	X	O
18	X	O	X	O	X				O	X	O	X	O
	X	O	X	O	X				O	X	O	X	O
17	X	O		O					O		O		O
	X											S
16	X											
	X											
15	X											
	X											
14	X											

1991

(B)

	1	2	3	4	5	6	7	8	9	10
30	X		X			X				
	X	O	X	O		X	O			
	X	O	X	O	X	X	O			
	X	O	X	O	X	O	X	O	X	
	X	O	X	O	X	O	X	O	X	O
25	X	O		O	X	O	X	O	X	O
	X		O		O		O		O	
	X								S	
	X								O	
									O	

(C)

	1	2	3	4	5	6	7	8
			X		X			
			X	O	X	O		
			X	O	X	O		
			X	O	X	O		
75	X		X	O	X	O	X	
	X	O	X	O	X	O	X	O
	X	O	X	O	X	O	X	O
	X	O	X	O	X	O	X	O
	X	O	X	O	X	O		O
70	X	O	X	O	X			O
	X	O		O				O
	X							S
	X							
	X							
65	X							
	X							
	X							
	X							

Figure 4-11

BEARISH SIGNAL REVERSED PATTERN

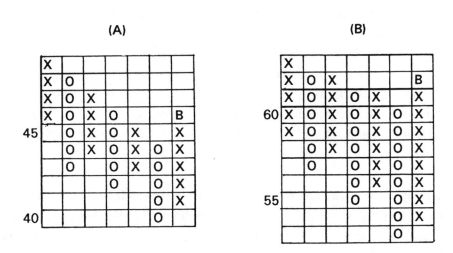

(A)

(B)

(C)

Figure 4-11 illustrates **the seven-column bearish signal reversed pattern**. In A, the first six columns display the classic bearish sign of lower tops and bottoms. However, in column seven an upmove surfaces and exceeds the previous top at 45. The penetration of one previous top reverses the bearish symptoms of the pattern and indicates a price reversal to the upside. Similar buy signals may be found at 62 and 38 in B and C respectively.

Figure 4-12 reveals **the bullish signal reversed pattern,** which represents the downside counterpart to Figure 4-12. Of the seven columns, the first six demonstrate higher tops and bottoms, symptomatic of bullish price trends. However, column seven contains a sharp downside price move which breaches the previous bottom from column five. Sell signals occur at 70, 37, and 35 in A, B, and C. The sell signal warns of a forthcoming price reversal to the downside.

Figure 4-13 simply illustrates a **triple top pattern with a pullback** following the initial breakout. The pullback allows the stock to pause before another upmove. Some chartists such as Blumenthal[3] propose that the upmove following the pullback contains a second successive buy signal because it carries beyond the first breakout. In A, an initial buy signal at 63 is followed by a pullback and then another advance which gives a buy signal and further confirms the uptrend at 64. Variations of follow-up buy signals after pullbacks appear in B, C, and D.

Triple bottom patterns with a pullback are illustrated in Figure 4-14. Both triple bottom continuation and reversal patterns appear in the illustration. However, the major significance of Figure 4-14 focuses on the penetration of two previous bottoms by a third downmove. A pullback then follows the initial sell signal and allows the stock a brief respite before another downmove that Blumenthal terms a second successive sell signal. In both triple top and bottom patterns, the interruption from the pullback should be regarded as temporary. Pullbacks must not alter the correct interpretation of a bearish signal and lower prices. Notice in B that the first downside breakout appears at 41, followed by a pullback and another or second sell signal at 37. Similar variations may be found in A, C, and D.

Figures 4-15 and 4-16 illustrate base patterns or extensions of triple top and bottom formations. In Figure 4-15 (A) and (B), the major difference is that multiple tops are exceeded rather than just two. The interpretation remains the same -- a move above a larger number of tops in a well-defined resistance area still furnishes a buy signal. Similar illustrations comprise Figure 4-16 (A) and (B). Multiple bottoms rather than tops are breached, while sell signals result.

Chart patterns represent only one aspect of traditional point and figure analysis. An integral part of evaluating chart patterns revolves around the proper construction and understanding of trend lines that accompany them. Conventional trend line construction is treated at length in Chapter 5.

Figure 4-12

BEARISH SIGNAL REVERSED PATTERNS

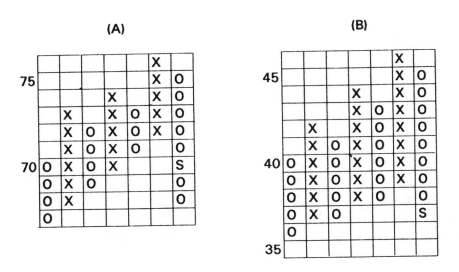

Figure 4-13

TRIPLE TOP PATTERN WITH A PULLBACK

(A)

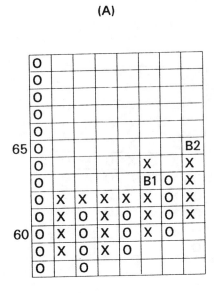

O							
O							
O							
O							
O							
65 O							B2
O					X		X
O					B1	O	X
O	X	X	X	X	X	O	X
O	X	O	X	O	X	O	X
60 O	X	O	X	O	X	O	
O	X	O	X	O			
O		O					

(B)

O							
O							
O							B2
O					X		X
O					X	O	X
30 O					B1	O	X
O	X		X		X	O	X
O	X	O	X	O	X	O	
O	X	O	X	O	X		
O	X	O	X	O	X		
25 O	X	O		O			
O							

(C)

					X		B2
					X		X
					X	O	X
					X	O	X
					B1	O	X
60 X					X	O	X
X	O	X			X	O	
X	O	X	O	X			
X	O	X	O	X			
X	O	X	O				
55 X	O						
X							
X							
X							
X							

(D)

						B2
				B1		X
45		X		X	O	X
X		X	O	X	O	X
X	O	X	O	X	O	
X	O	X	O	X		
X	O	X	O	X		
40 X	O			O		
X						
X						
X						
X						

56

Figure 4-14

TRIPLE BOTTOM PATTERN WITH A PULLBACK

(A)

(B)

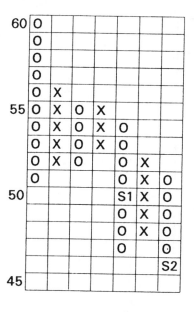

(C)

(D)

Figure 4-15

MODIFIED TRIPLE TOP FORMATIONS

(A)

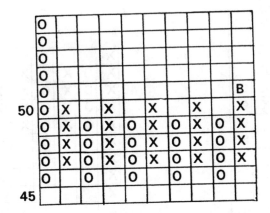

Triple Top or Breakout From a Base Pattern

(B)

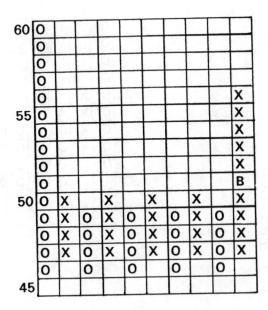

Figure 4-16

MODIFIED TRIPLE TOP FORMATIONS

(A)

35	X		X		X		X		X	
	X	O	X	O	X	O	X	O	X	O
	X	O	X	O	X	O	X	O	X	O
	X	O	X	O	X	O	X	O	X	O
	X	O		O		O		O		O
30	X									S
	X									
	X									
	X									
	X									

**Triple Bottom or Breakout
From a Base Pattern**

(B)

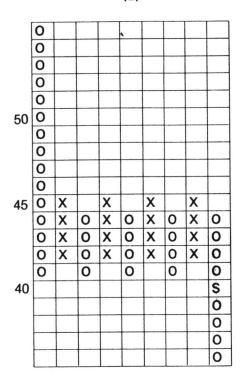

SUMMARY

The more advanced chart configurations in Chapter 4 are simply derivatives of basic formations treated in the preceding chapter. Although more complexities and subtleties are involved, the underlying rationale remains the same. Buy and sell signals still develop from breakouts above or below previous resistance and support levels and continue to indicate reversals or continuations of price trends.

ENDNOTES

[1]A.W. Cohen, <u>How To Use the Three-Point Reversal Method of Point and Figure Stock Market Trading</u> 9th ed. (New Rochelle, NY: Chartcraft, Inc., 1987), 38.

[2]Michael L. Burke, <u>The All-New Guide to the Three-Point Reversal Method of Point and Figure Construction and Formations</u> (New Rochelle, NY: Chartcraft, Inc., 1990), 98.

[3]See Earl Blumenthal, <u>Chart For Profit Point & Figure Trading</u> (Larchmont, NY: Chartcraft, Inc., 1975).

CHAPTER 5

THE IMPORTANCE OF TRENDLINES

Trend lines represent a vital part of technical analysis. Technicians subscribe to the view that stock prices move approximately along a straight line for considerable periods of time. This tendency for stock price movements to persist in a given direction along the path of a straight line remains dear to all chartists. If the trendline remains unimpaired, the stock's price movement should continue in that direction. Penetrations of the trendline warn that a major juncture is imminent.

THE BULLISH SUPPORT LINE

The major uptrend line in P & F charting is the **bullish support line.** To understand its construction, let's examine Figure 5-1. The illustrations disclose a variety of starting points to establish the major uptrend line. Avon Products provides an excellent starting point for illustration purposes. A buy signal evolves in April 1989, with an upside breakout at 29. When the buy signal takes place, the bottoming process concludes and an upturn begins. The buy signal warns of a bullish trend and justifies drawing the bullish support line. Immediately after the buy signal, P & F chartists drop one square below the lowest O in the bottom and draw a 45 degree trendline. The bullish support line connects successively higher corners on the graph rather than different low points or bottoms on the chart.

Enserch Corporation reveals multiple bottoms before the upmove begins. We register the final buy signal at 21 in February 1989, as the price moves above all previous tops. Once the buy signal occurs, we may establish the uptrend line. In the case of two or more bottoms, bullish support lines should be drawn by dropping one square below the most recent bottom and drawing the line at a 45 degree angle. All trend lines should extend across the entire page because they serve as a reference point for future areas of support and resistance.

The Enron Corporation chart provides an interesting example. A buy signal appears at 44, and the bullish support line may be drawn from one square below the most recent O in the base. Although the latest bottom is at 36 rather than 35 like its two predecessors, you should always choose the most recent part of the base pattern (or support level). If we do not select

Figure 5-1

CONSTRUCTING THE BULLISH SUPPORT LINE

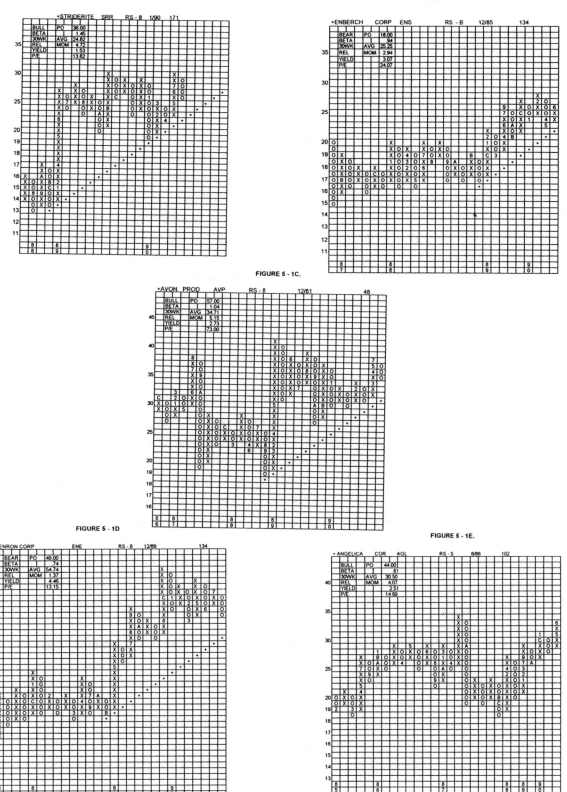

63

recent bottoms to draw the uptrend, the line would run through the base pattern and have little meaning.

Angelica provides a slightly different illustration because it entails multiple bottoms with one downside move below all others. The bullish support line may be drawn from one square below the lowest bottom once the buy signal occurs at 24. The Striderite, Enserch, and Avon charts show the inclination of stock prices to eventually move along the trendline, albeit in somewhat irregular fashion.

Figures 5-1 and 5-2 illustrate key ideas associated with trend line analysis. If we look at Striderite in 5-1, the stock's price drops and touches the trendline at $19\frac{1}{2}$ in January 1990. Bullish trend lines serve as potential points of support during retracements from major upmoves. Investors may regard price declines "bouncing off" the bullish support line as timely buying opportunities. Bullish support lines typically signal strength and downside resiliency. Avon stock could be prudently accumulated in the 30-31 area in January and February of 1990. Additions to portfolios could also be justified in Unilever (Figure 5-2) in March 1991, around 84. Readers will observe that the Unilever uptrend remains unbroken after steadily higher prices from 1988 to 1991.

Figures 5-1 and 5-2 also delineate another important concept of trend line interpretation. Let's examine the Enserch Corporation chart in May 1990, when a sell signal appears immediately above the bullish support line. A cardinal rule among P & F technicians says that sell signals occurring close to the bullish support line should be disregarded. As long as the bullish support line remains intact, analysts regard the long-term trend as bullish. Investors with intermediate and long-term investment horizons should not act on sell signals unless the bullish support line is breached.[1] We will focus on trend line violations shortly. Two sell signals in succession developed above the bullish support line in Striderite, but the decline ended on the trendline at $19\frac{1}{2}$ and was followed by a sharp upside price reversal.

Traditional theorists maintain that only short-term traders should act on sell signals above the bullish support line. These quick-term traders may capitalize on abbreviated price slides for short sales or put option purchases. However, their actions are based on inordinate risks.

The next step in conventional analysis focuses on whether "breaks" or penetrations of established trendlines are valid. To illustrate, let's look at Quick & Reilly. We construct the 45 degree trendline from one square below the lowest O in the base at the $11\frac{1}{2}$ square. A July downmove to $13\frac{1}{2}$ dips below the bullish support line by one square. However, no sell signal occurs. Since the downmove failed to exceed a previous bottom, the initial bullish signal continues. Therefore, the trendline break is not valid. For a reversal to occur, the bullish support line should be violated by more than one square with the downside move yielding a

Figure 5-2

A LONG-TERM BULLISH SUPPORT LINE

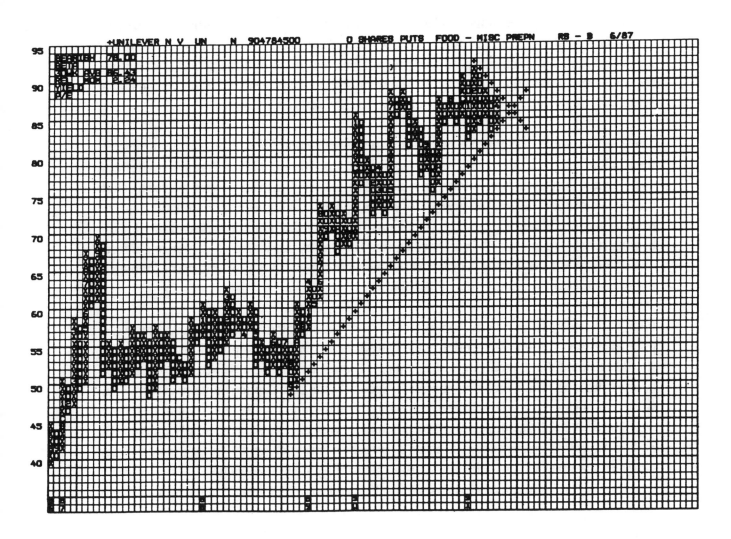

sell signal. Downside moves below bullish support lines are typically viewed as false or ostensible unless a sell signal occurs to confirm a trend reversal. When the stock price renews its advance, buyers may accumulate long positions.[2]

We can locate a similar example in Clayton Homes. Although there are multiple bottoms, the lowest O at $5\frac{1}{2}$ allows us to construct a clearly defined uptrend. A January downmove to 8 is not accompanied by a sell signal, so we disregard the break in the bullish support line. Further, the price only moved one square below the trendline. Since prices tend to move somewhat irregularly along defined trendlines, decisive price reversals are required.

The TRW example in Figure 5-3 provides an interesting contrast. A January decline carries the stock price to 45, one square below the bullish support line. No sell signal materializes, and we view the penetration as false. In June and July of 1990, a price decline moves through the bullish support line on the strength of a sell signal. A valid penetration results, and the primary trend of the stock turns bearish. Construction of the major downtrend line (or the bearish resistance line which is covered shortly) begins by drawing a 45 degree angle from one square above the highest X or last of the multiple tops. A major turning point follows in the stock and confirms a top area of distribution.

Figure 5-4 displays a long-term chart of Tuscon G & E. During the 1982-87 period of sustained price increases, Tuscon's stock price remains well above the bullish support line. Three things should be noted. First, recurring sell signals are routine during the advance but disregarded because the long-term trend remains bullish. Secondly, the bullish price movement carries the stock to a position considerably above the long-term uptrend line. When stock prices move well above the bullish support line, speculative buying excesses have usually entered the picture. Investors should anticipate a sharp correction or retracement to bring the stock price closer to the uptrend line. However, a third possibility may also occur. A series of rapid upside price moves frequently exhaust themselves and warn that the end of the bull market is near.

In the Tuscon illustration, the sideways distributional process concluded with a downside breakout below the bullish support line in July 1988. A bear market was triggered from the sell signal in the triple bottom formation in July. The decline reached 50 and was followed by a pullback in September to the old bullish resistance line at 54. Remember, old support becomes new resistance and vice versa. The sell signal at 54 confirmed a valid break of the uptrend line and marks a new resistance point for future rallies. This "pullback effect" does not change investor interpretations and should be viewed as temporary. When valid price reversals occur, investors must be cognizant of their permanence. Tuscon G & E shows a decline from 65 to slightly above 4 during a five-year period.

Figure 5-3

FALSE PENETRATIONS OF THE BULLISH SUPPORT LINE

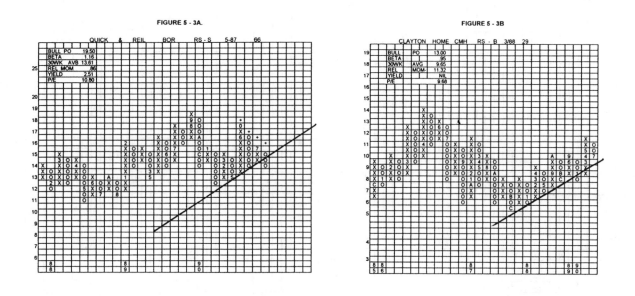

FIGURE 5 - 3A.

FIGURE 5 - 3B.

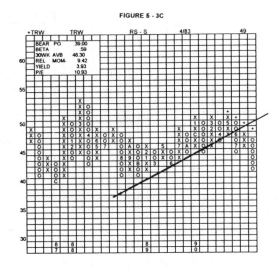

FIGURE 5 - 3C

Figure 5-4

REVERSING THE LONG-TERM UPTREND

Figure 5-5

STOCKS SWITCHING FROM BULLISH TO BEARISH

FIGURE 5 - 5A

STOCKS SWITCHING FROM BULLISH TO BEARISH

FIGURE 5 - 5B

STOCKS SWITCHING FROM BULLISH TO BEARISH

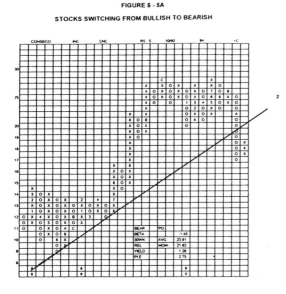

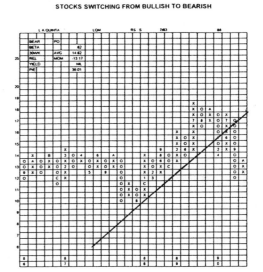

FIGURE 5 - 5C

STOCKS SWITCHING FROM BULLISH TO BEARISH

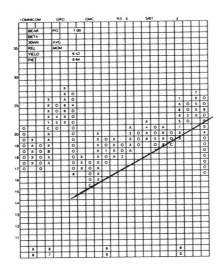

69

Figure 5-5 discloses three illustrations of stocks with valid price reversals. In Conseco, observe the broad topping area and distributional process completed by the October sell signal and penetration of the bullish support line. Conseco reveals the pullback effect with a return move toward the previous support area provided by the bullish support line. However, the stock continued its downmove to $8\frac{1}{2}$ in September 1990.

Both La Quinta and Omnicom reveal severe breakdowns in their chart patterns as stock prices violated bullish support lines with emphasis. La Quinta reveals an interesting concept, however. After the downtrend was confirmed, the attempted pullback moved slightly above the original bullish support line. However, the sell signal remained intact and suggests a defensive posture for the stock. La Quinta continued to display lower tops and bottoms despite strong pullback efforts. The only way to reverse the downside trend would be a buy signal.

Bullish Resistance Lines

Figure 5-6 illustrates the **bullish resistance line,** a companion supplement to the bullish support trendline. Bullish resistance lines are often called channel lines and do not command the attention or respect given to major trend lines. These minor lines simply provide a pathway or channel for stock price movements.

McDonalds experienced a price advance to 38 followed by a downside move back to original support near 30. The price fluctuations remained within the channel. If one channel line is broken, a second should be constructed. When two or more bullish resistance lines are broken, the stock is generally considered to be extended and vulnerable on the downside. Chartcraft calls minor lines corollary trendlines.

Let's determine how bullish resistance lines are drawn from the McDonalds illustration. Once a price advance exceeds previous tops, the stock's primary trend reverses upward and the bullish support line is constructed. The next step is to locate the "wall of O's" or large downside move to the left of the bottom formation. Such extended downside moves typically signal the end of the slide. Move one column to the right of the wall of O's to the square immediately above the highest X recording. Draw a 45 degree line parallel to the bullish support line. McDonalds continues a methodical advance within the channel defined by the bullish resistance line. Stocks which display gradual price moves remain within the channel more than their volatile counterparts.

The First American illustration in Figure 5-6 illustrates a different story. Consecutive buy signals at 42 and 43 in January 1988 indicate a trend reversal to the upside. After constructing the bullish support line, we identify the first lengthy column of O's (September 1987) to the left of the base pattern. We then move to the top of the adjacent column of X's in the 41

Figure 5-6

THE BULLISH RESISTANCE LINE

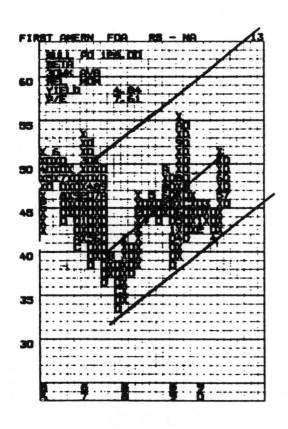

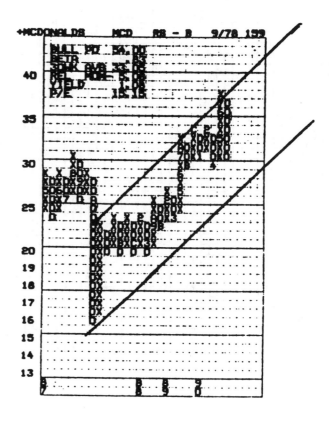

Figure 5-7

USING THE BULLISH RESISTANCE LINE TO IDENTIFY AN OVERPRICED STOCK

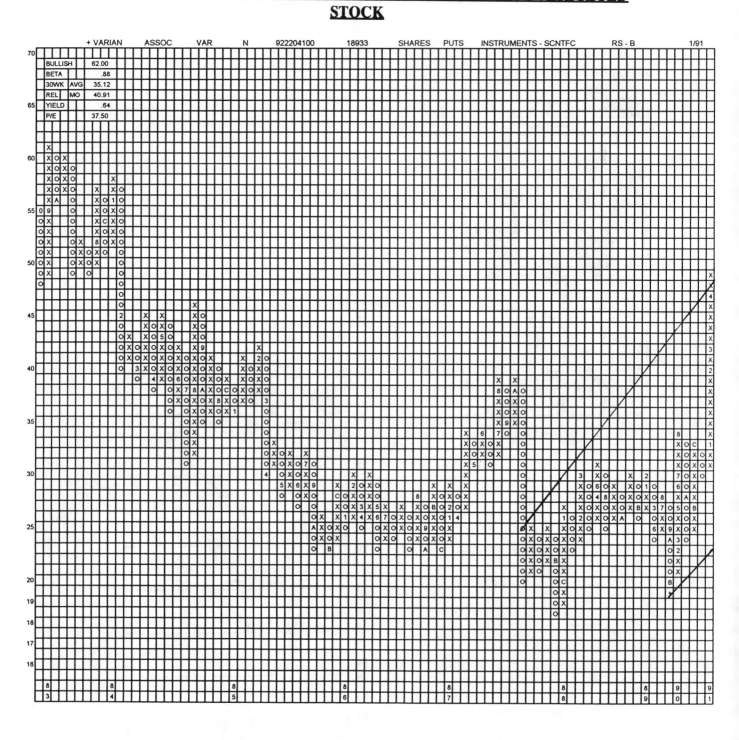

square and draw a 45 degree line across the chart. However, the first bullish resistance line is broken almost immediately. The closest available wall may be found in April and May of 1987. The wall of O's should protrude above all X's in the accumulation base at the bottom of the pattern. After finding the highest recording in the column to the immediate right, construct a second channel line from one square above the top X. A summer 1989 price increase carries to 56 but remains within the channel.

Figure 5-7 illustrates how bullish resistance lines help identify overpriced stocks. Varian advanced slightly above the channel line to 49. However, the stock retraced to 31 by December 1991. Moving beyond the established channel area signalled an extended stock in near term. Frenzied buying activity advanced the price too quickly. Speculative excesses were corrected with the downside retracement to original support at 31. Varian provides a good example of how old resistance becomes new support. The 30-31 area clearly indicated resistance from early 1988 until the buy signal at 32 in July 1990. Breaking one channel line signals a short-term overbought issue, but penetrations of two or more bullish resistance lines often mark the latter phases of the price runup.

THE BEARISH RESISTANCE LINE

The second major trendline in P&F charting is called the **bearish resistance line**, which represents the downside counterpart to the bullish support line. Figure 5-8 shows major downtrend lines are constructed in a diametrically opposite manner to long-term uptrend lines. Let's examine Anacomp and Eljer as a starting point. P&F chartists move one square above the highest X in the top area of distribution and draw a 45 degree downtrend line connecting successively lower corners of the graph. In the case of Jamesway with multiple tops, we locate the highest X near the end of the topping process at 11. A spread triple bottom sell signal develops in October 1989. Once a sell signal occurs, chartists go to the highest X in a single top (Anacomp and Eljer) or the most recent top (Jamesway) in a sideways price move. Only sell signals justify a downtrend line.

Several rules apply for proper interpretation of the bearish resistance line. First, chartists must regard buy signals close to the downtrend line cautiously. Secondly, buying below the bearish resistance line should be reserved for short-term traders looking for a quick profit on stocks or call options. And third, valid breaks of the downtrend line are realized only if a buy signal accompanies the penetration. All of these points are illustrated during the next few pages.

In Anacomp, what appears to be an evolving buy signal in July 1990, failed due to the presence of the bearish resistance line overhead. By January 1991, the stock had dipped to $\frac{1}{4}$ before launching an upmove. Jamesway makes repeated challenges to move above the downtrend line without success. Finally, in November of 1991, a pattern of lower tops

Figure 5-8

CONSTRUCTING THE BEARISH RESISTANCE LINE

FIGURE 5 - 8A

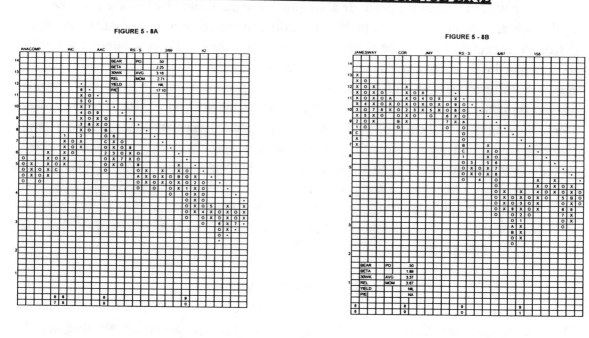

FIGURE 5 - 8B

FIGURE 5 - 8C

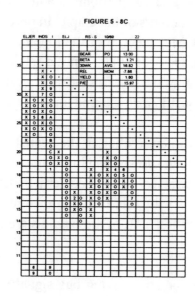

Figure 5-9

LONG-TERM BEARISH RESISTANCE AND SUPPORT LINES

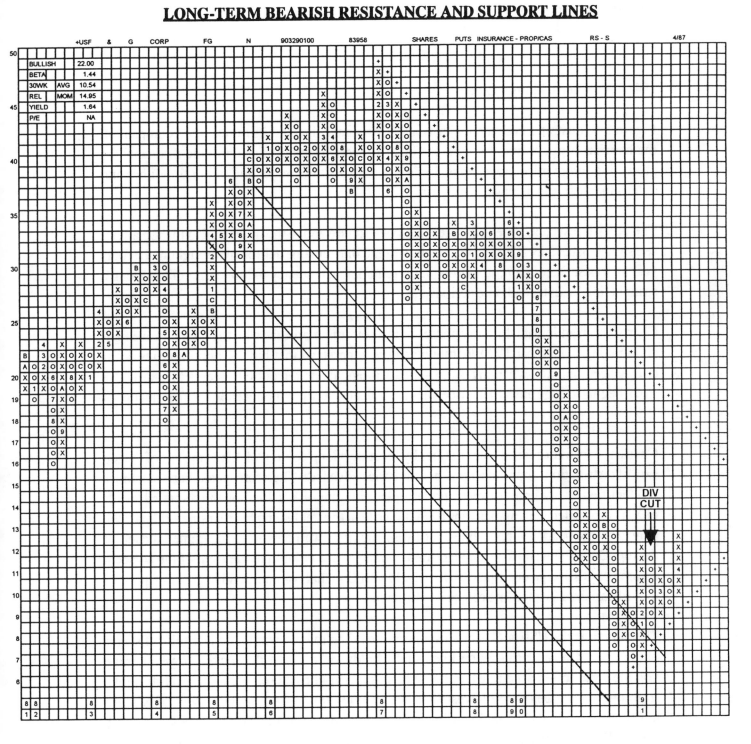

evolves. Descending tops confirm the failure of the rally attempts, and the stocks begin to drop toward previous support levels. A buy signal in Jamesway did occur close to the bearish resistance line in April 1991 but retreated to lower levels.

Using Another Channel Line

Figure 5-9 illustrates both the major bearish resistance line and its minor trend companion, the **bearish support line,** for USF & G Corp. Bearish support lines provide a channel for projecting future price movements. Let's examine both the major and minor trendlines and determine their role in long-term charts.

The bearish resistance line originates from one square above the highest X in the top after a sell signal materializes. The 45 degree downtrend line remains unbroken throughout the four-year analysis. Once again, stocks display a remarkable tendency to move irregularly along a straight line for extended time periods.

Chartists can anticipate the latter phases of the bottoming process with the lateral movement culminating in October 1990. Astute investors understand that buying opportunities occur during accumulation when investing appears illogical and the outlook seems bleakest. The stock begins to edge upward in price after a dividend cut was announced in the first quarter of 1991.

Chartists construct bearish support lines by locating a long column of X's to the left of the top area of distribution. Tops develop after rapid price advances. Therefore, peaks can sometimes be identified by one or more long, uninterrupted columns of X's. Finding the so-called "walls of X's" associated with market tops becomes critical to establishing bearish support lines. We may draw the bearish support line by locating the first "wall of X's" to the immediate left of the top. Once the wall has been identified, we move one column to the right of the adjacent column of O's and go one square below the lowest O in that column. A 45 degree line parallel to the bearish resistance line can be constructed.

The only time the USF & G bearish support line failed to hold was in the late sell-off stages of the stock. One bearish support line usually holds for less volatile stocks. However, more volatile issues often penetrate the first bearish support line and require a second line drawn from one square below the lowest O in the column adjacent to the next wall of X's. An unnecessary second channel line is included in USF & G for illustration purposes. Bearish support lines occupy a slightly more prominent role than bullish resistance lines because stock prices decline faster than they rise.

76

Figure 5-10

A CHANGING LONG-TERM TREND

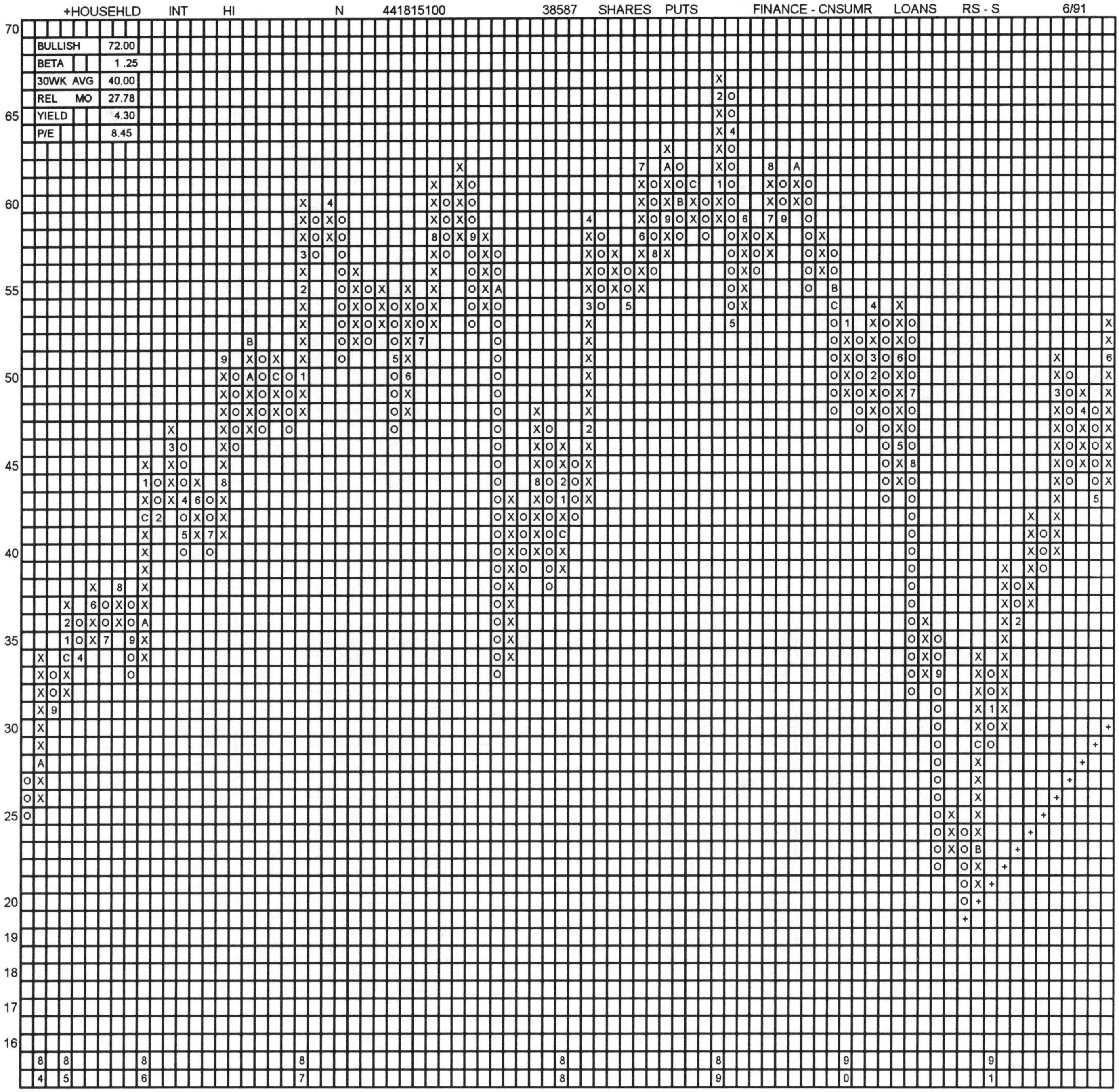

+HOUSEHLD INT HI N 441815100 38587 SHARES PUTS FINANCE - CNSUMR LOANS RS - S 6/91
BULLISH 72.00
BETA 1.25
30WK AVG 40.00
REL MO 27.78
YIELD 4.30
P/E 8.45

Figure 5-11

FALSE PENETRATIONS OF THE BEARISH RESISTANCE LINE

FIGURE 5 - 11A.

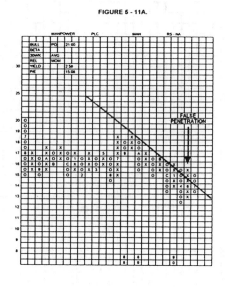

FIGURE 5 - 11B.

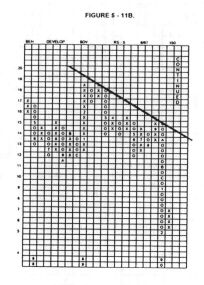

FIGURE 5 - 11C.

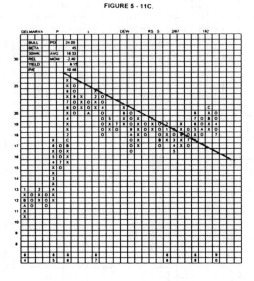

FIGURE 5 - 11D.

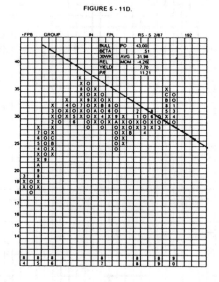

Figure 5-10 delineates a changing long-term trend after the bearish resistance line continued for two years. Attempted rallies nearly penetrated the downtrend line in October 1989 and June of 1990. However, a valid penetration develops in February 1991 at 42. The advance exceeds the trendline by more than one square with support from a buy signal. The price reversal was swift and consumed little time. However, short-term traders may acknowledge the buy signal at 25 in November 1991 because the stock was significantly removed from its downtrend line. Household's bearish support line essentially remains intact throughout the downmove.

Figure 5-11 includes four illustrations with false penetrations of the bearish resistance line. Manpower discloses a penetration of the downtrend by only one square with a sell signal still in force. No action would be taken, however. The pattern of progressively lower tops confirms a bearish trend.

General Development illustrates why trendline breaks must be approached cautiously. Although the stock achieved a short-term buy signal in September 1989 at 15, General Development ran into overhead supply (or previous resistance) at $15\frac{1}{2}$. A more definitive buy signal exceeding all tops in the base failed to materialize. The stock's failure to break out led to a downside move to 5 by February 1990.

Delmarva broke the bearish resistance line by one-square in June 1988. However, no buy signal accompanies the move. In July 1989, Delmarva registers a buy signal at $19\frac{1}{2}$ and the uptrend begins. A valid penetration confirmed the upmove.

FP&L Group has a one-square breach of the downtrend in November 1988. However, you would probably delay action until August 1989 when all adjacent tops are broken on a decisive triple top breakout. However, traders need to recognize future points of resistance at 34, 36, and 38 where past rally attempts have stalled. Each previous top represents a point of potential resistance. On downside moves, past bottoms similarly suggest possible areas of support.

Figure 5-12 integrates important concepts from the chapter. The downtrend line originates from one square above the highest X. A buy signal in February 1991 gives an upside breakout and valid trend reversal to complete the juncture. The bearish support line drawn from the wall of X's to the immediate left of the top remains unblemished. Also, an initial bullish resistance channel line is established next to the wall of O's on the left of the bottom area of accumulation.

Figure 5-12

CONFIRMING A JUNCTURE

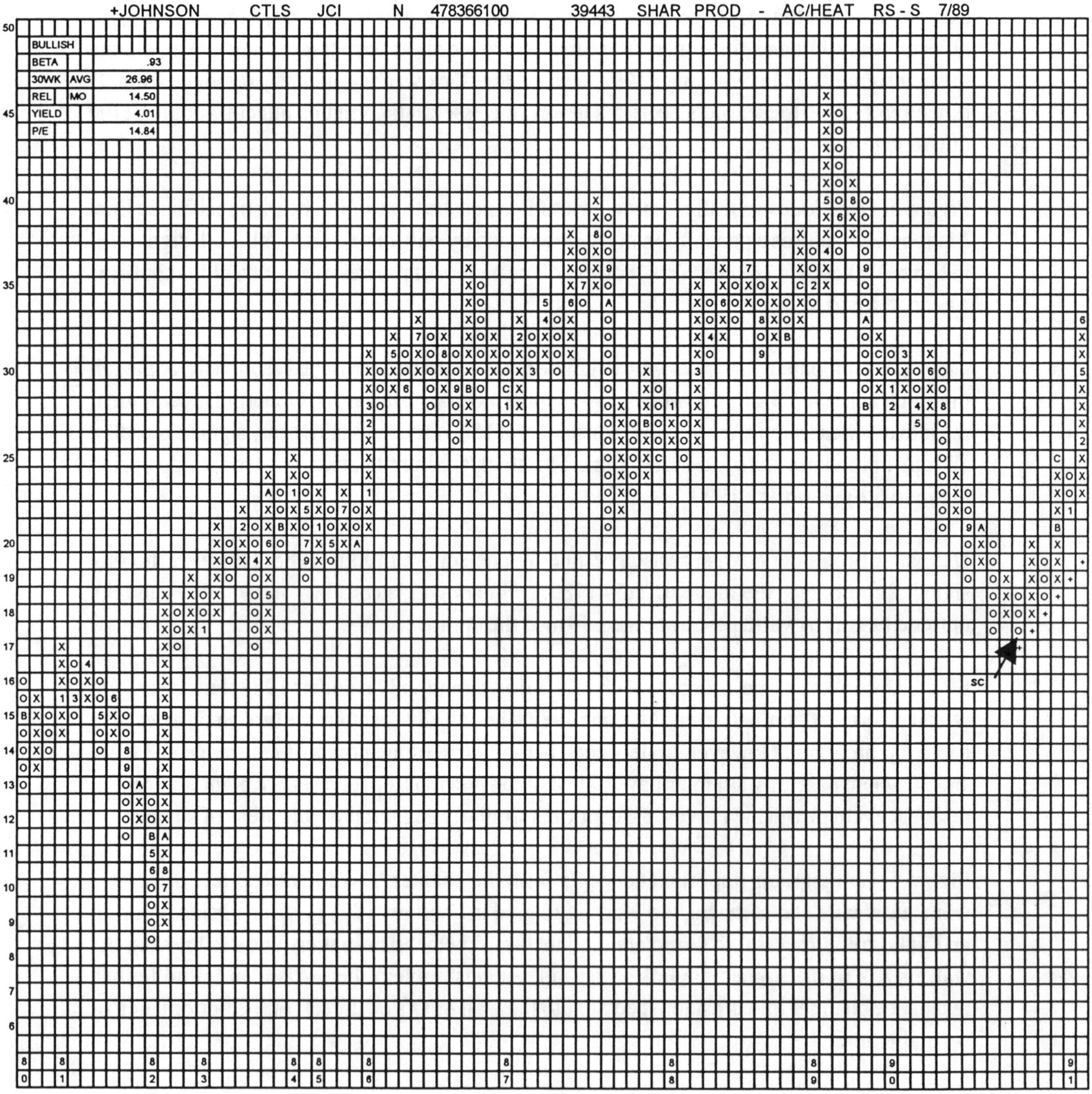

BULLISH		
BETA		.93
30WK	AVG	26.96
REL	MO	14.50
YIELD		4.01
P/E		14.84

Figure 5-13

TRENDLINES: A SYNTHESIS

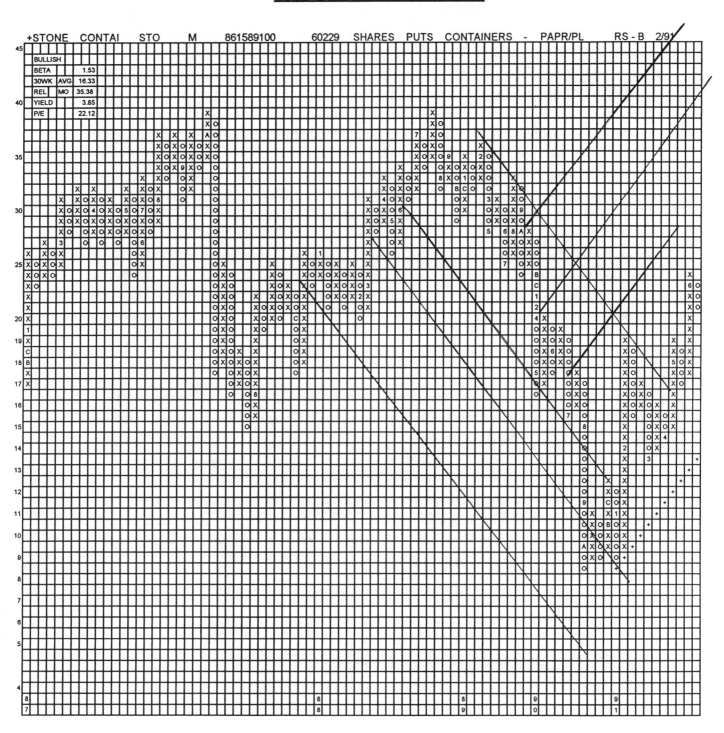

Figure 5-13 provides a synthesis of all trendlines covered in the chapter with a review of Stone Container. A breakout to the upside occurs in February 1989 at 36, but the trendline was not exceeded by more than one square. Therefore, another major downtrend line was constructed at the conclusion of the topping process and remained for two years before a penetration. Two channel lines or bearish support lines were penetrated during the decline. After a decline violates a second channel line, most stocks approach their final "blow-off" moves in either direction. For illustration purposes, a third bearish support line is included.

As Stone tries to reverse to the upside, the January-February 1990 upmove stops short of the bearish resistance line. After a retracement and consolidation follows, Stone's next advance breaks the downtrend. Three bullish resistance lines are drawn for instructional purposes after the reversal occurs and the bullish support line is established. Readers should closely examine the construction of all trendlines in the Stone Container chart.

Now that trendlines have been explored, we must now turn our attention to price objectives. Once accumulation and distribution are complete, it is essential that chartists gauge fixture price movements. Chapter 6 covers the traditional wisdom of forecasting price moves. Later in Section 3, we will add additional insights.

SUMMARY

Point and figure charts contain two major trendlines -- the bullish support line (uptrend) and the bearish resistance line (downtrend). The rationale underlying trendlines suggests that stock prices tend to move approximately along a straight line for long periods of time. Valid trendline penetrations warn of impending junctures and forthcoming price reversals.

The bullish resistance and bearish support lines represent two corollary or channel lines. Despite their merit, neither supplemental channel line commands the attention or respect received by major trendlines. However, channel lines delineate areas of support and resistance and serve to identify overvalued and undervalued stocks.

ENDNOTES

[1]Michael L. Burke, <u>The All New Guide to the Three-Point Reversal Method of Point & Figure Construction and Formations</u> (New Rochelle, NY: Chartcraft, Inc., 1990), 23-47.

[2]A.W. Cohen, <u>How to Use the Three-Point Reversal Method of Point and Figure Stock Market Trading</u>, 9th ed. (New Rochelle, NY: Chartcraft, Inc., 1987), 43-54.

CHAPTER 6

FORECASTING PRICE MOVEMENTS

Sophisticated investors argue that knowing when to sell is more difficult than learning when to buy. P & F charts offer an important tool for decision making. Even vertical bar chartists find P & F essential in locating selling opportunities. There are two different approaches to estimate price moves -- the **horizontal count** and the **vertical count**.

THE HORIZONTAL COUNT

Chartists utilize the horizontal count to obtain intermediate-term price objectives. We may learn to calculate the horizontal count by reviewing Figure 6-1. Base patterns begin with the "wall of O's" or "wall of X's" at the extreme left of the formation. Remember, any extended price move in the form of a wall of O's or X's indicates a strong down or upmove, respectively, and suggests the stock may be overdue for a reversal, correction, or consolidation. Horizontal counts can be used to forecast all types of interim price moves.

The horizontal count depends on the width of the base formation. Most chartists initially locate the line with the most recordings (i.e., the line with the least number of unoccupied squares). In Figure 6-1, both the 9 and the $9\frac{1}{2}$ price levels are complete with recordings. The letters "HC" indicate the line(s) where the horizontal count may be taken. The underlying theory of the horizontal count suggests that lateral patterns with more width have greater price potential. Conversely, more narrowly defined sideways base patterns and consolidations usually offer less potential.

The base pattern in Figure 6-1 is 10 squares (columns) wide from start (wall of O's) to finish (the buy signal suggesting a price reversal). The estimated price move may be found by multiplying the width of the pattern times the reversal rule for the particular chart. Since the price lies between 5 and 20, each square represents $.50 or $\frac{1}{2}$ point. A three-square reversal thus requires a $\frac{1}{2}$ point price move, so we have a $1\frac{1}{2}$ point chart.

By multiplying 10 (width of base) x $1\frac{1}{2}$ (reversal rule for individual chart), we have a product

Figure 6-1

THE HORIZONTAL COUNT

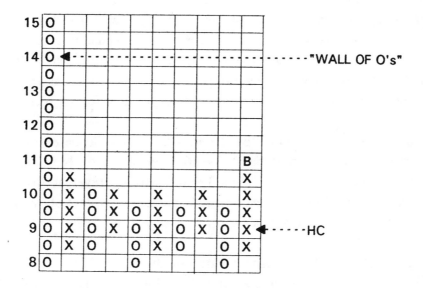

PRICE OBJECTIVE (PO)		WIDTH OF BASE	X	REVERSAL RULE
PO	=	10 Squares	X	1 1/2 PT Chart
PO	=	15		
		+ 8	(lowest O)	
PO	=	23		

of 15. The next step involves locating the lowest O in the base pattern at 8. We add the lowest O to the product to arrive at a projected price move to $23 (i.e., 8 + 15 = 23). Traders should think of liquidating positions as the stock approaches 23. However, an interesting point should be made about selling the stock. Technicians using P & F charts arrive at a price target of 23. To be safe, consider selling about 22 $\frac{1}{2}$, 22 $\frac{3}{4}$, or 22 $\frac{7}{8}$. Although the stock may move to 23-23+, heavy selling will probably occur near the target area and possibly depress the stock price over the near term.

Investment firms provide their customers with suggested sales or purchase prices. Brokerage price targets usually come from P & F charts. Technicians with investment firms command considerable influence in the market. You will ordinarily find it in your best interest to sell or buy slightly before the stock reaches the recommended price from your brokerage firm. You may avoid the rush, stand a better chance of getting your order filled, and escape unexpected price reversals caused by large-scale selling or buying from brokerage recommendations.

Two more illustrations appear in Figure 6-2. Part A reveals a wider base with greater potential price movement. We count across the 21 line 16 squares from the breakout or column with the buy signal to the wall of O's. Using a 3-point chart and reversal rule, multiply the 16 square width times the 3-point reversal rule. We obtain a product of 48 and add it to the lowest O at 19$\frac{1}{2}$ to get an intermediate-term price objective of 67$\frac{1}{2}$.

Part B indicates a base pattern 8 squares wide with the 28 and 29 lines used to establish the horizontal count. By adding the product of 24 (8 x 3 = 24) to 26 (the lowest O), we reach a target of 50. Intermediate price forecasts do not suggest the end of the move or imply the stock will not exceed 50. Intermediate targets indicate price areas where stocks may undergo corrections or consolidations -- much needed interruptions needed to ensure a continuation of the major trend. Bull and bear markets cannot be sustained without brief interludes to rekindle the sentiment associated with major uptrends and downmoves.

Figure 6-3 illustrates the horizontal count on low-priced and more expensive issues. Part A includes a stock priced at less than $5. Each square below 5 equals $\frac{1}{4}$ point, so a three-square reversal is $\frac{3}{4}$ point (3 x $\frac{1}{4}$ = $\frac{3}{4}$). To establish the horizontal count, we may read the 2$\frac{1}{2}$ line from the wall of O's to the breakout column. The base formation contains 12 squares multiplied by a reversal rule of $\frac{3}{4}$ (12 x $\frac{3}{4}$ = 9) to get a product of 9. By adding 9 to the lowest O of 1$\frac{1}{2}$, the price objective is 10$\frac{1}{2}$.

Figure 6-2

MORE ON THE HORIZONTAL COUNT

(A)

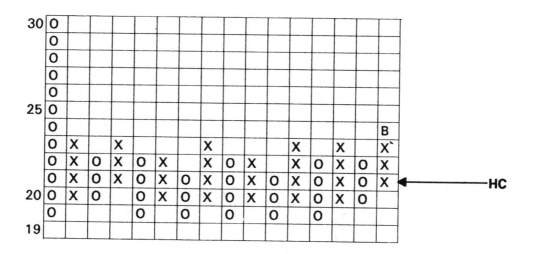

PO = 16 SQS Wide x 3 PT Chart
   = 48 + 19 1/2 (lowest O)
PO = 67 1/2

(B)

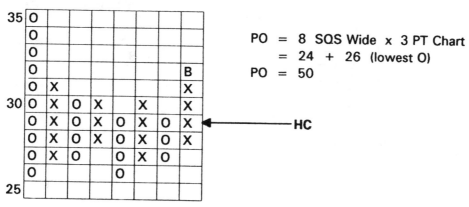

PO = 8 SQS Wide x 3 PT Chart
   = 24 + 26 (lowest O)
PO = 50

Figure 6-3

APPLYING HORIZONTAL COUNTS TO 3/4-POINT AND 6-POINT CHARTS

(A)

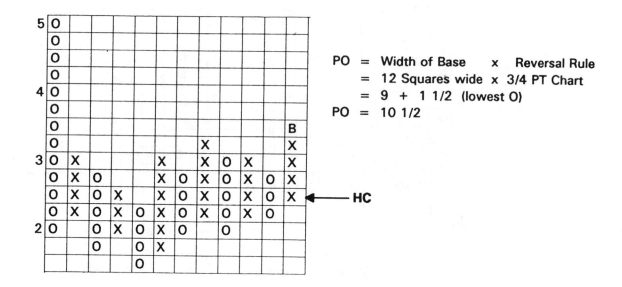

PO = Width of Base   x   Reversal Rule
     = 12 Squares wide   x   3/4 PT Chart
     = 9 + 1 1/2 (lowest O)
PO = 10 1/2

(B)

PO = 6 SQS wide   x   6 PT Chart
     = 36
PO = 36 + 112 (lowest O)
     = 148

88

Figure 6-4

HORIZONTAL COUNTS AND DOWNSIDE MOVES

(A)

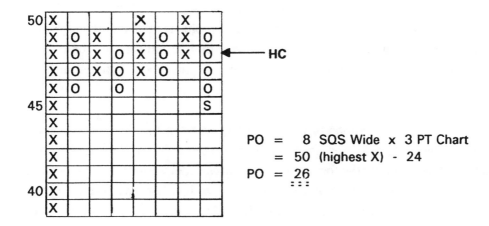

PO = 8 SQS Wide x 3 PT Chart

  = 50 (highest X) - 24

PO = 26

(B)

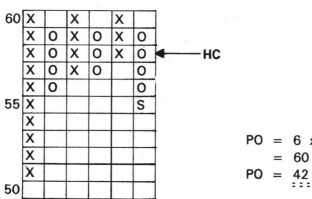

PO = 6 x 3

  = 60 - 18

PO = 42

89

Part B illustrates a issue priced at more than $100. Each square equals $2, so a three-square reversal requires a 6-point move in the opposite direction. The base is 6 squares wide and should be multiplied by a 6-point reversal rule to yield a product of 36. By adding 36 to the lowest O at 112, the expected price move is 148.

Concluding Observations on the Horizontal Count

Most published material on price objectives centers on bullish or upside forecasts. Given the long-term bias in the market toward higher prices, such emphasis appears logical. However, stock prices decline more rapidly than they advance. Some attention must be devoted to downside targets for closing out short sales, taking profits in puts, and accumulating stocks at reduced prices.

Figure 6-4 provides two illustrations of downside targets from the horizontal count. The procedure remains basically the same. In A, we measure the width of the base by counting across the 48 line. After learning the formation is 8 squares wide, we multiply the width times the reversal rule for the 3-point chart (8 x 3 = 24). The product is then subtracted from the highest X (at 50) in the top area of distribution. By subtracting 24 from 50, we receive a downside price objective of 26. Similarly, a formation 6 columns wide exists in B. We arrive at a price objective of 42 by implementing the same techniques used in A.

Another key point is emphasized in Figure 6-5. At times, a triple top, spread triple top, or more protracted base pattern develops with price recordings on two different scales. In Figure 6-5, both Moore and Raychem have price recordings below and above 20. The question arises as to which reversal rule to use. We would make one fundamental suggestion. The count should always be used conservatively; overstated price forecasts can be expensive. You will not suffer irreparable damage from taking acceptable profits.

In examining the Moore chart, let's figure a horizontal count from the 19 line. The base width totals 11 squares. We multiply by the lower reversal rule from the $\frac{1}{2}$ point chart. The product of 15 is added to the lowest O in the base at $16\frac{1}{2}$. Our target is $31\frac{1}{2}$. In July 1989, Moore reached 33 and underwent a correction back to the 20 area. Two points should be noted.

P & F chartists who adhere to their strategy sold long positions at $31\frac{1}{2}$ to 32 and were out of the stock prior to the downmove. Further, once the stock turned down, we would expect support in the 20 area. The original buy signal occurred at 21 in December 1988 and eliminated the previous resistance level at 20.

Figure 6-5

USING PRICE FORECASTS CONSERVATIVELY

FIGURE 6 - 5A.

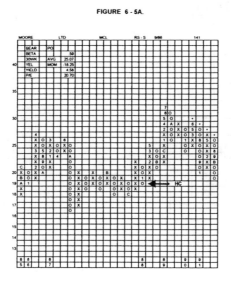

FIGURE 6 - 5B.

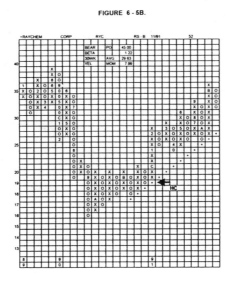

Figure 6-6

HORZONTAL COUNTS ON REVERSAL AND CONTINUATION PATTERNS

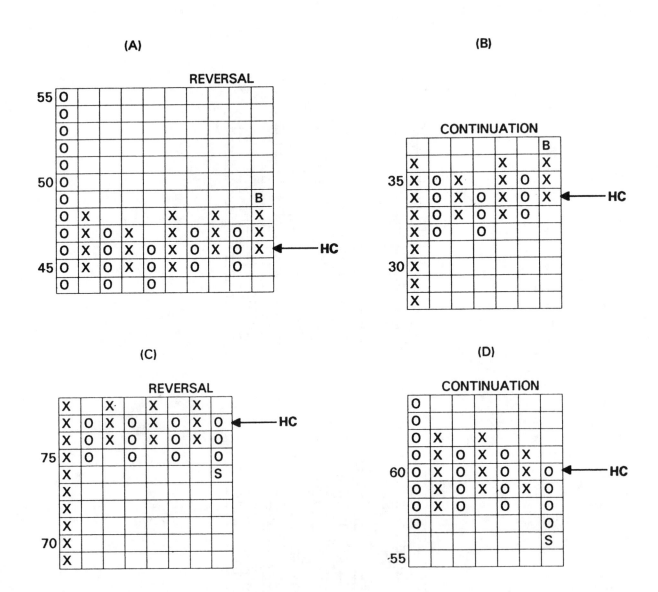

Raychem gives a buy signal at 21 in 1990. Counting across the formation from the first wall of O's to the buy signal column, there are eight squares. Multiplying 8 times the more conservative $\frac{1}{2}$ point reversal rule equals 12 which is added to the low point of 16 for a price objective of 28. Raychem hovered between 28 and 29 and then declined back to 24 over a two-month period. The stock did not go lower because the 24 recording approached the long-term bullish support line. In each illustration, the conservative use of the count accurately forecasted the move. In the case of Moore LTD, we were also spared the loss of all profits previously earned. Liberal use of price projections leads to distorted targets which in turn result in excessive optimism and potential timing errors.

Figure 6-6 lends some clarification to the literature. Most chartists believe that upside horizontal counts should begin with the wall of O's on the left. They further feel that downside horizontal counts must be calculated from the wall of X's on the left. However, most conventional literature fails to make our earlier distinction between reversal and continuation patterns. Such an oversight means that original ideas regarding the starting point for horizontal counts may need modification. We need to distinguish whether horizontal counts are calculated for reversal or continuation patterns.

In Figure 6-6(A), we have a stock in a decidedly bearish trend. However, the buy signal at 49 marks a reversal of the stock's trend. The horizontal count should be determined by counting across the 46 line. Chart 6-6(B) indicates a base pattern continuation of the current uptrend. The stock has paused or consolidated briefly and then resumed its upmove. The horizontal count is taken from the 34 line, but the starting point is the wall of X's on the left hand side. For upside price moves, horizontal counts begin with the wall of O's during reversal patterns (i.e., at junctures). However, continuation patterns start with a wall of X's, which marks the beginning of another upmove.

In 6-6(C), the downside horizontal count begins with the wall of X's on the left because the pattern reveals a juncture and impending price reversal. Counts may be gauged by examining the 76 and 77 lines. However, 6-6(D) discloses a stock in a bearish trend accentuated by another sell signal at 56. In this continuation pattern, the horizontal count starts from the wall of O's at the extreme left of the chart. The horizontal count may be calculated from either the 60 or 59 price lines. For downside moves, horizontal counts initiate with the wall of X's during reversal patterns (i.e. at junctures). However, continuation patterns begin with a wall of O's, which marks the start of another downmove.

THE VERTICAL COUNT

The vertical count provides an ultimate or final price estimate. Rather than an intermediate projection, the vertical count approximates a long-term price objective. Vertical counts are to

Figure 6-7

THE VERTICAL COUNT

(A)

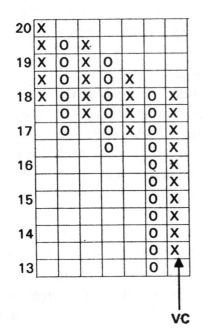

20	X						
	X	O	X.				
19	X	O	X	O			
	X	O	X	O	X		
18	X	O	X	O	X	O	X
		O	X	O	X	O	X
17		O			O	X	O	X
				O		O	X
16						Q	X
						O	X
15						O	X
						O	X
14						O	X
						O	X
13						O	↑

VC

PO = 10 Squares x 1 1/2 PT Chart in 1st Upmove
   = 15 + 13 (lowest O)
PO = 28 (ultimate price objective)

(B)

35	O			X
	O			X
	O			X
	O			X
	O			X
30	O			X
	O			X
	O			X
	O	X		X
	O	X	O	X
25	O	X	O	X
	O		O	↑

VC

PO = 11 Squares x 3 (Reversal Rule) in Breakout Leg
   = 34 + 24 (lowest O)
PO = 57 (final or ultimate price forecast)

Figure 6-8

THE DOWNSLIDE VERTICAL COUNT

(A)

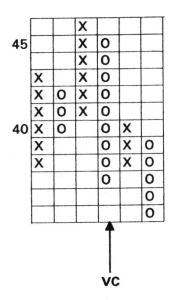

PO = 9 (Squares in 1st Downmove) x 3 (Reversal Rule)
   = 46 (highest X) - 27
PO = 19

(B)

PO = 10 (SQS in Breakout Leg) x 3 PT Chart
   = 77 (highest X) - 30
PO = 47

95

be calculated in one of two ways. First, count the number of squares in the breakout leg (i.e., the column with the buy or sell signal) and multiply that total by the appropriate reversal rule. Secondly, count the number of squares in the first upmove following the lowest O (or final bottom) and multiply by the reversal rule that applies to each individual chart. Figure 6-7 contains an illustration of each.

In 6-7(A) a final bottom appears at 13 and culminates the downtrend. There are 10 squares in the first upmove. The product of a 10 square vertical upmove multiplied by a reversal rule of $\frac{1}{2}$ equals 15 and a price objective of 28 (15 + 13, the lowest O). Until we reach Section 3, the projection of 28 should be regarded as the final, long-term price move for the stock. Once the move carries close to 28, investors should anticipate a change in the direction for the stock.

Whereas 6-7(A) concentrates on counting the number of vertical squares in the first upmove after the final bottom, Figure 6-7(B) focuses on counting the number of squares in the breakout leg. A double top pattern yields a buy signal at 28 and contains 11 squares in that column. Multiplying 11 x a reversal rule of 3 equals 33, which is added to the lowest 0 at 24. You should expect the stock price to reach 57 over the long-term.

Figure 6-8 illustrates the downside vertical count, which is determined in an opposite manner from its upside counterpart. We count the number of squares in the first downmove following the highest X or final top, or take the number of recordings in the breakout leg that includes the sell signal. The stock in Part A registers 9 squares in its first downmove. Multiplying 9 times 3 gives a product of 27, which is subtracted from the highest X at 46. The final downside price objective should fall in the 19 area. Part B illustrates a breakout leg containing 10 squares with a sell signal at 73. The product of 30 (10 squares in breakout leg x a reversal rule of 3 = 30) is subtracted from the highest X at 77 to give a downside price estimate of 47.

Figure 6-9 furnishes some actual examples of the vertical count. In Kaufman and Broad, the first upmove following the bottom is 8 squares which should be multiplied by a reversal rule of $\frac{1}{2}$. The resulting product of 12 is added to the lowest O to yield a target of 17 to $17\frac{1}{2}$. Kaufman and Broad reached 17 in June 1991 and immediately retraced to 10. By liquidating positions with a limit order near 17, you would be spared a 40%+ retracement in the stock. The Kaufman and Broad example confirms our earlier suggestion to use the count conservatively and consider selling slightly before price objectives are reached. Technicians at major brokerage firms wield inordinate amounts of influence, and their buy and sell recommendations give too many people the same advice simultaneously. Beat the crowd and ease out of positions without trying to sell at the exact target. We will discuss modified vertical counts in Section 2.

Figure 6-9

SOME ACTUAL EXAMPLES OF THE VERTICAL COUNT

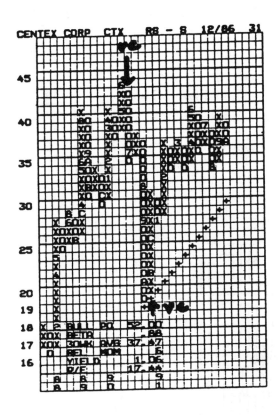

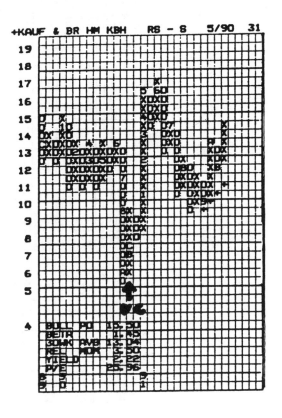

Figure 6-10

TAKING A VERTICAL COUNT ON CHANGING SCALES

(A)

25			
			X
24 O			X
23 O			X
20 O			X
O			X
19 O			X
O			X
18 O			X
O			B
17 O	X		X
O	X	O	X
16 O	X	O	X
O	X	O	
15 O			

↑
VC

PO = (Squares below 20) x 1 1/2
= 8 x 1 1/2 (Reversal Rule) = 12
+ (Squares 20 & above) x 3 +
4 x 3 = 12
PO = 12 + 12 + 15 (lowest O) + 15
PO = 39

(B)

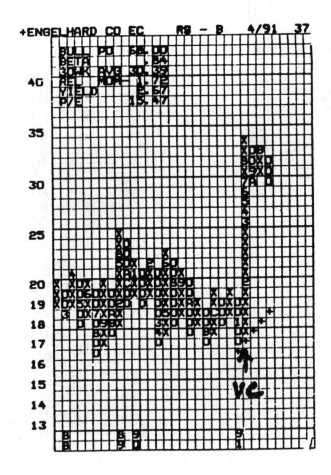

Figure 6-11

THE VERTICAL COUNT: A SYNTHESIS

FIGURE 6 - 11A.

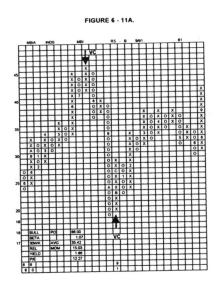

FIGURE 6 - 11B.

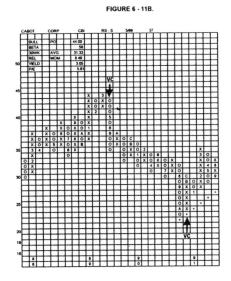

FIGURE 6 - 11C

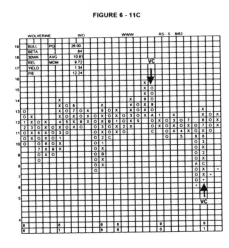

FIGURE 6 - 11D

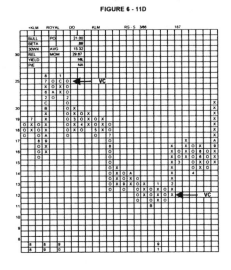

In Centex Corporation, let's examine two individual vertical counts. June 1990 marked a peak in the advance and the first downmove totaled 9 squares. By multiplying 9 squares x 3 (reversal rule), we arrive at a product of 27 to be subtracted from 44. Our downside price objective is 17. Notice that Centex bottoms at $19\frac{1}{2}$ in October 1990. The downside price estimate was accurate and allowed investors to accumulate shares in the bottom area. As in the case with selling, do not attempt to pick precise bottoms. It is better to pay a little more and own the stock earlier in the general vicinity of the bottom. Don't hope for "one more decline" to the exact price forecast and miss the entire buying opportunity. Bernard Baruch once said that, "Only fools and liars buy at exact bottoms and sell at precise tops."

The first upmove in Centex after the bottom totaled 12 squares. The product of 12 squares x a reversal rule of 3 is 36, which we add to $19\frac{1}{2}$. Our final, long-term price forecast falls in the 55 - $55\frac{1}{2}$ area. We realized the price objective in February 1992 when Centex hit 55 and immediately began to slide. Technicians utilizing P & F charts probably contributed to the decline with selling. A second issue on the Centex chart requires mentioning. The 40-41 area has proven to be a major point of resistance as indicated by the number of prior tops. As a chartist, our long-term objective was $55\frac{1}{2}$. However, an intermediate or shorter-term price objective would be the 40-41 area because it is a resistance level. Traders would possibly sell at 40, which we could consider as our initial target.

Figure 6-10 illustrates vertical price recordings on two different scales. The breakout leg includes 12 recordings, with eight below 20 and 4 at 20 or above. The 8 squares below 20 are multiplied by a reversal rule of $1\frac{1}{2}$ for a product of 12. The 4 squares above 20 should be multiplied by a reversal rule of 3 for a separate product of 12. Since the sum of the two different products equals 24, it is added to the lowest 0 at 15. The final price objective reaches 39 from the calculation adjusted for two different scales.

Figure 6-11 includes several examples which should integrate vertical count fundamentals. Two vertical counts appear on the MBIA chart, where the stock tops out at 45. The first downmove is 9 squares, which gives a product of 27 (9 sqs. x 3 reversal rule = 27). After subtracting 27 from 45, a downside forecast of 18 results. The lowest recording in the bottom falls in the $19\frac{1}{2}$ square. A first upmove registers an advance of 10 squares on the three-point chart. The product of 30 is added to $19\frac{1}{2}$ to suggest a price objective at $49\frac{1}{2}$ (i.e., the 49 - 50 area). However, you may wish to consider a resistance level in the 44 - 45 area as indicated by previous tops at 44 and 45. For those who are not greedy, a reduced target of the mid-40's seems appropriate. Those holding for maximum gains should not gamble on prices beyond 49 to 50.

The KLM Royal Dutch chart contains 9 squares in its breakout leg with the buy signal achieved in February 1991 at $13\frac{1}{2}$. A stronger buy signal at 15 confirms the uptrend and gives chartists more conviction concerning an upside price reversal because all near-term tops are penetrated. A product of $13\frac{1}{2}$(9 sqs. X$1\frac{1}{2}$ reversal rule = $13\frac{1}{2}$) plus 11 (the lowest O) totals $24\frac{1}{2}$ for a final price expectation. Previous tops occur at 19, $19\frac{1}{2}$, and 20 and suggest that KLM will encounter overhead supply or resistance in the 19 - 20 area. A shorter-term target would appear to be around 20, with long-term prognostications in the mid-20's.

The MBIA and KLM examples illustrate when the two vertical count rules should be implemented to obtain price objectives. In the MBIA chart, the stock experiences an uninterrupted price slide as evidenced by a string of O recordings. We will refer to these long, consecutive price moves in either direction as **"upside or downside spikes"** which reflect speculative excessives. They will be treated in more depth in Section 2 of the book.

However, large spikes typically precede a rather sharp counter price move up or down. These so-called "bounces" provide a means of correcting excessive speculation from extreme optimism or pessimism. In the case of charts with spikes, the vertical count can usually be gauged by measuring the extent of the first up or downmove following the bottom or top. Conversely, KLM shows a basing formation which succeeds a downmove in price. With base patterns, the first significant upmove typically occurs with the breakout leg. Vertical counts are taken from base patterns by counting the number of recordings in the column with the buy or sell signal.

Using the Downside Vertical Count Conservatively

The rationale underlying the vertical count stems from the thesis that major bull and bear market movements occur during the course of three approximately equal up or downmoves known as "legs." Therefore, multiplying the number of price recordings in either the first major up or downmove or the breakout leg by a reversal rule using three should approximate the entire 3-leg bull or bear market move.

However, investors function in a market environment where prices have displayed an upward bias for the long term. Persistently higher price trends over time suggest that multiplying by three may overstate downside price objectives. Pessimistic forecasts can pose a problem because many downside price moves assume the form of a sharp correction rather than a full-fledged bear market decline. To accommodate the problem of unrealistically low price objectives, Chartcraft suggests taking downside vertical counts by multiplying times 2.[1] However, a twofold approach to downside vertical counts may be more appropriate. First, multiply the number of squares in the downmove by 2 initially to obtain a preliminary target. Secondly, however, if the downmove exceeds the first estimate, a second vertical count should be determined with a full 3-square reversal rule multiplication process. To illustrate, let's examine Cabot Corporation.

Cabot completes a top at 45 and the breakout leg shows 10 squares. The vertical count may be conservatively calculated by multiplying 10 x 2 = 20, which is subtracted from 45. The downside price objective suggests a low of 25, and the stock actually bottoms at 23. A full downside vertical count would have estimated $15, which would have been used had the stock price continued to decline. By using a fraction equal to $\frac{2}{3}$ of the normal reversal rule, we have essentially made allowances for both a deep price correction and a less severe bear market. An upside vertical count may be run for Cabot on the first upmove following the bottom at 23. A column of 7 squares multiplied by 3 equals 21, which must be added to 23 to give us an estimate of 44. The 44 estimate seems logical because strong resistance appears at 45. Cabot will probably at best consolidate in the mid-40s before another advance. Use charts conservatively at every opportunity.

The process of using $\frac{2}{3}$ of the normal multiplication rule may also be applied to lower priced issues. Wolverine reaches a top at $15\frac{1}{2}$, and a 9-square downmove follows. Recordings between $5 and $20 dictate a $\frac{1}{2}$ point chart. However, $\frac{2}{3}$ of $\frac{1}{2}$ points equals 1 point. If we multiply 9 x 1, the product of 9 can be subtracted from $15\frac{1}{2}$ to give a target of $6\frac{1}{2}$, the exact spot the decline was terminated. Another vertical count can be determined from the next upmove. The 13-square initial upmove also serves as the breakout leg in the Wolverine example. By multiplying 13 times $\frac{1}{2}$, we get a product of $19\frac{1}{2}$ added to $6\frac{1}{2}$ for an upside estimate of 26.

Conventional wisdom for estimating price objectives has been explored. We are ready to redirect our efforts to Section 2, which seeks to improve P & F charting. New patterns and formations, additional trendlines, new price objectives, relative strength, and technical indicators will be introduced.

SUMMARY

Most experienced professionals maintain that knowing when to sell is more difficult than understanding when to buy. A principal advantage afforded by P & F charts centers on gauging the extent of future price moves. The two primary techniques to forecast price moves are the horizontal count and the vertical count. The horizontal count furnishes an intermediate-term price objective, while vertical counts provide a final or more permanent target. All forecasting techniques should be used conservatively in arriving at price estimates.

ENDNOTES

[1]A. W. Cohen, <u>How to Use the Three-Point Reversal Method of Point and Figure Stock Market Trading</u>, 9th ed. (New Rochelle, NY: Chartcraft, Inc., 1987), 60.

Figure 6-12

THE VERTICAL COUNT: A SYNTHESIS

FIGURE 6 - 12A.

FIGURE 6 - 12B.

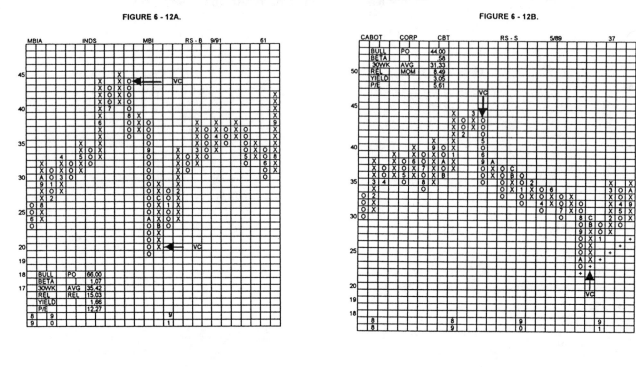

FIGURE 6 - 12C.

FIGURE 6 - 12D.

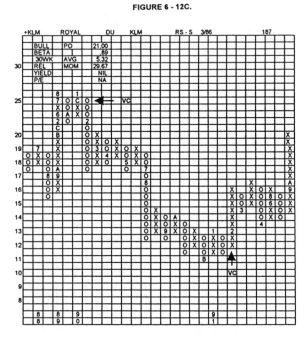

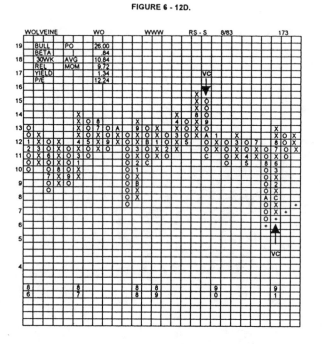

104

SECTION 2
SOME CONTEMPORARY VIEWPOINTS ON P & F CHARTS

Section I includes the conventional thoughts relating to P & F charting. However, technical analysis remains a relatively undeveloped discipline in need of continual change. P & F charting is certainly no exception.

Section 2 explores new techniques relating to trendlines, price objectives, and relative strength, among others. An objective of this section is to focus more on traders and shorter-term investment strategies. Another thrust of this section centers on profit preservation. By giving chartists earlier sell signals, profits may be enhanced from quicker liquidations. Returns may also be improved from buying sooner at lower price levels. Coverage in Section 2 offsets many existing criticisms concerning Chartcraft's 3-square reversal method of P & F charting.

CHAPTER 7

P & F CHART PATTERNS REVISITED

Investment tools become less effective when they are generally recognized. When a majority becomes familiar with certain approaches, successful investors abandon these ideas for surrogate techniques. Investors cannot afford the luxury of commonplace thoughts and approaches. Refreshing, innovative methods of analysis must be introduced on a continuing basis.

Point and Figure charting falls into the category of a generally accepted discipline in need of change. Formerly reliable techniques may now result in abysmal failures. Trustworthy patterns must be renovated to ensure success. Let's examine some new and/or modified chart patterns.

SOME NEW PATTERNS

Earl Blumenthal[1] introduced the **high pole formation** to P & F chart analysis. By definition, a high pole forms on an upside breakout when a column of X's exceeds one or more previous tops by at least three squares. The following column of O's then retraces more than 50% of the advance in the breakout column. This relationship is called a pole formation. Graphically speaking, the stock moves quickly higher and reaches a price level with no other near-term recordings. The last column of X's stands uniquely tall as if it were a pole.

Although the high pole formation may be overlooked, its proper recognition is essential. If a high pole pattern occurs during strong bull markets, it suggests near-term weakness and a possible correction in the individual stock. However, a high pole formation during bear markets usually warns of a "topping process" in the stock.

Figure 7-1 provides several illustrations of high pole formations. One of the key criteria concerns the correction of more than 50% of the previous advance. Stocks with strong upside momentum ordinarily enjoy brief interruptions or small setbacks. When price declines begin retracing more than one-half of a prior advance, technical deterioration may be in the formative stages. When a stock advances above previous resistance levels and then retraces most of the gains, suspicions of introductory technical weakness are spawned.

Figure 7-1

BLUMENTHAL'S HIGH POLE FORMATION

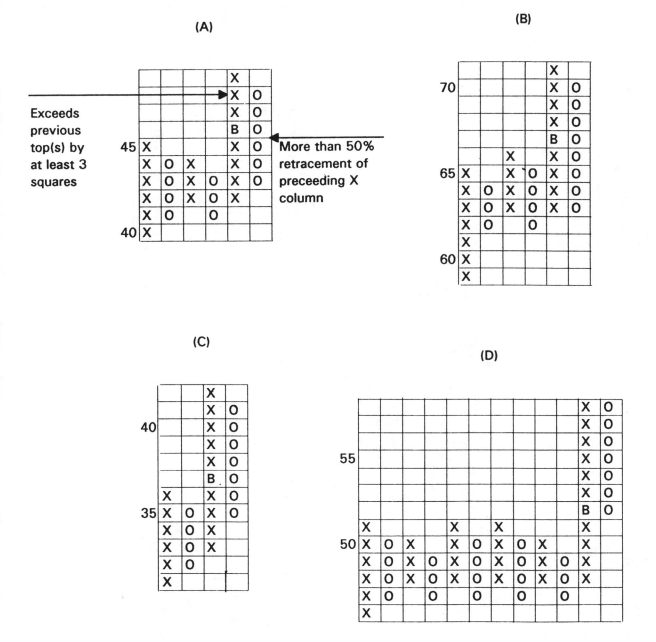

Figure 7-2

ACTUAL ILLUSTRATIONS OF THE HIGH POLE

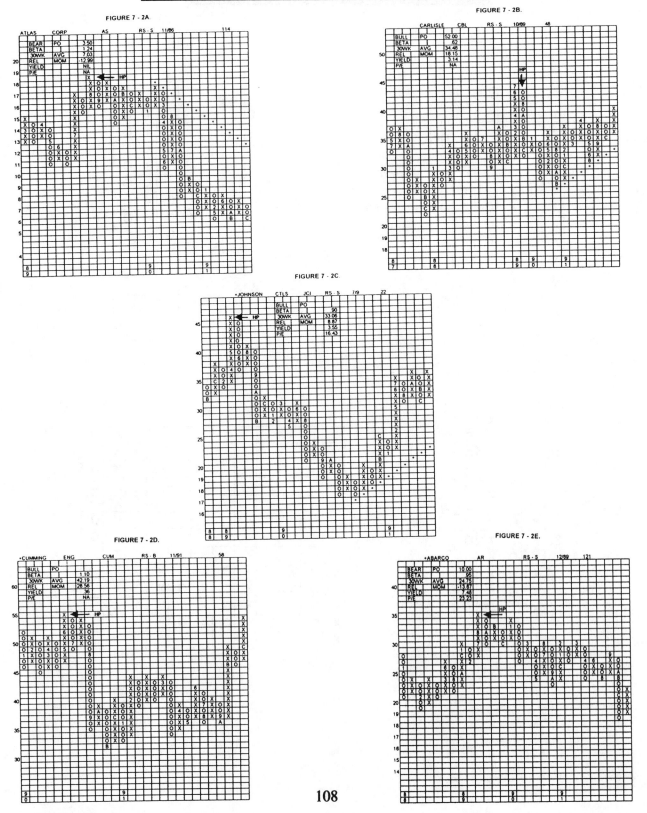

FIGURE 7 - 2A.

FIGURE 7 - 2B.

FIGURE 7 - 2C.

FIGURE 7 - 2D.

FIGURE 7 - 2E.

Figure 7-2 illustrates varying degrees of technical deterioration in different stocks with high poles (HP). In Atlas and Asarco, declines tended to be more gradual once the formation was complete. However, Cummins Engine, Carlisle, and Johnson Controls suffered precipitous drops. As a general rule, the more elongated the pole formation, the more volatile the downside price reversal.

A cursory comparison of Atlas Corporation and Carlisle supports such a generalization. Similarly, Asarco versus Johnson Controls provides another illustration. Charts with smaller, subtle high poles tend to yield more gradual downmoves.

In each illustration, the 50%+ retracement gives the pattern a "churning" or "toppy" appearance and indicates shares of stock are changing hands rapidly. By its very nature, the high pole formation indicates a "tired" or overbought stock which needs time before another price advance. Whether high poles result from penetrating one or multiple tops, the technical significance and downside implications remain the same.

However, there is one distinction that should be made between high pole formations. When high poles occur after extended upmoves in price, they tend to be more distributional in nature and lead to larger downside price moves. However, high poles that occur early in an uptrend or in breakouts from large base patterns imply small downside corrections. In effect, high poles are more bearish when they follow large price advances. High poles are less bearish early in the advance and/or on breakouts from large base formations.

The high pole formation affords a distinct timing advantage which rebuffs a criticism of the P&F discipline. Critics maintain that sell signs are received late. With the high pole, however, chartists need not wait for the penetration of one or more previous bottoms to implement strategies. Once the 50%+ retracement occurs, short sales, purchases of puts, and sales of long positions can take place. P&F chartists may make strategy decisions comfortably before a sell signal is realized.

Michael Burke[2] followed Blumenthal's lead and sought to use **low pole formations** to identify stocks under accumulation. According to Burke, a low pole forms on a downside breakout when a column of O's exceeds one or more previous bottoms by at least three squares. The following column of X's then retraces more than 50% of the decline in the breakout column. The retracement feature provides early evidence of strength in the stock for speculators who engage in "bottom fishing." The 50%+ retracement usually warns of an oversold stock in the bottoming phase of downmove. Figure 7-3 shows how low pole formations form.

Figure 7-3

BURKE'S LOW POLE FORMATION

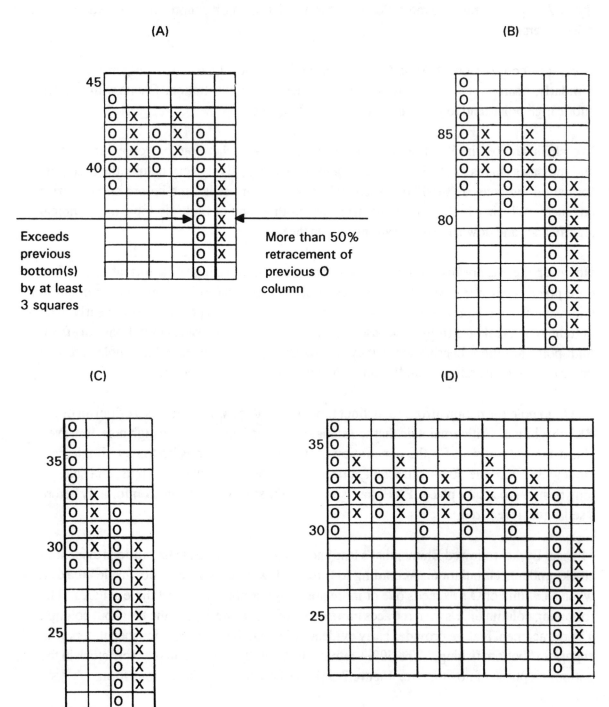

(A)

Exceeds previous bottom(s) by at least 3 squares

More than 50% retracement of previous O column

(B)

(C)

(D)

Figure 7-4

ACTUAL ILLUSTRATIONS OF THE LOW POLE

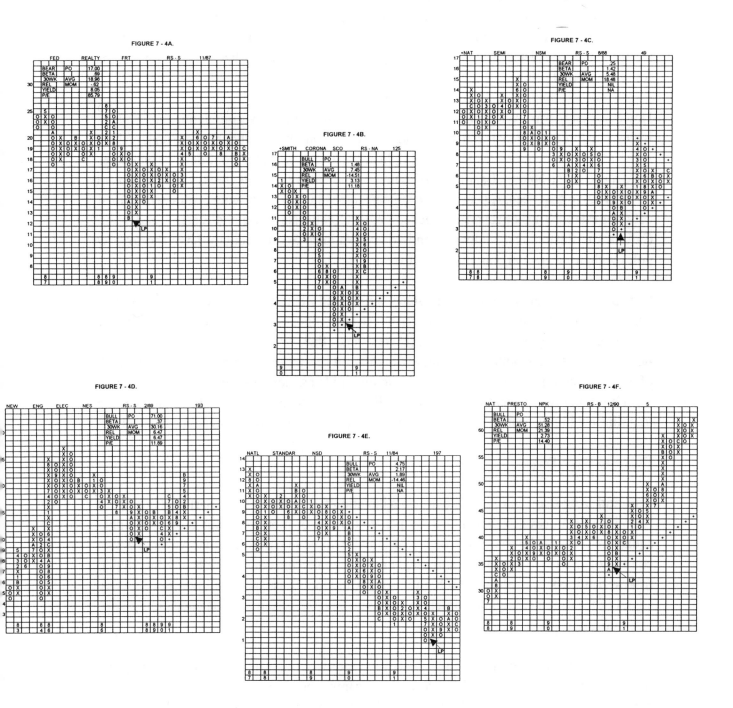

FIGURE 7 - 4A.

FIGURE 7 - 4B.

FIGURE 7 - 4C.

FIGURE 7 - 4D.

FIGURE 7 - 4E.

FIGURE 7 - 4F.

A low pole formation in a stock during bull markets should be considered bullish. You may expect a stronger price move in the stock. However, low poles developing in bear markets may signal a correction.

Figure 7-4 reveals some actual illustrations of low pole formation. Although low poles do not pinpoint the precise timing for an upmove, they generally indicate the worst of the slide is over. A timing advantage emerges because chartists may buy stocks or calls once the 50%+ retracement is completed. Don't wait for buy signals. Scalpers may utilize low pole formations for several point gains.

However, long-term investors may also gain a timing advantage by accumulating undervalued issues with low poles at market bottoms and during rising markets. Although these undervalued issues may not undergo a marked advance right away, investors can feel confident the purchases were made near a bottom. Examples in Figure 7-4 indicate varying degrees of acceleration in the respective advances. A general rule appears to be that low poles with protracted vertical columns establish upside reversals quicker. Federal Realty, New England Electric, and Smith Carona are illustrations. National Standard and National Semiconductor have shorter low poles with more gradual bottoming processes.

High pole formations should be particularly scrutinized when stocks attempt to change from bearish to bullish by penetrating the bearish resistance line. Figure 7-5 shows Blumenthal's high pole formation occurring at the bearish resistance line. According to Blumenthal, **a high pole at the bearish resistance or major downtrend line** represents one of the most bearish of all chart patterns.[3] The breakout from the high pole cannot be sustained, and weakness from a sizable retracement counters the bullish implications. High pole formations at the trendline are highly bearish because they describe a stock's inability to sustain a reversal.

Bull and Bear Traps

Bull and bear traps in Figure 7-6 are an adaptation from vertical bar chart analysis.[4] Bull traps include an advance which usually penetrates two or more previous tops by a single square and deludes investors into believing a major upmove will follow. However, the next column of O's reverses quickly and yields a sell signal. This combination of a buy signal followed quickly by a sell signal is highly bearish and fools unsuspecting investors. The buy signal exhausts remaining limit orders (purchases), and the sell signal fills outstanding stop-loss orders.

Bear traps contain a decline which ordinarily exceeds two or more previous bottoms by one square and convinces investors that a downmove is imminent. The next column of X's reverses quickly, however, and furnishes a buy signal. The combination of a sell signal followed by an

Figure 7-5

HIGH POLE AT THE BEARISH RESISTANCE LINE

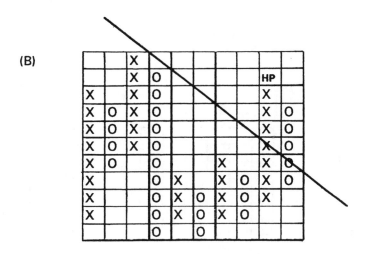

Figure 7-6

BULL AND BEAR TRAPS: AN ADAPTION FROM VERTICAL BEAR CHARTS

Bull Traps

(A)

```
            B
      X     X  O
 X    X  O  X  O
 X O  X  O  X  O
40 X O X  O     O
 X O           S
 X
```

(B)

```
            B
 X    X     X  O
 X O  X  O  X  O
55 X O X  O  X  O
 X O     O     O
 X             S
               O
```

(C)

```
            B
 X          X  O
 X O  X     X  O
70 X O X  O  X  O
 X O  X  O  X  O
 X O     O     O
 X             S
```

Bear Traps

(A)

```
 O
 O                B
 O  X             X
 O  X  O  X       X
 O  X  O  X  O    X
25 O    O  X  O    X
       O     O    X
                S
```

(B)

```
 O
 O                B
 O  X     X       X
 O  X  O  X  O    X
30 O X  O  X  O    X
 O    O     O    X
                S
```

(C)

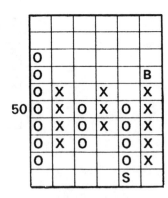

```
 O
 O                B
 O  X     X       X
50 O X  O  X  O    X
 O  X  O  X  O    X
 O  X  O     O    X
 O          O    X
                S
```

114

Figure 7-7

SOME ACTUAL BULL TRAP PATTERNS

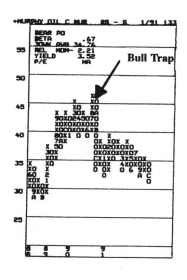

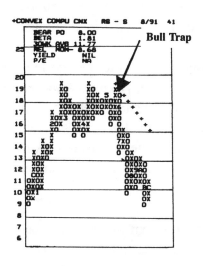

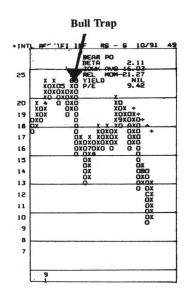

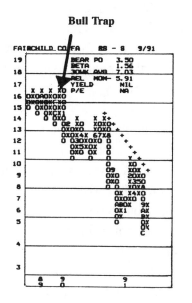

115

immediate buy signal has strong bullish implications and confuses investors. The sell signal leads to the execution of protective stops, while the buy signal fuels limit purchase orders from chartists anticipating an upside breakout.

An interesting facet of both trap patterns is the subtlety with which they occur. Figure 7-7 illustrates the potential devastation from bull trap patterns.

Bull traps may lead to both corrections and major downmoves. Despite the innocence of their appearance, you must always be conscious of trap patterns to escape vulnerability and to improve timing in investment decisions. Bull traps may complete distributional periods by providing the final downside breakout. The Murphy Oil and International Rectifier chart patterns show these stocks breaking out of a base to apparent new highs for the moves. Without warning, the succeeding column of O's gives a sell signal by penetrating several previous bottoms.

Downmoves from bull traps may be less volatile than those from some high pole formations. However, a greater sense of permanence or finality seems to be linked to bull traps. For example, let's refer again to Murphy Oil. A sell signal appears at 39 from a breach of multiple bottoms, and the chart warns that old support becomes new resistance. The 39 - 40 area represents potential selling or overhead supply. Murphy makes several unsuccessful attempts to move above 39 - 40, and the stock begins to decline. Bull traps disclose an important concept of charting. The further along a stock moves in a bull market, breakouts become less trustworthy. Further, chartists who calculate additional price objectives must use forecasts more conservatively.

Another bull trap illustration appears with USX in Figure 7-8. Two basic principles should be recognized. First, the 35 - 40 area indicates a resistance zone which has held for the last 10 to 11 years. USX reverses with the peak of the bull trap appearing at 39 in October 1989, as the stock enters the resistance area or overhead supply. Bull traps tend to form in resistance zones. Secondly, bull traps are more likely to form after stocks undergo an appreciable advance and/or when they approach all-time highs. After the subtle occurrence of the bull trap at an 11-year high, USX drops to the mid-twenties where well-documented levels of support exist. Interestingly enough, the last seven columns of the chart indicate a bearish signal reversed formation. The correction enters its final stages in the heart of past support zones.

Figure 7-9 confirms the value of bear trap formations in timing purchases. Before we examine individual patterns, two points should be emphasized. Bear traps form as stocks approach all-time lows or the end of a downmove. In addition, bear traps develop in areas of well-defined support where buying appears likely. Downside breakouts are less dependable as the stock

Figure 7-8

ANOTHER BULL TRAP

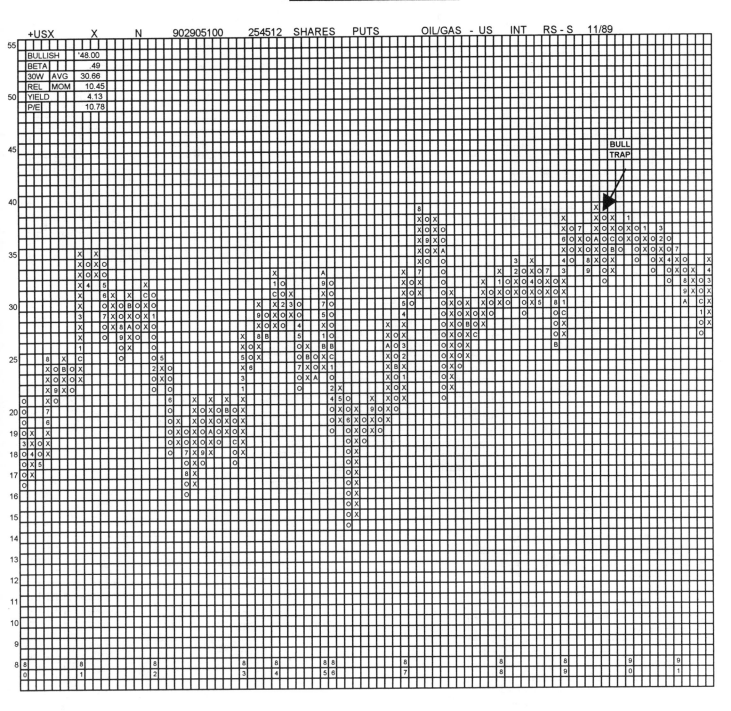

Figure 7-9

ILLUSTRATIONS OF BEAR TRAPS

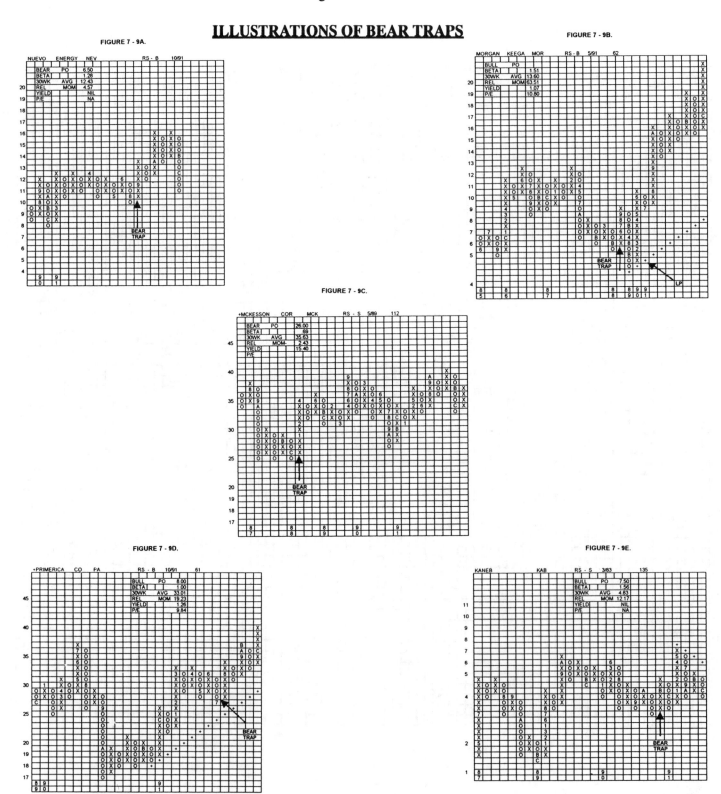

FIGURE 7 - 9A.

FIGURE 7 - 9B.

FIGURE 7 - 9C.

FIGURE 7 - 9D.

FIGURE 7 - 9E.

moves further down a bear market decline. Thus bear traps may be depicted not only as subtle reversals but patterns which can generate explosive upside price moves.

Morgan Keegan enters a support near $5 in the 1989-1991 period. A third column of O's penetrates two previous bottoms and a buy signal results from the next column of X's. An unusual development corroborates the bottoming process. A low pole pattern follows and unveils the final panic selling prior to a huge bull market advance signaled initially by the bear trap formation. A bear trap also forms nicely in McKesson in November-December1987, and a major uptrend emerges. In October 1990, a correction in McKesson concludes with a low pole formation that sets the stage for another advance. Bear traps formed in well-established support areas for Kaneb and Primerica and advise the next move will be to the upside. Bear traps developing in proven bottom areas can be highly profitable.

Spikes

Upside and downside spikes are lengthy, vertical price advances or declines with no interruption. The basis of spike formations is that speculation reaches a point of excess. Once price moves become extreme in either direction, the probability exists for a correction. In other words, expect a retracement of this extended price movement. Speculative excesses cannot be sustained and price reversals result. Rules of thumb have evolved over the years to generate trading ideas for spike formations. For example, Blumenthal warned investors to be careful once uninterrupted advances approximated 20 squares. Burke proposes that continuous upmoves will carry 17 to 20 squares before speculative excesses are corrected. However, Burke and Blumenthal agreed that long, unbroken price declines occupying a similar number of squares were a "long tail" down and had bullish implications. Perhaps a broader theorem may be advanced when continuous downside price moves of 15 to 25 squares appear on a stock's P & F chart. The decline may constitute a selling climax if two conditions are met. First, the general market must be deeply oversold and set for a rally. Secondly, the individual stock has been in a downtrend and ready for a reversal. If these two criteria are satisfied, climactic selling has concluded and set the stage for a solid price advance. The downside spike has bullish overtones, so chartists can begin purchases.

The upside spike of 15 to 25 squares must also be evaluated on the basis of the aggregate market and the trend of the individual stock. If a stock has been in an long-term uptrend and the general market appears overbought, the initial decline following the upside spike may trigger a bear market. However, if both the individual stock and general market are in the relatively early stages of an advance, the first recording of O's following an upside spike probably suggests a correction. Figure 7-10 illustrates the downside spike pattern. In Figure 7-11, the charts of both King World and IBM reveal downside spikes which represent selling

Figure 7-10

THE DOWNSIDE SPIKE

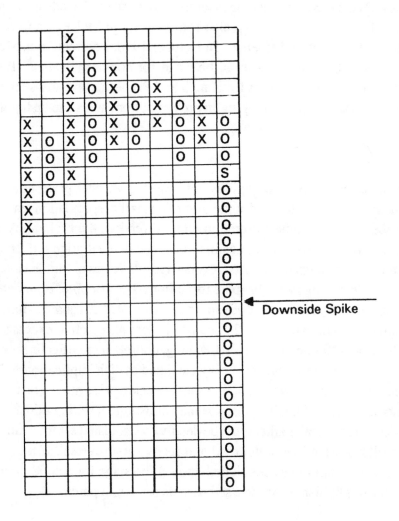

Downside Spike

120

Figure 7-11

ILLUSTRATING THE DOWNSIDE SPIKE

FIGURE 7 - 11A.

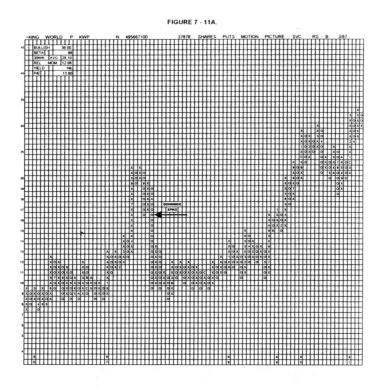

FIGURE 7 - 11B.

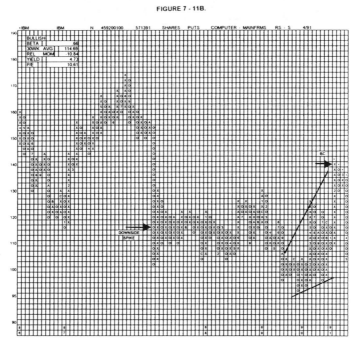

Figure 7-12

THE UPSIDE SPIKE

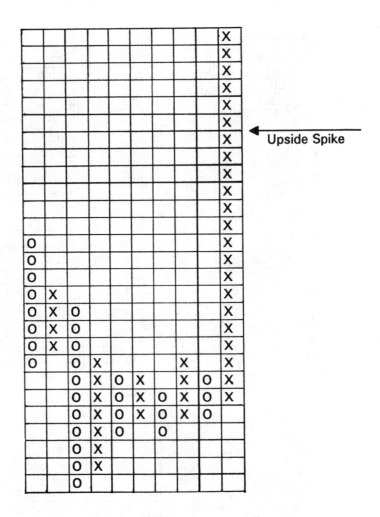

Upside Spike

Figure 7-13

SOME UPSIDE SPIKES

FIGURE 7 - 13A.

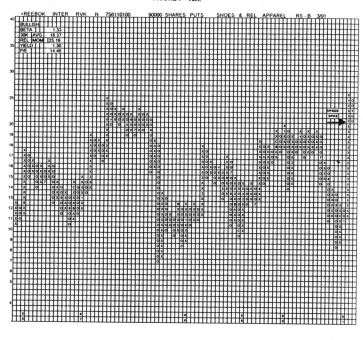

FIGURE 7 - 13B.

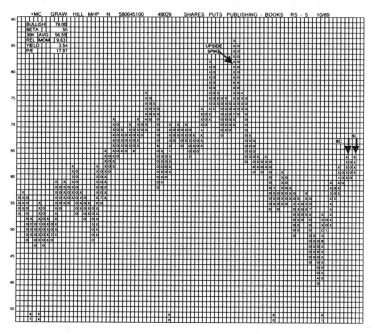

climaxes. The "long tail down" created the base pattern by forming the "wall of O's" on the left.

Figure 7-12 provides an example of the upside spike formation with the long, unbroken column of X recordings. Charts for Reebok and McGraw Hill appear in Figure 7-13 and evoke two contrasting patterns. In the case of Reebok the stock shows a sharp decline in 1987, followed by a rally attempt which fizzles in the 20 area.

The old support from 1987 became the new resistance level in 1989 and 1990. However, an upside spike pattern took place in January 1991 and became the first "leg up" in the bull market. The general market's uptrend was also in its embryonic stages. When a stock undergoes an early advance in conjunction with a young market, sophisticated conjecture tells us the pullback should amount to little more than a routine correction. Since a breakout occurred at 21, a pullback would logically dip to the 17-20 area because old resistance becomes new support.

McGraw Hill advances steadily from 1987 through most of 1989 and essentially doubles in price. A high pole formation results from an upside spike at the end of the move followed immediately by a large retracement. Since the market was not unusually strong, we would suspect a larger downside move. An extended stock price accompanied by a deteriorating general market portends of price weakness. McGraw Hill confirmed these suspicions.

Charts in Figure 7-14 reinforce the basic principles of spikes. Like most issues, McDonnell Douglas encountered some difficulties during the September-October 1987 period. A downside spike helped the stock lose one-half of its value. However, an upside spike formed a low pole formation and warned the stock had bottomed. McDonnell Douglas exhibits three distinct upside spikes, each of which represents a "leg" in the bull market. Weakness appears toward the end of the third leg when the stock seems overbought and the general market tired. Nashua Corporation provides classic examples of upside spikes forming the first two legs in a bull market. The stock undergoes a healthy consolidation or correction at the end of each spike.

Triple Bottom and Top Reversals

Figure 7- 15 indicates a modification of the bear trap called the **triple bottom failure**. Chartcraft, Inc. developed this formation and refers to it as a bear trap. However, we treated the bear trap somewhat earlier in the chapter with a different approach. For our purposes, the triple bottom failure (TBF) signal is a modified triple bottom formation with the sell signal immediately followed by a three-square reversal to the upside. Although a buy signal may or may not result, doubts are cast concerning the validity of the popular triple bottom pattern.

Figure 7-14

SPECULATIVE EXCESSES

FIGURE 7 - 14A.

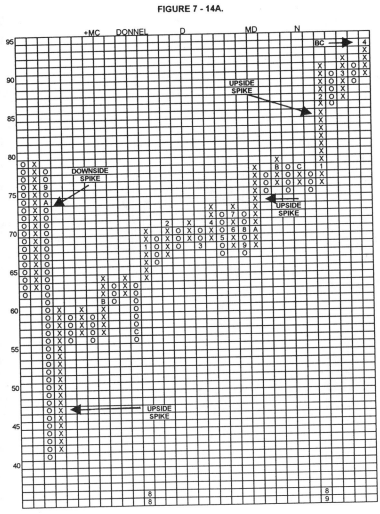

FIGURE 7 - 14B.

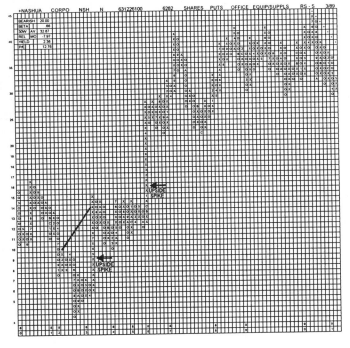

Figure 7-15

CHARTCRAFT'S TRIPLE BOTTOM FAILURE SIGNAL

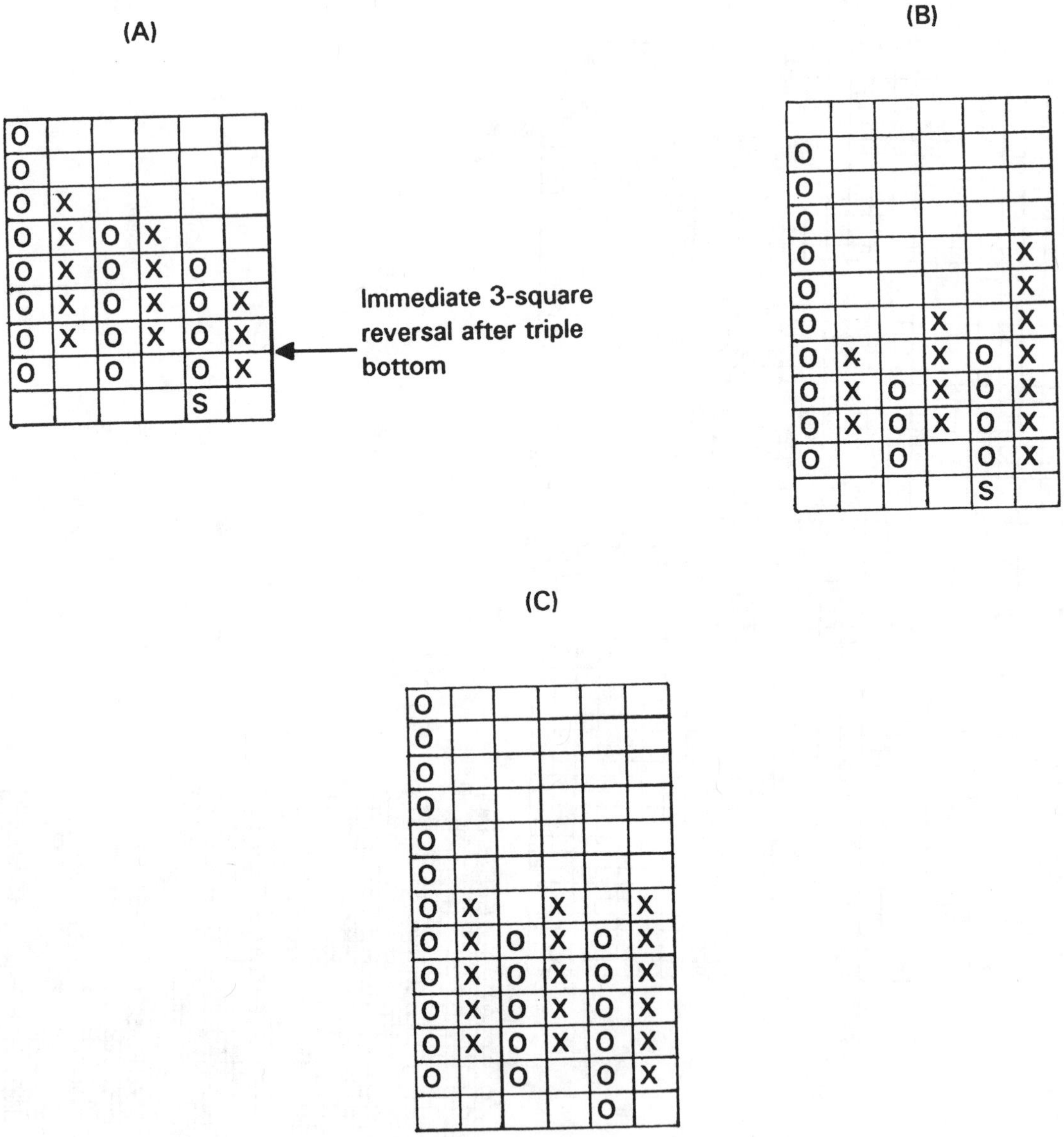

(A)

Immediate 3-square reversal after triple bottom

(B)

(C)

Figure 7-16

TRIPLE BOTTOM FAILURE EXAMPLES

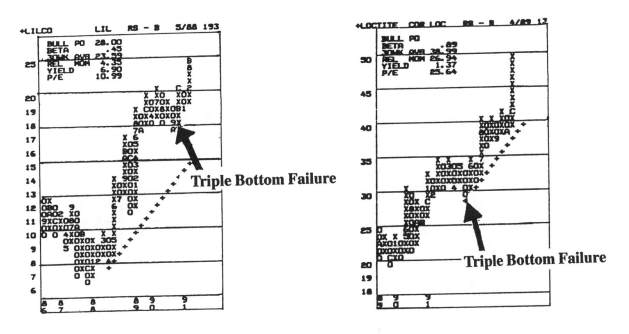

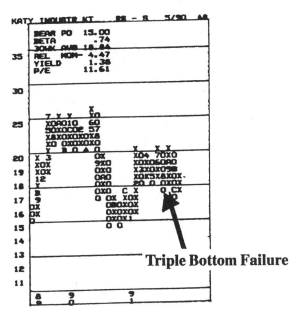

Figure 7-17

CHARTCRAFT'S TRIPLE TOP FAILURE SIGNAL

(A)

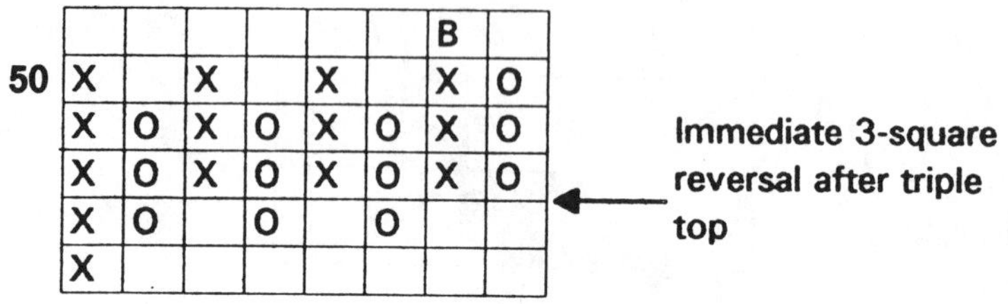

				B	
50	X		X		X		X	O
	X	O	X	O	X	O	X	O
	X	O	X	O	X	O	X	O
	X	O		O		O		
	X							

← Immediate 3-square reversal after triple top

(B)

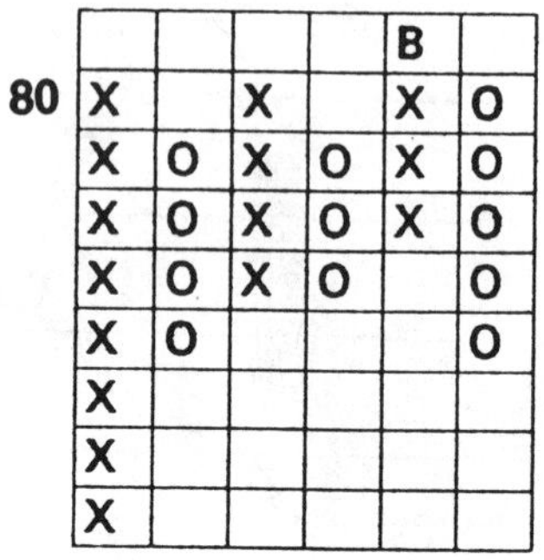

				B	
80	X		X		X	O
	X	O	X	O	X	O
	X	O	X	O	X	O
	X	O	X	O		O
	X	O				O
	X					
	X					
	X					

(C)

				B	
40	X		X		X	O
	X	O	X	O	X	O
	X	O	X	O	X	O
	X	O	X	O		O
	X	O				O
	X					
	X					
	X					
	X					

128

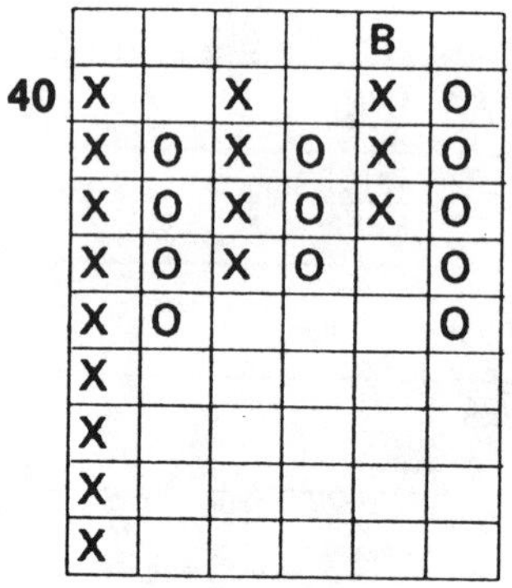

Figure 7-18

TRIPLE TOP FAILURE EXAMPLES

FIGURE 7 - 18A.

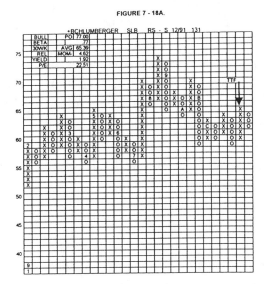

FIGURE 7 - 18B.

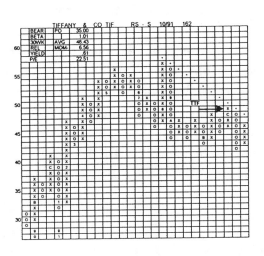

FIGURE 7 - 18C.

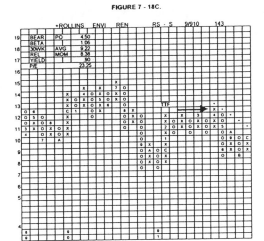

FIGURE 7 - 18D.

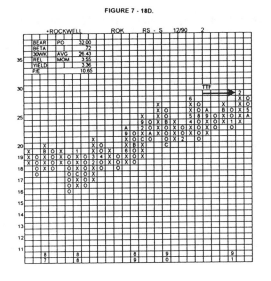

This TBF pattern cogently implies that the quick reversal offsets the sell signal and makes the intensity of the downmove questionable.

Figure 7-16 contains three examples of sell signals from the conventional triple bottom pattern. After the breakout exceeds previous bottoms by one square, a quick reversal of at least three squares materializes. Triple bottom failure patterns cryptically signal the end of either a major downmove or a correction, although the reversal may require some time to complete.

Figure 7-17 illustrates the **triple top failure signal** (TTF), which is a derivative of the basic triple top formation. Chartcraft, Inc. developed this formation and terms it a bear trap. However, our bear trap formation coverage differs and appeared earlier in the chapter. A buy signal exceeds previous tops by one square and precedes an immediate pullback of at least 3 squares. The pullback cancels the buy signal and makes investors wary of the conviction behind the expected upside move. Figure 7-18 presents several variations of triple top failures. Price reversals develop subtlety and give little or no warning.

SUMMARY

Technical analysis must constantly be refurbished by new techniques. Without fresh ideas, investors become complacent and too comfortable with the generally accepted. Success appears to be reserved for the creative minority with stout hearts and bold, new approaches.

Chapter 7 recognizes the need for change in P & F charting. Current thoughts are introduced on such configurations as high poles, low poles, spikes, traps, and triple top and bottom failures. These patterns are designed to combat criticism of P & F charts. Such advanced formations provide timing advantages to investors and counteract charges of late signals or warnings. Perhaps the most visible characteristics of the new patterns are their subtlety in developing, their innocuous appearance, and their interrelationship with the general market in-determining the extent of price moves.

ENDNOTES

[1] Earl Blumenthal, <u>Chart For Profit Point and Figure Trading</u> (Larchmont, New York: Investors Intelligence, 1975), 43.

[2] Michael L. Burke, <u>Three-Point Reversal Method of Point & Figure Construction and Formations</u> (New Rochelle, New York: Chartcraft, Inc., 1990), 70-71.

[3] Earl Blumenthal, <u>Chart For Profit Point and Figure Trading</u> (Larchmont, New York: Investors Intelligence, 1975), 43.

[4] William L. Jiler, <u>How Charts Can Help You In the Stock Market</u> (New York: Trendline Corporation, 1965).

CHAPTER 8

CHART PATTERNS: THE FINISHING TOUCHES

A foundation for expanding P & F charting was established in Chapter 7. Additional patterns are introduced in Chapter 8 with an emphasis on deceptively developing configurations. A common failure of technical analysis lies in investors becoming comfortable with the obvious because that requires less effort. However, resourcefulness epitomizes continued market success. Let's expand P&F analysis by evaluating some new ideas on chart analysis.

RECURRING HIGH POLES

In the preceding chapter, we established that a high pole formation usually signaled lower prices for individual stocks. If one high pole has negative implications, a series of these formations probably is more bearish. The Hughes Chart in Figure 8-1 provides an insightful starting point. The stock makes three unsuccessful attempts to move above overhead supply (resistance) in the low 20's. In each case, the rally failed with a high pole formation (HP on the graph). Three high pole formations lead to a major downmove in 1990.

The Lotus Development chart divulges three high poles in quick succession as the stock declines from 38 to 15. Recurring high poles are distributional in nature and warn traders to sell holdings. When a stock rallies followed by 50%+ retracements, large amounts of stock usually change hands. Informed traders dispose of their shares by selling to credulous members of the uninformed public.

We may take the Lotus example one step further. When charts have patterns of large price runups followed in the next column by declines which retrace more than one-half of the gain, distribution normally takes place. In other words, price runups may not have to form high pole formations in the purest definitional sense to indicate market weakness. However, recurring high pole formations provide the strongest evidence of a distributional climate. This pattern of large price advances followed by significant retracement typically occurs near the end of an extended upmove.

Figure 8-1

RECURRING HIGH POLES SIGNAL DISTRIBUTION

FIGURE 8 - 1A.

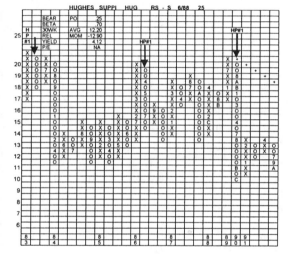

FIGURE 8 - 1B.

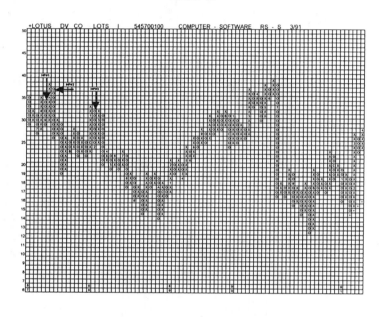

Figure 8-2

TECHNICAL DETERIORATION FROM REPEATED
HIGH POLE FORMATIONS

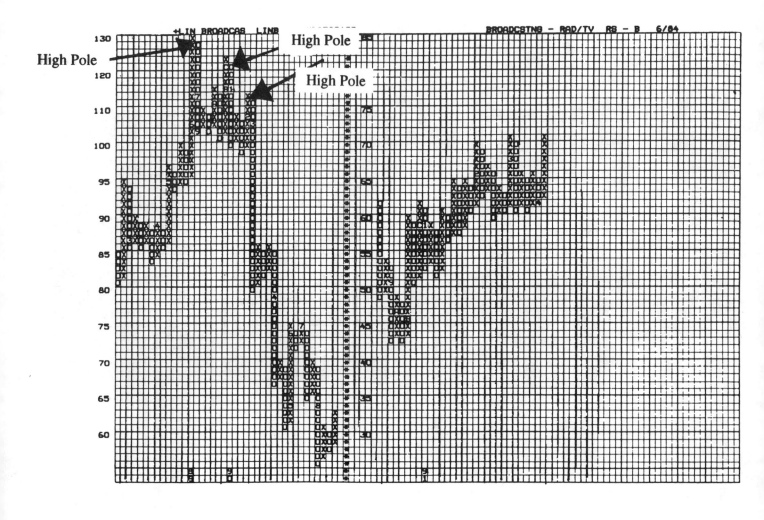

Figure 8-3

A SERIES OF LOW POLES SIGNALS ACCUMULATION

FIGURE 8 - 3A.

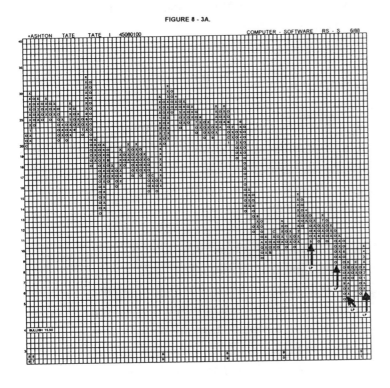

FIGURE 8 - 3B.

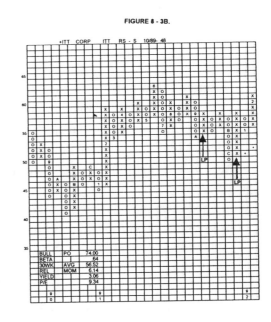

FIGURE 8 - 3C.

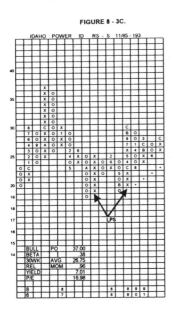

FIGURE 8 - 3D.

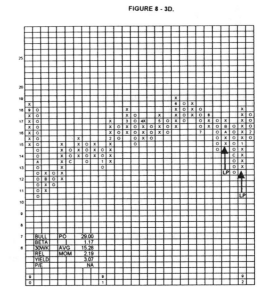

Figure 8-2 reveals a series of three high pole formations at the conclusion of an uptrend by LIN Broadcasting. The stock ultimately plummeted from 130 to 43 in the midst of a decline triggered by recurring high poles. LIN's pattern is more bearish because the high pole series reveals successively lower tops and bottoms. When a second high pole formation appears after a sustained advance, liquidate positions. High poles occurring in succession warn the stock is struggling to move higher. You can find other stocks with fewer problems.

RECURRING LOW POLES

A series of low pole formations suggests the stock is searching for a bottom. Two or more low poles occurring close together normally indicate a stock under accumulation. In figure 8-3, Ashton Tate experienced an appreciable price increase following the final low pole in 1990-1991. IT&T Corporation completed its correction bottom in 1991 when the second of two low pole formations lead to an upside breakout at 59 in January 1992.

Idaho Power indicates two low poles with the first establishing support at 19 in October 1987. A second low pole reached $19\frac{1}{2}$ in August 1988 and preceded an upside breakout at 27 in July 1989. The Federal Mogul chart shows the first low pole reaching bottom at $14\frac{1}{2}$ in August 1991. A second low pole follows a sharp sell-off that carries the stock to $12\frac{1}{2}$ in December 1991. In each of the illustrations, a series of two or more low pole formations indicates accumulation prior to the inception of a price advance. In Figure 8-4, MCI Communications gives an excellent picture of two well-defined low pole formations that mark the end of a price slide from 28 to 5. A series of low pole formations advises the bottom is near, and the stock may be accumulated.

OTHER SUBTLE PATTERNS

Figure 8-5 represents a vertical bar chart adaptation from work previously developed by William Jiler. [1] The **weekly key reversal bottom** contains a combination of a new low for the decline coupled with a gain for the week. The weekly gain is seen from the different level of the closing price (perpendicular slash) on the vertical bars on the left of the upper graphic. Price recordings appear on the P & F chart in a similar manner to the right hand side of the top illustration. An O dips below previous bottoms followed by an upside price movement.

Weekly key reversal bottoms force investors to ask why a stock reaches a low level during the week and fails to close at or near the low point. Questions arise as to the underlying strength responsible for at least a short-term reversal of the downtrend. Key reversal bottoms are selling climaxes (SC in illustrations) that can lead to either a temporary or major upmove.

Figure 8-4

LOW POLES AND MARKET BOTTOMS

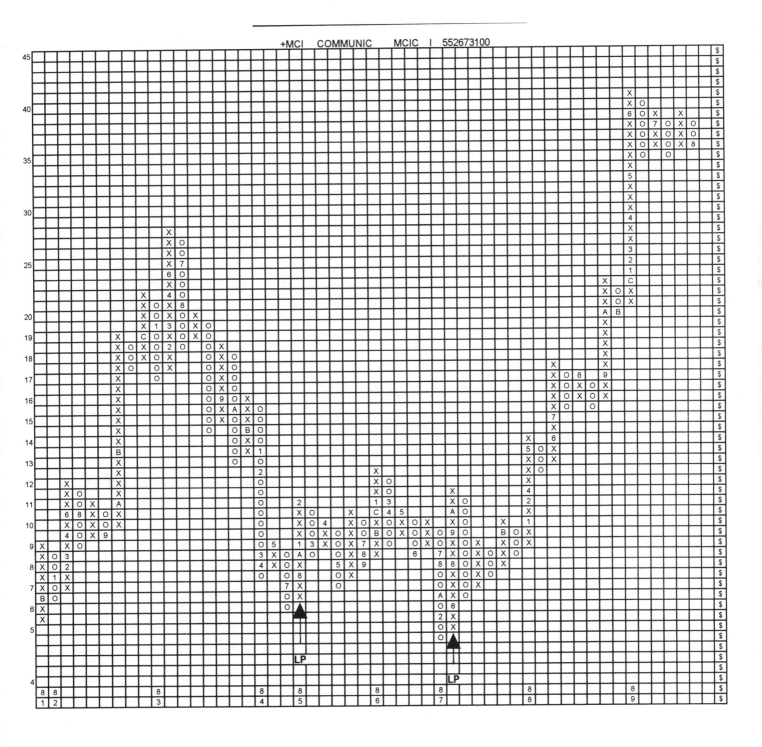

Figure 8-5

JILER'S KEY REVERSAL BOTTOMS AND TOPS

(A) **Weekly Key Reversal Bottom**

New low for the decline combined
with a gain for the week

O					
O					
O					
O (25)	X				
O	X	O			
O	X	O	X		X
O		O	X	O	X
		O	X	O	X
		O		O	X
				O	X
				O	

Weekly High Reversal Top

(B)

New high for the advance combined
with a loss for the week

				X	
				X	O
		X		X	O
		X	O	X	O
X		X	O	X	O
X (40)	O	X	O		O
X	O	X			
X	O				
X					
X					

138

Weekly key reversal tops demonstrate a new high for the advance combined with a loss for the week. Graphic presentations for vertical bar and P & F charts appear in the bottom portion of Figure 8-5. In a key reversal top, investors must ask why a strong stock hits a peak level and fails to stay there. Short-term traders should wonder why weakness enters the picture and reverses the uptrend. Key reversal tops are buying climaxes (BC in examples) which lead to a short-term correction or a major decline.

Figure 8-6 includes examples of key reversal tops and bottoms. The Morgan Stanley chart indicates a series of three successive key selling climaxes which precede a bottom. A series of key reversal bottoms or selling climaxes have bullish overtones. However, these weekly key reversal bottoms often lack the duration and underlying strength of major upturns inaugurated by a series of low poles.

The Medtronic chart indicates three different key reversal tops, each of which marks the beginning of a correction. Buying and selling climaxes signify speculative excesses. As stated earlier, bull and bear markets depend on corrections or retracements to ensure their continuation. Buying and selling climaxes during strong stock markets usually suggest a correction; however, these weekly key reversals in weak markets often indicate a more forceful price change.

Shakeouts

Earl Blumenthal[2] always argued that investors should ignore the first sell signal in a bull market. Michael Burke[3] refined Blumenthal's efforts and termed this first sell signal a **shakeout formation.** Simply stated, bull markets originate in the depths of despair and pessimism. New bull market beginnings depend on the mechanics of disbelief. A sell signal early in the uptrend casts more doubts about the staying power of the advance. A sell signal in the formative stages of a market advance merely supports the majority view that higher prices could not possibly result given the debilitated economic climate.

Figure 8-7 provides two illustrations of shakeout formations early in a bullish move. Frequently, the first sell signal declines to new support levels where the upside breakout penetrated prior resistance points. In Figure 8-8, each shakeout (SO) illustration creates skepticism concerning the uptrend. Traders sell on shakeout formations and stocks become oversold quickly. Then astute investors enter purchase orders and drive prices upward. Shakeout formations should be regarded as either an initial or additional buying point for individual stocks. Purchases can be made at the first sign of higher prices following the sell signal.

Shakeouts frequently conclude their downmoves either at new support levels or near the newly established bullish support line. In either case, shakeouts preclude investors from being entrenched in bullish sentiment too early in the move. Most bull markets begin without notoriety

Figure 8-6

<u>KEY REVERSAL TOPS AND BOTTOMS</u>

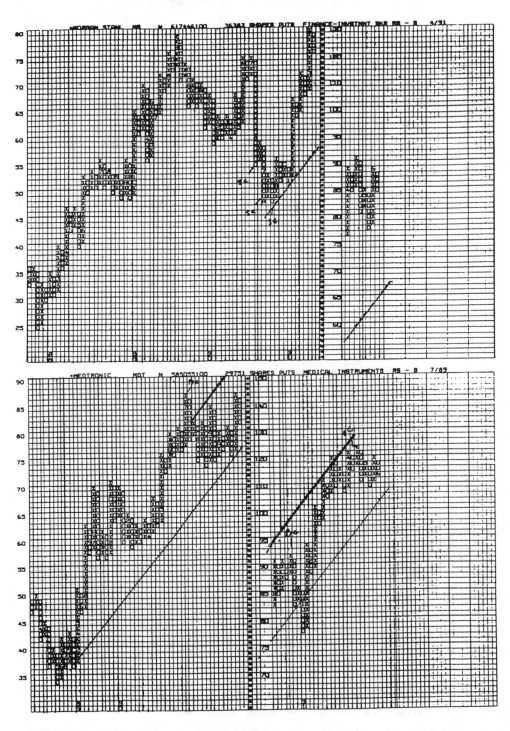

140

Figure 8-7

CHARTCRAFT'S SHAKEOUT FORMATION

(A)

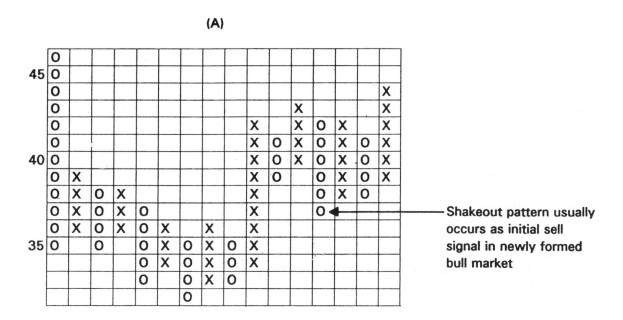

Shakeout pattern usually
occurs as initial sell
signal in newly formed
bull market

(B)

Shakeout

Figure 8-8

THE "SHAKEOUT" ILLUSTRATED

FIGURE 8 - 8A.

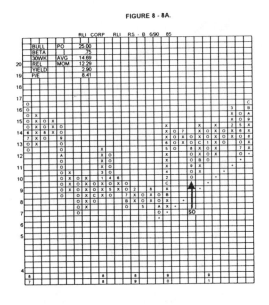

FIGURE 8 - 8B.

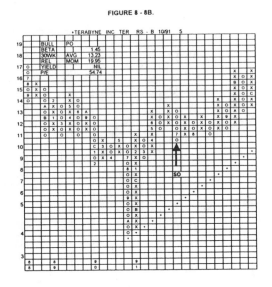

FIGURE 8 - 8C.

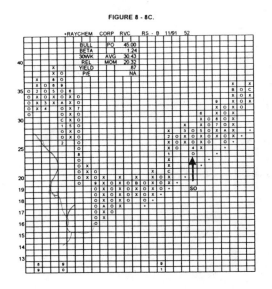

FIGURE 8 - 8D.

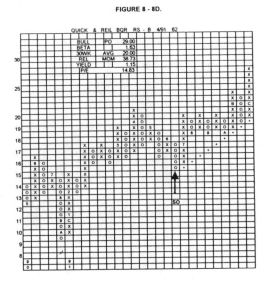

and flow smoothly until investors become cognizant of stocks from media attention. When stock market developments make front page news, the bull market is reaching maturity.

COMPARING STOCK AND GENERAL MARKET TRENDS

As we learned in Chapter 1, investors should display a preference for strong stocks in good industry groups during rising markets. By selecting individual issues which satisfy such criteria, the probability of success should be markedly higher. Conversely, weak stocks in poor industry groups should be sold or sold short during declining markets.

Simply, when the stock market increases, most stocks also rise in price and improve an investor's chances to make money. We may select increasing stocks in a rising market with a single approach. Both individual issues and the aggregate market must display higher tops and-higher bottoms.[4]

Figure 8-9 affords a comparison between a bullish 1991 stock market and some individual stocks with a pattern of lower tops and bottoms. Individual stock trends do not confirm the movement in the market as a whole. Technicians term this non-confirming action **divergence,** which warns of technical weakness in the individual stocks. Just as the term confirmation is used in the Dow Theory, the principle of non-confirmation or divergence must also be understood. Judicious investors should avoid Coastal, Kerr McGee, Federal Express, and Clark Equipment in making purchase decisions. When stocks fail to participate in the underlying strength of the overall market, they are technically weak and not likely to perform in the near future. Such stocks typically underperform the market in both up and down markets.

Figure 8-10 shows some stocks with higher tops and bottoms to illustrate the concept of **confirmation**. The price action in individual stocks confirms higher highs and higher lows in the general market and suggests that such issues may keep pace or outperform the market in the coming months. Confirming issues provide the largest appreciation potential during bull markets. Some unusually strong stocks appear in Figure 8-11. In the upper left hand corner of the example, we observe a declining stock market during 1990. However, three individual stocks show a pattern of persistently higher tops and higher bottoms. The combination of higher individual stock trends and simultaneously lower aggregate market movements may be termed **convergence.** Convergence in a down market warns that rising individual stocks are strong and embrace unusual profit potential for both the near term and for the longer-term market uptrends. On a relative basis, individual stocks are outperforming the market.

Figure8-9

DIVERGING STOCK AND MARKET TRENDS

FIGURE 8 - 9A.

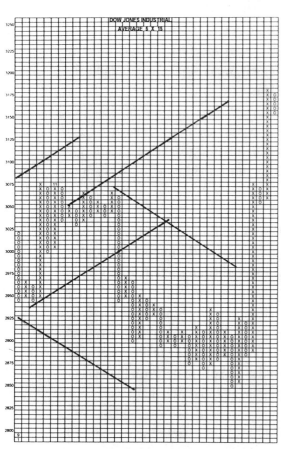

FIGURE 8 - 9B

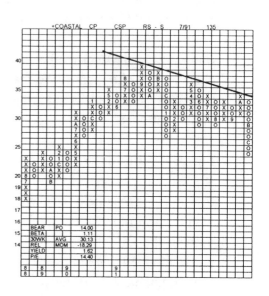

FIGURE 8 - 9C.

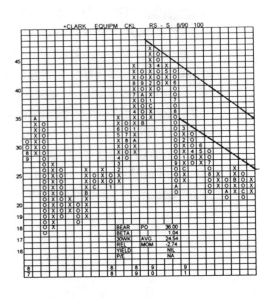

FIGURE 8 - 9D.

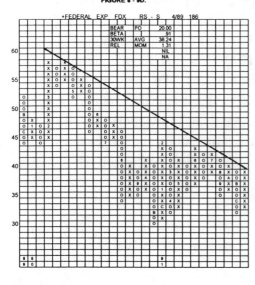

Figure 8-10

CONFIRMING STOCK AND MARKET TRENDS

FIGURE 8 - 10A

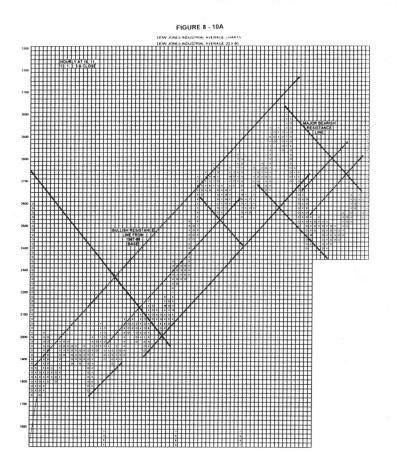

FIGURE 8 - 10B.

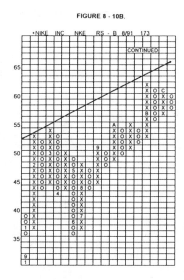

FIGURE 8 - 10C.

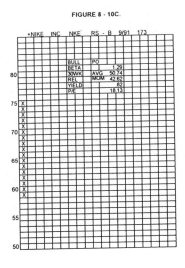

FIGURE 8 - 10D.

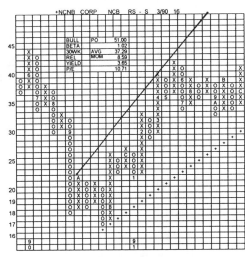

Figure 8-11

CONVERGING STOCK AND MARKET TRENDS

FIGURE 8 - 11A.

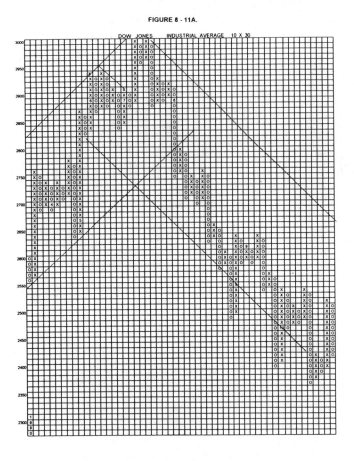

FIGURE 8 - 11B.

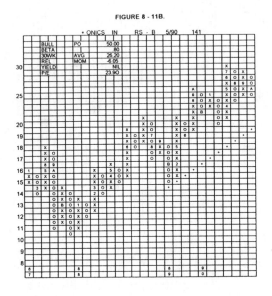

FIGURE 8 - 11C.

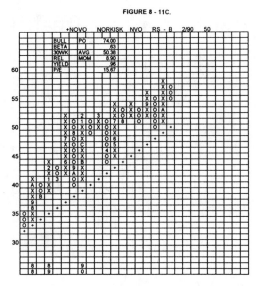

FIGURE 8 - 11D.

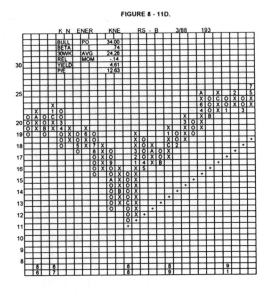

Figure 8-12

USING THE MOVING AVERAGE LINE TO BUY A POTENTIAL SUPPORT

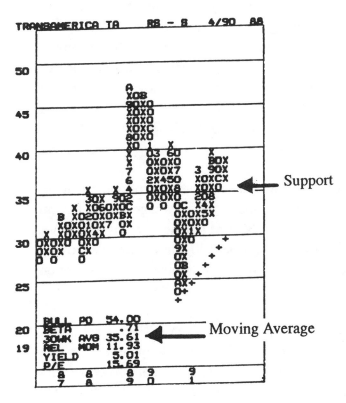

Support

Moving Average

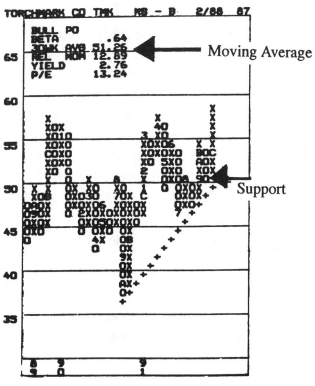

Moving Average

Support

MOVING AVERAGE DATA

Chartcraft maintains a **30-week moving average** of the weekly closing price for all charted stocks. Arrows in Figure 8-12 locate 30-week moving averages P & F charts from Chartcraft. Transamerica advances to 40 but pulls back to 36 in December 1991. As the stock concludes its correction at 36, a glance at the chart tells us the 30-week moving average is 35.61. Downside price moves often find support at or near the moving average. Similarly, Torchmark dips to 51 in November 1991, during a correction following an upside breakout. The 30-week moving average happens to be 51.26. Once again, the downside move found support on the moving average line. Two points should be made. First, support areas for declining stocks are normally found close to moving average lines. Secondly, additional buying opportunities stem from resilient stocks rallying from moving averages.

Figure 8-13 illustrates how rising stocks encounter resistance as they approach the moving average line. In the case of American Electric Power, the moving average for the last 30 weeks registers 30.35. A line of resistance forms in the 30 area as evidenced by a series of tops from 1986 to 1990. The tendency of the stock to stay near 30 implies that the moving average will also be close to 30. Almost five years of lateral price movement and consolidation were required to achieve the upside breakout above the 30-30+ area.

Let's assume speculators acquire some trading interest in American Express. Short-term traders will have an interest for several reasons. First, two bottoms were reached in the $18-18\frac{1}{2}$ area in the last quarter of 1991. Secondly, the bottoms at 18 and $18\frac{1}{2}$ correspond to previously established support at $17\frac{1}{2}$ in October 1990. And third, American Express declined sharply in the final quarter of 1991 from tax selling. Stocks which undergo sell-offs during the last quarter of a year have often been poor performers. Investors typically choose to unload them in the last three months of the year and apply the losses to tax returns. Stocks victimized by tax selling are oversold and primed for a short-term rally. Traders could assume positions near the 18 support area and play for a move to roughly $22\frac{1}{2}$. Even though American Express enjoys an upside breakout at 21, knowledgeable traders would sell in the 22 to $22\frac{1}{2}$ area because the moving average rests at 22.56. Speculators should regard the 30-week moving average as potential resistance and a place to take profits. If a breakout occurs, however, traders normally have a chance to re-enter the stock as it pulls back to the 30-week moving average or to new support from old resistance levels.

ROUNDED BOTTOMS AND TOPS

We derive **rounded bottom and top patterns** from saucer formations used in vertical bar charts. Rounded bottoms are highly bullish configurations which hint that stocks need a

Figure 8-13

USING THE MOVING AVERAGE LINE TO IDENTIFY RESISTANCE

FIGURE 8 - 13A.

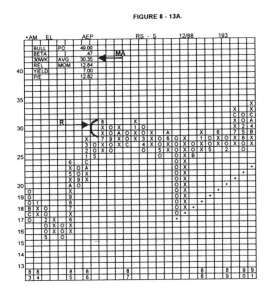

FIGURE 8 - 13B.

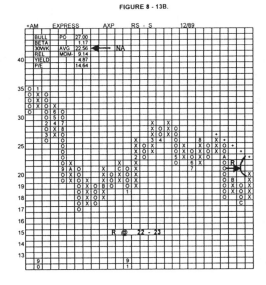

gradual effort to reverse the downtrend. Figure 8-14 includes several examples of rounded bottoms. In the case of Eastern Utilities, a several-year bottom concludes during 1990. The saucer or rounding effect means the dissolution of lower bottom trends and furnishes evidence of a reversal with higher bottoms on the right-hand side of the pattern.

Rounded bottoms often generate explosive advances. To illustrate, let's examine Genentech, a stock known for its volatility. Despite all of its press as a "mover and shaker," Genentech gradually completes a rounded bottom formation over a one-year period. However, the stock immediately doubles in price. Bristol Myers ends a retracement with a rounded bottom formation that renews the uptrend. Finally, Mattel builds a 12-month base pattern with rounding bottoms that finalize the accumulation process. The stock doubles in value once the pattern is completed.

Several things should be kept in mind regarding the rounded bottom. Bases form after a protracted downtrend with stocks disclosing a pattern of lower bottoms. When one bottom reaches a low point in the base, it typically marks the end of a selling climax as in Eastern Utilities and Mattel (August 1990). If two or more bottoms reach low points in the base, these multiple bottoms generally mark a support level for successful retests of the bottom. Genentech and Bristol Meyers illustrate multiple bottoms. A second reminder concerns the rounding of bottoms. The rounding bottoms will not be perfectly symmetrical in most cases. Although the points forming the saucer bottom may not be a perfect fit with a compass, enough rounding exists to identify the formation. The rounded bottom pattern incorporates first lower bottoms, then one or more downside thrusts which represent selling climaxes and support levels, respectively, and finally a series of higher bottoms to confirm the end of the price slide.

Rounded tops ordinarily spell the end of a sustained price advance and offer the potential for rapid downside price moves. The left side of the rounding begins with rising columns of X's. One or more tops stand alone as buying climaxes and levels of resistance. A price decline follows and precedes a later rally attempt on the right-hand side of the pattern. However, the rallies fall short of the high points, and the price begins to slide again. The failure of the final rally to make previous highs confirms the topping process of the rounded top and prepares chartists for lower prices.

Figure 8-15 shows a chart of Fieldcrest Cannon. Once the rounding of the top concludes, downside price action begins. The vertical count taken from the first downmove following the highest X gives a downside target of 8 (10 squares x 2 + 2 squares x 1 = 22, then 30 - 22 = 8 for PO). By using $\frac{2}{3}$ of the normal reversal rule to multiply by the number of squares on the 3-point and $1\frac{1}{2}$ point charts, the modified counting technique accurately forecasts the bottom at $8\frac{1}{2}$.

Figure 8-14

BUYING FROM A ROUNDED BOTTOM PATTERN

FIGURE 8 - 14A.

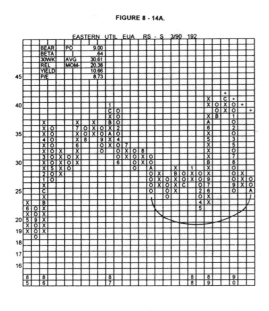

FIGURE 8 - 14B.

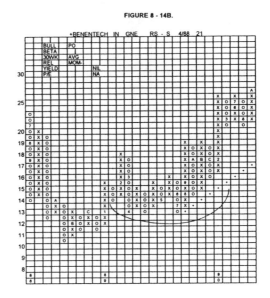

FIGURE 8 - 14C.

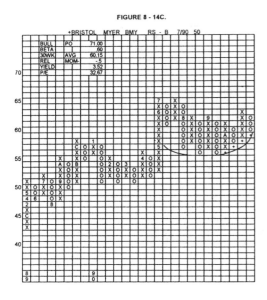

FIGURE 8 - 14D.

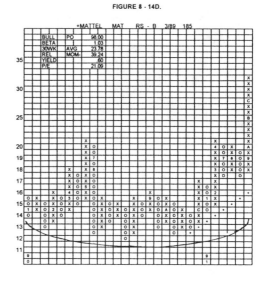

Figure 8-15

THE ROUNDED TOP FORMATIONS

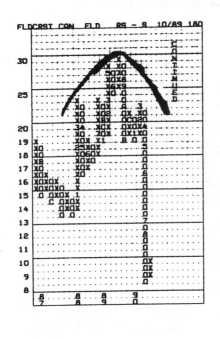

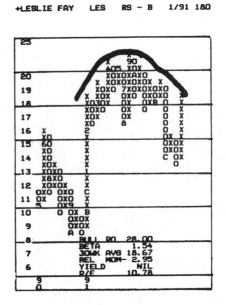

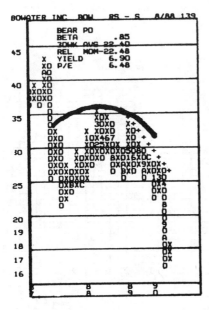

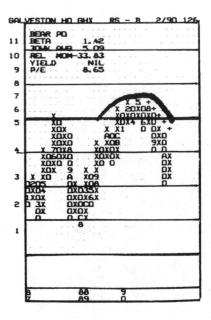

152

A more gradual rounded top appears in the Leslie Fay Chart. Bowater and Galveston Houston offer slightly different versions of the rounded top, but in each case results are the same. Rounded tops share the same fundamental characteristics as do rounded bottoms but in diametrically opposite fashion. The same reminders apply.

Now that a variety of new chart patterns has been introduced, we may proceed to other changes in P & F chart analysis. The subject of traditional trendlines has already been introduced. However, a number of steps may be taken to make these tools more sensitive. Earlier buy and sell signals should result and profits will be preserved.

SUMMARY

Chapter 8 introduces additional chart patterns and serves as an extension of Chapter 7. P & F charts can no longer be regarded as an ultra mechanical approach without some creativity and analysis. Recurring high and low pole formations, shakeouts, rounded tops and bottoms, key reversals, and moving averages are introduced. Vertical bar chart adaptations are found to be helpful to and consistent with P & F charts.

Decisions made on individual stocks should entail a comparison between stock trends and general market price moves. Furthermore, subtlety developing patterns continue to play increasingly important roles in investment strategy and in our efforts to revise the common body of knowledge in P & F chart analysis.

ENDNOTES

[1] William L. Jiler, <u>How Charts Can Help You In the Stock Market</u> (New York: Trendline Corporation, 1965).

[2] Earl Blumenthal, <u>Chart For Profit Point and Figure Trading</u> (Larchmont, New York: Investors Intelligence, 1975), 37.

[3] Michael L Burke, <u>Three-Point Reversal Method of Point & Figure Construction and Formations</u> (New Rochelle, New York: Chartcraft, Inc., 1990), 54-55.

[4] Michael L. Burke, <u>Three-Point Reversal Method of Point & Figure Construction and Formations</u> (New Rochelle, New York: Chartcraft, Inc., 1990), 68-69, 96-97.

CHAPTER 9

MAKING TRENDLINES MORE SENSITIVE

Critics argue that trendlines are a major weakness of P & F charts. Long-term bullish support and bearish resistance lines are drawn at 45 degree angles. The most objectionable feature of traditional wisdom centers on outdated and insensitive trendlines as prices fluctuate too far above or below the line. Conventionalists argue that major trendlines do not require revision until penetrated. Traditional thought has no quarrel with stock prices being removed from trendlines. The fact that trendlines may no longer be sensitive to current price levels fails to shake the faith of those entrenched in the early roots of P & F charts.

Our position argues that trendlines are useful only if they stay current. Sensitivity to constantly changing price levels makes trendlines effective. Furthermore, continually revised trendlines serve to combat the principal indictment of P & F charting; that is, buy and sell signals develop too late and prove costly to investors.

In Chapter 9, we discuss how major trendlines can be revised. Further, introducing short-term and intermediate-term trendlines makes P & F charts a better option for traders. The end result means current trendlines ideally suited for both speculators and long-term investors.

REVISING THE BULLISH SUPPORT LINE

Earlier, we left the bullish support line (BSL) in its original form as long as it remained unbroken. However, bullish support lines should be revised when a sell signal occurs above the major uptrend. Figure 9-1 illustrates a stock which fluctuates away from the BSL in a bullish mode. To keep the major uptrend line responsive to current market conditions, we identify sell signals during the advance. New bullish support lines commence from one square below the lowest O in the sell signal column. A line is then drawn connecting successively higher corners of the graph at a 45 degree angle.

Interpretation of each revised bullish support line remains consistent with the treatment in Chapter 5. The primary advantage of revised BSLs concerns earlier warnings of price reversals. Trendline penetrations occur sooner and at higher price levels because of the revisions.

155

Figure 9-1

REVISING THE BULLISH SUPPORT LINE

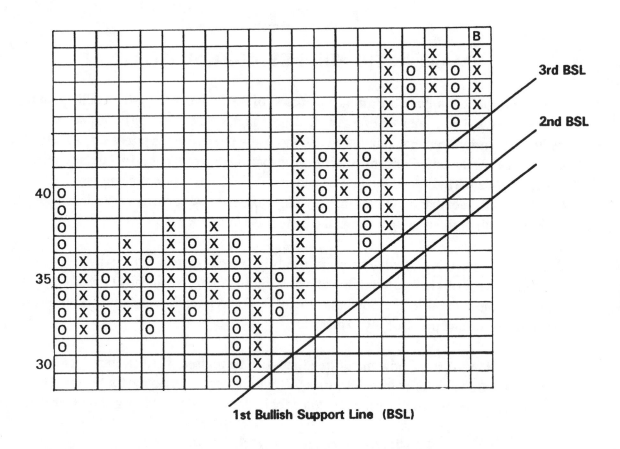

1st Bullish Support Line (BSL)

Figure 9-2

REVISING THE MAJOR UPTREND LINE

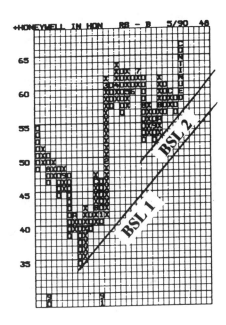

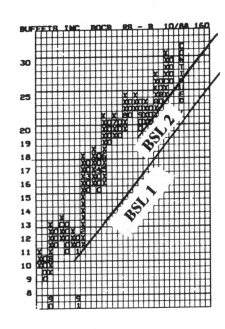

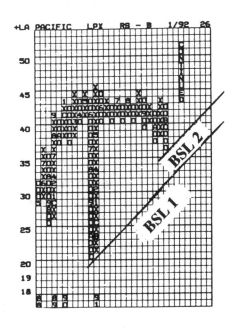

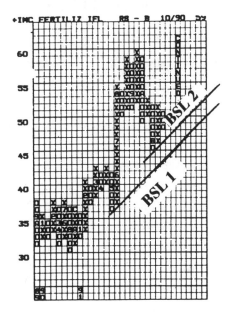

Investors can do a better job of preserving profits and entering protective stops because warnings surface at higher price levels.[1]

Figure 9-2 furnishes some key illustrations of timely BSL revisions. The Honeywell chart shows a sell signal in August 1991 with a successful retest of support at 53. When multiple bottoms form in conjunction with sell signals, bullish support line revisions originate from one square below the most recent bottom in the base. Buffets, Inc. experiences a price advance which quickly outdistances the 45 degree trendline. Both charts demonstrate the need for updating and revising trendlines. Otherwise, stocks need to undergo drastic price declines before investors detect a juncture. Original trendlines would incur breaks at lower levels and give belated efforts to warn of a forthcoming trend reversal.

The Louisiana Pacific chart reveals a downside spike followed by a sharp advance that becomes removed from the bullish support line. Revised BSLs ensure that investors are more attuned to current developments in the stock. IMC Fertilizer also allows for a revision of the major uptrend line at the conclusion of a price correction at 46. In each illustration, investors receive earlier warning signals from updated bullish support lines.

The Mobil chart in figure 9-3 shows an original BSL that endures for approximately four years before a break in the last quarter of 1990. However, a sell signal in January 1990 permits chartists to establish a revised trendline which is broken earlier in the price slide. Liquidation should take place on penetration of the revised BSL because a sell signal exists. Since the trendline violation is valid, a major juncture evolves. The previous BSL now becomes resistance. Although the pullback in Mobil moved above the new resistance line, the stock dipped into the 50's by April 1992. Pullbacks toward trendlines simply emphasize a stock's tendency to move along a straight line for long periods of time. However. the trendline violation ultimately contributed to a major downturn in the stock.

VERTICAL BAR CHART TRENDLINES

Vertical bar chart trendlines function as an interesting contrast to their P & F counterparts. From Figure 9-4 we learn that three points establish vertical bar chart trendlines. In the case of an uptrend, we draw the line connecting low points of daily or weekly sessions. With uptrends, point 1 marks the beginning of the upmove while point 2 concludes that "leg" or portion of the primary advance. Point 3 marks the end of the correction. The uptrend contains higher bottoms and higher tops consistent with Dow's original works. The uptrend line represents support at points along the trend.[2]

The downtrend consists of lower tops and lower bottoms with the trendline connecting high points of daily or weekly sessions. As in uptrend lines, points 1 - 2 show the primary downmove

Figure 9-3

REVISING AND PENETRATING THE BULLISH SUPPORT LINE

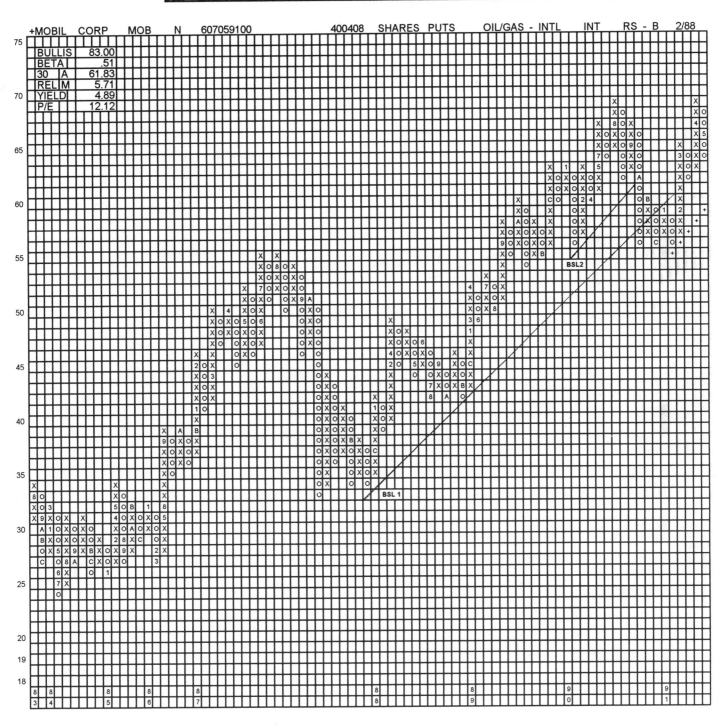

Figure 9-4

<u>VERTICAL BAR CHART TRENDLINES</u>

UPTREND

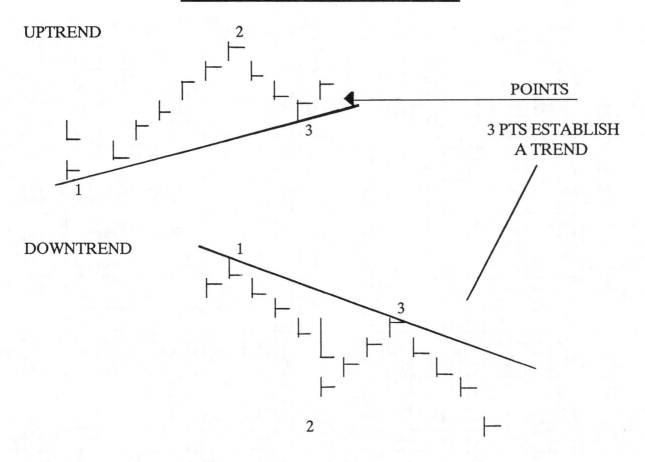

POINTS

3 PTS ESTABLISH
A TREND

DOWNTREND

SIDEWAYS TREND

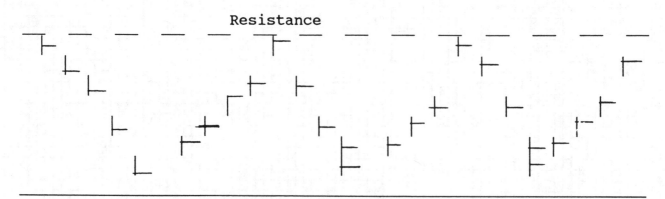

Resistance

Support

or "leg". The correction ends at point 3 and the downtrend resumes. Once again, three points establish a trend.

Sustained price declines exhibit persistently lower tops and lower bottoms and fit the Dow definition of a bear market. The downtrend line expresses potential resistance at all points.

From Dow's studies, the major move in either direction constitutes the primary movement, while the retracement represents the secondary move. Secondary moves or corrections tend to retrace from one-third to two-thirds of the primary movement. Some technicians employ a 50% rule to estimate corrections because a retracement of one-half is the midpoint of the range from $\frac{1}{3}$ to $\frac{2}{3}$.

To illustrate, let's assume the uptrend in Figure 9-4 moves from 20 (point 1) to 41 (point 2), a primary move of 21 points. The secondary move or retracement could carry from 34 (41 - 7 where $\frac{1}{3}$ x 21 = 7) to 27 (41 - 14 where $\frac{2}{3}$ x 21 = 14). A one-third retracement amounts to 7 points, while a two-thirds retracement equals 14 points. The 50% rule means the stock would undergo a correction of 10 to 11 points (50% x 21 = 10.5) and suggests the stock on average would drop to the 30 - 31 area.

The sideways trend suggests a base-building process within the context of lateral price movements discussed earlier. Numbered points do not appear on the sideways trend, although they could easily be inserted. Points are not included simply because sideways trends may occupy long periods of time and can be identified rather routinely. Trendlines connect the bottoms of the recordings, while channel lines appear at the top. Trendlines indicate bottoms, and channel lines denote resistance. Breakouts in either direction are usually meaningful, with the more protracted sideways movements offering larger price potential in either direction.

Figure 9-5 provides an extension of the concepts from Figure 9-4. Whereas three points establish a trendline, five points confirm the trend. Confirmation of a trendline means a better defined trend and one less likely to be broken. Established trendlines fail to show the permanence of confirmed trends. With five points, the argument can be made that two legs in a primary move already exist.

SHORT-TERM AND INTERMEDIATE-TERM UPTREND LINES

P & F trendlines can be adapted to short-term traders by modifying what we have learned from vertical bar charts.[3] Long-term trends in the form of bullish support and bearish resistance lines have been fully explored. However, traders and investors with brief investment horizons need to be apprised of short-term changes which alter their strategies.

Figure 9-5

CONFIRMING BAR CHART TRENDLINES

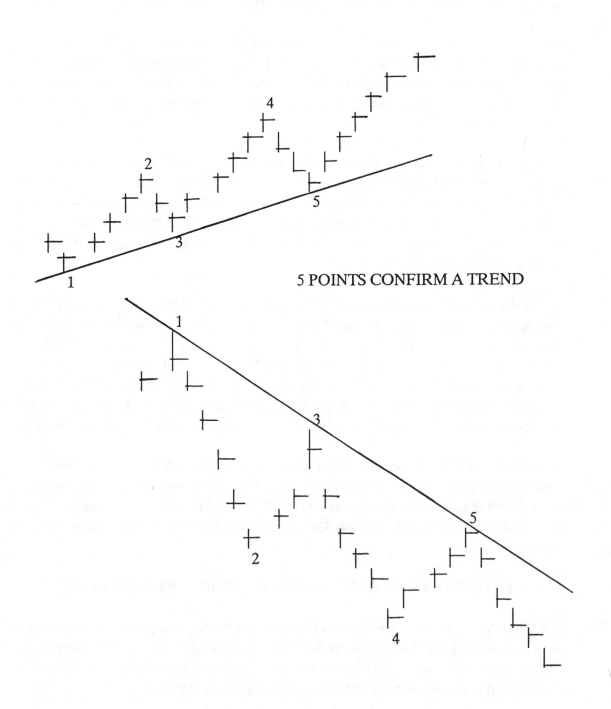

5 POINTS CONFIRM A TREND

Figure 9-6

THE SHORT-TERM UPTREND LINE

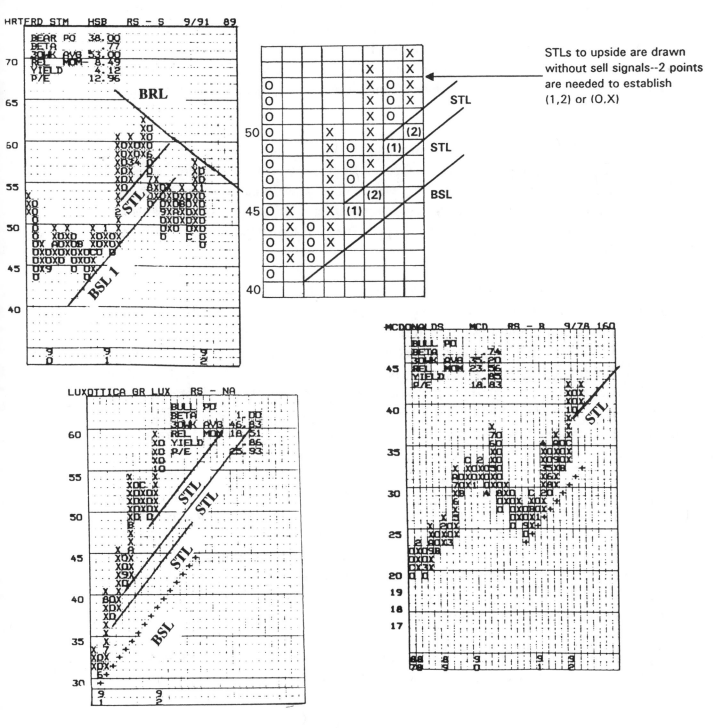

STLs to upside are drawn without sell signals--2 points are needed to establish (1,2) or (O,X)

163

Figure 9-6 illustrates a stock with an upside reversal from a bullish signal formation. The stock advances high above the bullish support line with no opportunity for major trendline revision. We may adjust for the fast pace, however, by using short-term uptrend lines formed by two points labeled 1,2 for illustration purposes. The two points must be in succession and can be identified by an O,X from a pair of columns that end a decline and start another upmove. Revision of the bullish support line (BSL) occurs after a downside breakout occurs. Short-term uptrend lines do not include a sell signal but merely two points O,X that resume the uptrend after a correction or retracement. Two short-term uptrend lines (STL) appear in the hypothetical illustration in Figure 9-6. Both lines proceed from brief price drops without a sell signal. STLs are drawn by moving one square below the lowest O in the correction column and drawing a 45 degree line intersecting successively higher corners of each square on the graph.

From Figure 9-6, we observe the Luxottica and McDonalds' charts where bullish support lines (BSLs) receive timely updates from companion short-term uptrend lines. Luxottica benefits from two quick STLs because the stock advances rapidly. McDonalds also experiences a sharp price rise, so investors have an STL to gauge near-term support. STLs assist chartists in guarding against downside vulnerability. To appreciate short-term trendlines, let's review the Hartford chart.

After a BSL is drawn, the stock rises in almost vertical fashion. A February 1991 correction back to 55 permits a short-term trendline (1,2 or O,X) which is broken in June 1991. Chartists received advance warning to sell Hartford as the STL break warns of a short-term top. Penetration of the short-term uptrend line occurs in June 1991, while the major bullish support line holds until September -- three months later. Hartford shows a pullback to the original BSL, but a high pole formation prompts another downside move immediately after touching the new resistance line (BRL). Old support becomes new resistance. For purposes of illustration, we insert a bearish resistance line (BRL) to acknowledge the sell signal and warn that the stock turns from bullish to bearish.

Figure 9-7 illustrates an intermediate uptrend line (ITL). ITLs require four consecutive points (1,2,3,4 or O,X,O,X) in a 45 degree straight line for confirmation. Drop one square below the initial O and draw the line connecting successively higher corners of the graph. ITLs have more permanence than STLs. Thus a penetration of an ITL carries greater significance than does a break of an STL and warns of a steeper decline. A penetration of an intermediate uptrend line indicates an intermediate top. Like STLs, ITLs develop after pullbacks or retracements and form without a sell signal.[4]

Figure 9-8 contains several actual examples of intermediate uptrend lines. Mesa Royalty illustrates the endurance of ITLs as a line formed in 1986 continues until the end of 1990.

Figure 9-7

THE INTERMEDIATE-TERM UPTREND LINE

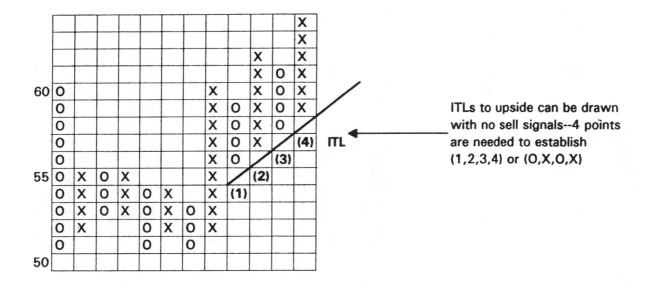

ITLs to upside can be drawn
with no sell signals--4 points
are needed to establish
(1,2,3,4) or (O,X,O,X)

165

Figure 9-8

SOME EXAMPLES OF INTERMEDIATE UPTREND LINES

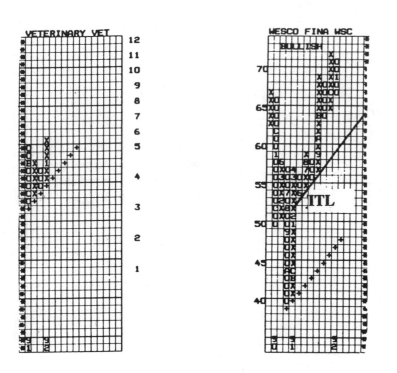

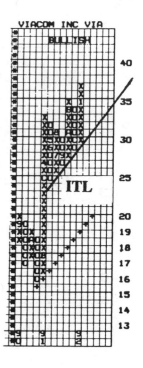

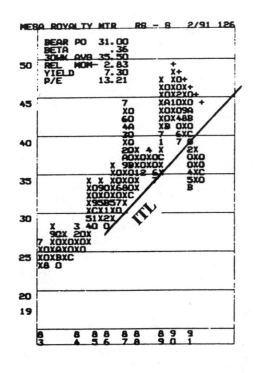

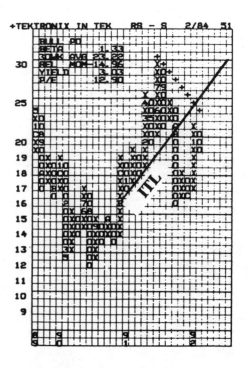

166

Figure 9-9

REVISING THE BEARISH RESISTANCE LINE

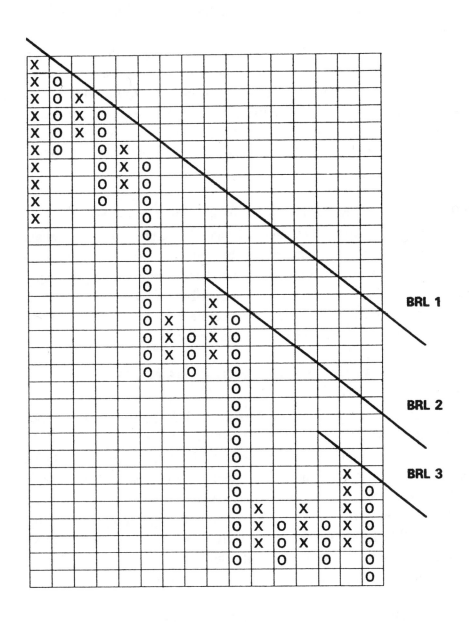

Two points merit attention. In July 1988, a downmove from a sell signal touches the ITL and resumes the uptrend. Secondly, a sell signal in February 1991 breaks below the ITL and completes a four-year top area of distribution. The same trendline interpretation rules apply to both ITLs and STLs. Sell signals occurring immediately above the ITL should not be accepted unless a valid penetration occurs. Valid breaks result when sell signals accompany the downmove.

The Veterinary and Viacom charts in Figure 9-8 display beautifully formed intermediate uptrends. Viacom particularly needs updating because the price rises almost vertically with little consolidation. Wesco Financial reveals a downside spike followed by a steep rally in the form of a low pole formation. A correction appears high above the bullish support line, so investors are removed from the stock without an ITL. If the current rate of advance is maintained, sell signals will emerge from violations of STLs and ITLs long before the original bullish support line is breached.

The Tektronix chart perfectly illustrates how minor trendlines provide early signs of technical deterioration and cause investment strategy changes. November 1991 sell signals occur at 21 and $19\frac{1}{2}$ and the ITL formed in January is exceeded. If investors waited for the unrevised BSL to be broken, reversals would happen much later. An important point should be made regarding the Tektronix chart. The top area of distribution formed quickly considering the stock lost about 50 percent of its value in the decline. When junctures form quickly, minor trendlines (ITLs and STLs) represent a valuable timing tool due to quicker signals.

REVISING THE BEARISH RESISTANCE LINE

Figure 9-9 illustrates the revision of bearish resistance lines (BRL). Revising major downtrend lines can be accomplished in an opposite way to bullish support line updates. Until now, the BRL has been left in its original form. However, BRLs should be revised when a buy signal takes place below the major downtrend. To make sure the major downtrend line remains current with market conditions, we identify buy signals during the price decline. New bearish resistance lines may be drawn from one square above the highest X in the buy signal column or correction top. When multiple tops form on buy signals, BRL revisions originate from one square above the highest X in the most recent column. A line may then be drawn connecting successively lower corners of the graph at a 45 degree angle.

Analysis of revised BRLs is consistent with guidelines from Chapter 5. The principal objective of revised downtrend lines concerns securing earlier signs of price reversals. Violations of trendlines take place earlier and at lower price levels by using revisions. Investors may gain an advantage from buying at lower prices, while speculators may close out short positions and put option purchases earlier.

168

Figure 9-10

REVISING THE MAJOR DOWNTREND LINE

FIGURE 9 - 10A

FIGURE 9 - 10B

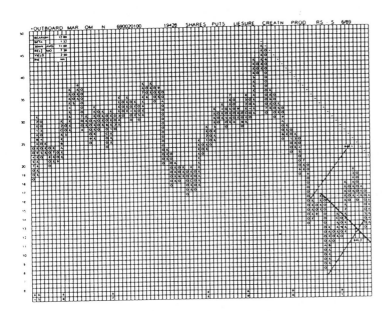

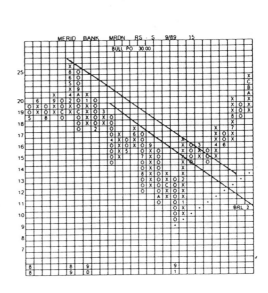

FIGURE 9 - 10C.

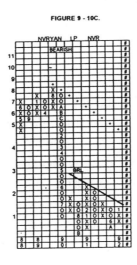

Figure 9-10 provides three examples of how the bearish resistance line can be revised. In the Outboard Marine Chart, notice the price descent after the original BRL . In November 1990, a buy signal emerges in a correction base, but the advance fails to materialize because the price is below the revised downtrend line. An initial buy signal from a bullish signal formation appears at 13, but the price turns down again after confronting the downtrend line. However, a second buy signal surfaces at $14\frac{1}{2}$ in February 1991 and penetrates the revised BRL. Chartists using the revised line receive timing advantages because they can buy the stock at cheaper prices. With a buy signal and the revised BRL break at $14\frac{1}{2}$, prices have still not reached the original downtrend line. Readers should note the pullback after the first sell signal in the newly formed bull market. First, the price carries back almost to the revised BRL, which is now new support. And secondly, the decline also reaches previous breakout levels where additional support enters the picture.

The Meridian Bank Chart shows a buy signal below the original downtrend line in June 1990 at $17\frac{1}{2}$. We draw a revised BRL (BRL2) from one square above the highest (and last) X. However, the BRL revision offers potential timing benefits in the Nuryan chart. The stock falls straight downward without interruption until a buy signal appears in February 1991. Once the revised BRL is penetrated, the buy signal will offer significant benefits in terms of timing and potential profits.

THE SHORT-TERM DOWNTREND LINE

You will recall that short-term trend lines (STLs) require two points for construction. With STLs in downtrends, points 1,2 or X,O are used. STLs develop after brief corrections and cannot be linked to sell signals. Although short-term downtrend lines do not carry the permanence or significance of major downtrends, a penetration nevertheless signals a short-term reversal. Points 1,2 serve to illustrate the line's origination and appear over X,O. Notice the X,O points appear in a straight, 45 degree angle line connecting successively lower corners of the graph.

The hypothetical stock in Figure 9-11 begins a steep slide interrupted by two brief corrections. At the end of each rally, an X,O forms and provides the basis for an STL to the downside. In the Mid Maine chart, an STL appears below the main downtrend and develops at the end of a retracement bounce. A February 1991 buy signal takes place immediately below the STL and fails to break out on the upside. The price decline then resumes. The Mid Maine chart reinforces our view that all trendline interpretations remain the same. STLs and ITLs are no different than primary lines when we interpret penetrations, support, resistance, and buy and sell signals.

Figure 9-11

THE SHORT-TERM DOWNTREND LINE

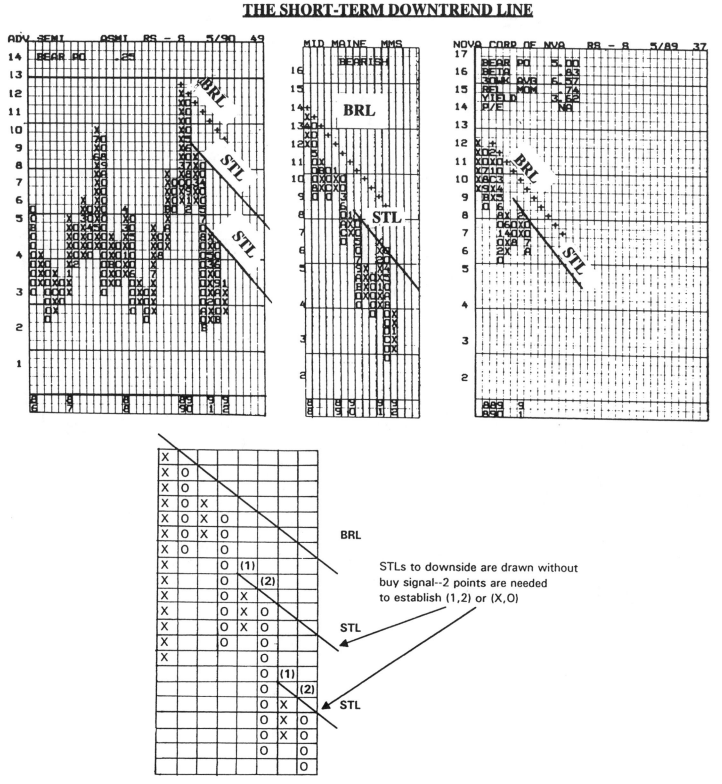

STLs to downside are drawn without
buy signal--2 points are needed
to establish (1,2) or (X,O)

Figure 9-12

INTERMEDIATE DOWNTREND LINE EXAMPLES

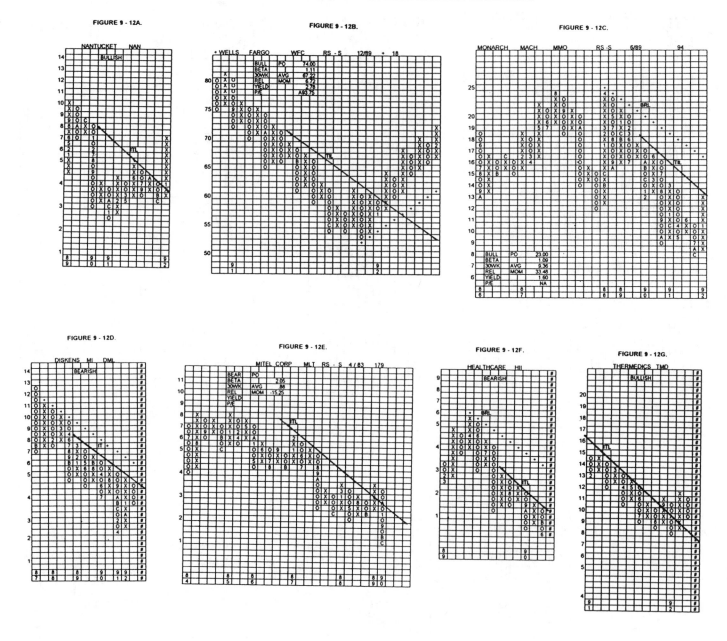

172

Nova Corporation forms a base pattern during the 1990-91 downmove, with an STL updating the main downtrend. Notice the STL originates from one square above the last X because multiple tops are involved in the sideways price movement. A timely update results.

The Advanced Semi chart makes two attempts to rally following a steep downmove. In both cases, the new STLs benefit chartists. Warning signals of an early reversal are assured because of the steep decline in the stock's price.

INTERMEDIATE DOWNTREND LINES

Figure 9-12 gives an example of an intermediate downtrend line (ITL). ITLs need four successive points (1,2,3,4 or X,O,X,O) in a 45 degree straight line to construct an intermediate downtrend line. By moving one square above the highest X, we may draw the line connecting successively lower corners of the graph. When multiple tops are involved during a correction, draw the line from one square above the most recent X. ITLs are less permanent than major trendlines, but they should be considered more significant than STLs. A penetration of an intermediate downtrend line signals an intermediate bottom. Intermediate-term reversals are more lasting than short-term bottoms but less protracted than major turning points.

Let's examine the Wells Fargo chart in Figure 9-12. The ITL (X,O,X,O) suffers a valid penetration in January 1992 and signals an intermediate-term bottom. Consequently, an earlier buy signal evolves. The Thermedics example shows a valid upside break of an ITL with a pullback to the trendline after the buy signal. Mitel Corporation reveals a penetration of the ITL with no buy signal to accompany it. Therefore, the validity of the break remains questionable. Mitel promptly reverses and continues downward.

The Nantucket chart also shows a valid upside breakout and intermediate trend reversal. Both Diskens and Healthcare have ITLs that remain intact throughout the chart and force the patterns to continue with lower tops and lower bottoms. Monarch shows an ITL still intact but faces a rising price with a buy signal. If the stock continues upward, penetrates, and then pulls back to form a high pole formation at the ITL or BRL, bearish implications arise. If the stock retraces from 13, consolidates, and then makes another rally attempt, chances are probably better for a valid upside reversal. Patterns with corrections and consolidations maintain their upside (downside) momentum better than do issues which attempt to move straight up (or down).

Trendlines now constitute a more viable technical tool for formulating investment strategies. Our philosophies make trend lines more sensitive and assist investors in earlier purchases and sales. Two key areas must be included, however, for a more successful trading strategy.

These topics encompass a better approach to arriving at price objectives and the use of relative strength to eliminate false and misleading signals. In other words, we are continuing to seek more accurate decisions. Let's turn our attention to some improved price objectives.

SUMMARY

Traditionalists contend that trendlines should remain in their original form without revision until a penetration occurs. However, trendlines often become removed from current price levels, particularly when volatile stocks are plotted. A more realistic view suggests that revised trendlines keep chartists apprised of current developments in the stock. Chapter 9 proposes that major trendlines be revised and updated whenever possible. Investors receive earlier warning signs of price reversals with current trendlines.

Short-term and intermediate-term trendlines also prevent the loss of unrealized profits. Trendline breaks for these minor trendlines do not signal a major turning point, but they do warn of near-term damage in the stock. Investors receive quicker warnings of price junctures and enjoy more sensitive charts.

ENDNOTES

[1]A. W. Cohen, <u>How To Use the Three-Point Reversal Method of Point and Figure Stock Market Trading</u>, 9th ed. (New Rochelle, NY: Chartcraft Inc., 1987), 43-54.

[2]William L. Jiler, <u>How Charts Can Help You In The Stock Market</u>, (New York: Trendline Corporation, 1965).

[3]Earl Blumenthal, <u>Chart For Profit Point and Figure Trading</u> (Larchmont, New York: Investors Intelligence, 1975), 43.

[4]Earl Blumenthal used the term "support level moves up" in describing what appears to be the first experiment with minor trendlines in P & F analysis. However, Blumenthal confined most of these efforts with minor trends to commodity futures. A definitive niche exists for minor trendlines in common stocks, however. With the advent of large institutional investors, larger trading volume, and increased price volatility, making more sensitive, updated P & F charts more imperative. See Earl Blumenthal, <u>Chart for Profit Point and Figure Trading</u> (Larchmont, New York: Investors Intelligence, 1975), 92.

CHAPTER 10
IMPROVING PRICE OBJECTIVE FORECASTS

P & F chart analysis needs better price forecasts. Horizontal and vertical counts were introduced earlier. As time passes, however, the risk of these approaches becoming stagnant increases. With a few adjustments, existing techniques might be enhanced and made useful for all traders. With a view toward more sensitive price forecasts for short-term traders, let's build on the body of knowledge from Chapter 6.

ANOTHER LOOK AT THE VERTICAL COUNT

Figure 10-1 includes several charts with vertical count illustrations. Let's begin with the Morgan Keegan example. We measure the extent of the first upmove following the lowest O. The first column of X's contains 13 squares with one square on the $\frac{3}{4}$ point chart and 12 squares on the $1\frac{1}{2}$ point chart. If we add $18\frac{3}{4}$ (i.e., $1 \times \frac{3}{4} + 12 \times 1\frac{1}{2} = 18\frac{3}{4}$) to $4\frac{1}{2}$ (lowest O), a price move to $23\frac{1}{4}$ can be estimated. The stock's ultimate price move should carry to the 23-24 area. Morgan Keegan reaches 24 in January 1992. However, the stock dropped to the 13 area by April of 1992.

Magnetek's first upmove after the lowest O also represents the breakout leg, so both vertical count rules pertain to the same column of X's. Eighteen squares appear on the $1\frac{1}{2}$ point chart for the vertical count (VC 1). Therefore, an initial estimate of the stock's ultimate price move is 34 ($18 \times 1\frac{1}{2} = 27 + 7 = 34$). However, it is prudent at this point to revise price forecasting. Each time a sell signal appears during an uptrend, a revised vertical count may be established.

We calculate a revised price objective for the vertical count with the same rules. First, measure the number of recordings in the breakout leg when a new buy signal reaffirms the stock's bullish trend and negates the recent sell signal. Or secondly, count the recordings in the first upmove following the lowest O once a buy signal confirms the uptrend continuation. Remember, retracements, consolidations, lateral prices moves, or corrections are all different terms for the same thing -- an interruption in the primary trend of the stock. Such pauses renew the vigor of the move.

Figure 10-1

THE VERTICAL COUNT REVISITED

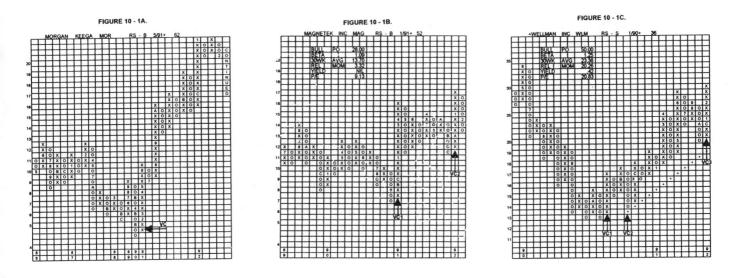

FIGURE 10 - 1A.

FIGURE 10 - 1B.

FIGURE 10 - 1C.

We establish another vertical count (VC 2) by counting 11 squares in the first upmove (and breakout leg). The price forecast occurs on the $1\frac{1}{2}$ point chart since recordings are between 5 and 20. A revised price forecast equals 28 (11 sqs. x $1\frac{1}{2}$ = $16\frac{1}{2}$ + $11\frac{1}{2}$ = 28). The revision reminds chartists of a cardinal rule relating to price forecasts: use price objectives conservatively. A compromise target, such as 30 to 31, might be appropriate, but a better suggestion would be to lend added weight to the latest target. Chartists may regard 28 as a final objective with a goal of holding the stock for higher prices if strength in the stock persists. Caution in the 28 area must be exercised.

The Wellman chart in Figure 10-1 gives a comprehensive view of vertical count revision. The first vertical count measures 8 squares on the $1\frac{1}{2}$ point scale. A first price objective suggests a move to 25 (8 sqs. x $1\frac{1}{2}$ = 12 + 13 = 25). Wellman then indicates a sell signal from a shakeout formation in November 1990. A second vertical count forecasts a move to 26 (8 sqs. x $1\frac{1}{2}$ = 12 + 14 = 26) and essentially confirms the first vertical count.

At this point, chartists should anticipate a price move to the 25-26 area and sell positions. In April 1991, Wellman hits 25 and corrects sharply to $18\frac{1}{2}$. The stock eventually struggles higher but then retraces to 20 in October on the strength of a sell signal. However, a buy signal surfaces in February 1992. The upside breakout cancels the earlier sell signal and provides a basis for another vertical count. A first upmove (also the breakout leg) counts 10 squares on the 3-point chart to forecast a target of 50(10 sqs. x 3 =30+20=50).

This second revised count hints of underlying strength and additional price potential in Wellman. Chartists with long-term orientations can modify their targets and anticipated holding period. A word of caution is needed at this point. Revised vertical counts should be evaluated more conservatively after stocks undergo considerable price moves in either direction. Protective stops should be utilized at all times, with specific emphasis placed on positions having substantial paper profits.

Figure 10-2 furnishes two more vertical count examples. CSX loses approximately 50% of its value in a bear market decline in late 1987. We measure 8 squares in the breakout leg of the base (VC 1) to arrive at an initial forecast of 47 [8 x 3 = 24 + 23 (lowest O) = 47]. However, a sell signal prompts the stock to reverse back to 26, where we measure 13 squares in the first upmove. This breakout leg furnishes a new buy signal to cancel the downtrend. We run a second vertical count (VC 2) for another forecast of 65 [13 x 3 = 39 + 26 (lowest O) = 65].

Since the stock is in the early stages of a trend, more credence should be given to the revised objective. In the latter stages of a well-defined trend, we would generally attach more importance to earlier forecasts. Chartists must use revised counts judiciously when stocks remain in a trend for long periods. In the first quarter of 1992, CSX remains in an uptrend with the stock

Figure 10-2

PINPOINTING THE TOP WITH SEPERATE VERTICAL COUNTS

FIGURE 10 - 2A.

FIGURE 10 - 2B.

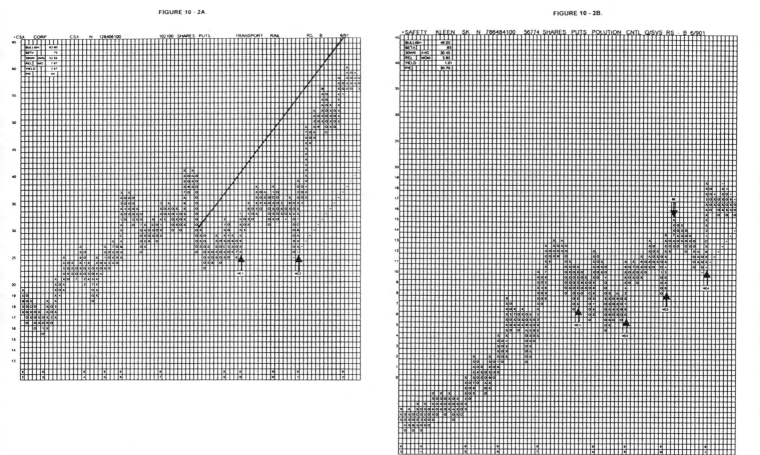

reaching 60. A revised vertical count prevented chartists from selling too soon and losing sizable profits.

A vertical count may be determined with Safety Kleen from the first upmove after the bottom at $11\frac{1}{2}$ in October 1986. Nine squares on the $1\frac{1}{2}$ point chart provide a price objective of 25 (9 x $1\frac{1}{2}$ = $13\frac{1}{2}$ + $11\frac{1}{2}$ = 25). The upmove culminates at 26 in October 1987, and begins a retracement. Another vertical count may be calculated (VC 2) in January 1989. The breakout leg has 8 squares on the $1\frac{1}{2}$ point chart (8 x $1\frac{1}{2}$ = 12) in addition to 3 squares on the 3 point chart (3 x 3 = 9). The price objective equals $35\frac{1}{2}$ [21 +$14\frac{1}{2}$ (lowest O) = $35\frac{1}{2}$]. A price advance should reach 35-36. Safety Kleen reaches 36 twice in 1991. The stock began to retreat from 36 and reached 22 in March/April 1992.

Two more vertical counts are included (VC 3 and VC 4) to illustrate earlier warnings about late price revisions. The third vertical count forecasted a price move to the 46 - 47 area, while the fourth predicted a move to 69. Meanwhile, the stock has declined to 22. The sell signal that resulted in a selloff to 22 cancels the vertical count and indicates a downtrend. Chartists must view price revisions late in the trend with a jaundiced eye. Stocks are prone to experience sell signals late in upmoves and buy signals in the latter stages of a decline.

Price estimates used conservatively are valuable. Forecasts made with reckless abandon have less value than no estimate at all! You should not completely disregard the third and fourth vertical counts. However, they are suspect and do not have the credibility of earlier revisions. As a stock moves further along a trend, assign more weight to earlier forecasts. Allocate less weight to revised predictions made late in a trend.

Figure 10-3 illustrates both upside and downside vertical counts. In the Kimberly Clark example, the first vertical count yields an upside price objective of 64 (8 x 3 = 24 + 40 = 64). The stock reaches the 64-65 area and then retraces to 54 after a sell signal. A second vertical count (VC 2) provides a forecast of 87 [11 sqs. x 3 = 33 + 54 (low O) = 87]. Kimberly Clark reaches the 90 area in the first quarter of 1991 and undergoes a slight correction. Although the stock edged slightly higher, points beyond the forecasted price could be attributed to a stock split announcement.

In the Cincinnati Milacron illustration, two vertical counts should be discussed. The initial vertical count totals 13 squares from the first downmove after the stock's peak. If a full vertical count were taken, the price objective would equal 0 because there are 13 squares on the 3 point chart. However, begin by using downside vertical counts with a $\frac{2}{3}$ reversal rule (i.e., $\frac{2}{3}$ x 3 = 2). Multiplying 13 times 2 gives a product of 26, which is subtracted from the highest X at 39 for a price estimate of 13. The stock drops to $15\frac{1}{2}$ followed by a low pole. The vertical count afforded traders and long-term investors good buying opportunities.

Figure 10-3

VERTICAL COUNTS UP AND DOWN

FIGURE 10 - 3A

FIGURE 10 - 3B

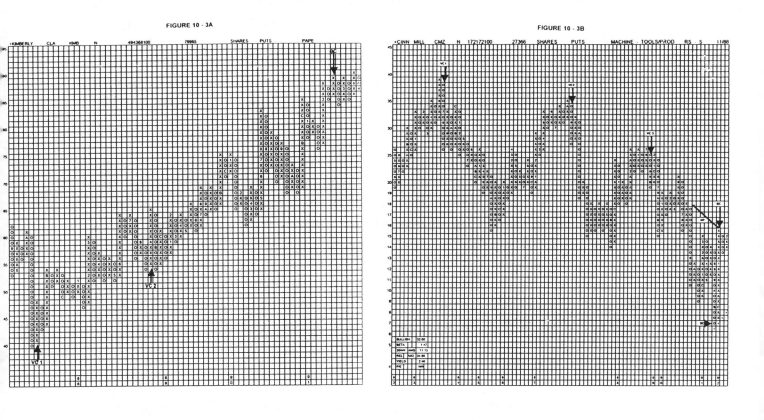

Remember another pivotal rule in using price forecasts. Buy or sell slightly ahead of forecasted price objectives due to the influence of investment firm technicians. When everyone receives similar advice, not everyone can act precisely at a certain price. In this case, buying began before 13 at the $15\frac{1}{2}$ area. The recommendation to buy early carries the same emphasis as an earlier suggestion to sell before targets are reached. A low pole formation confirms our strategy. The stock advances to 35 and requires a second downside vertical count. When Cincinnati Milacron fails to reach the first top at 39, another downmove begins. The long-term trend is down with lower tops from the stock's failure to move above 39. Using a $\frac{2}{3}$ reversal rule, the second vertical count is 19 (8 sqs. x 2 = 16, 35 - 16 = 19). Once the downmove exceeds 19, implement the full vertical count by multiplying 8 times 3 to arrive at 24. By subtracting 24 from 35, the price objective equals 11. However. the stock reversed slightly before the downside target at 14.

Buy signals in 1988 reverse the downtrend as the stock corrects back to 26. A third vertical count may be calculated from the downside breakout in the last four months of 1988. There are seven recordings in the breakout leg with six on the 3-point chart and 1 on the 1-point chart. Using a full reversal rule, we find the price objective to be $6\frac{1}{2}$ [6 x 3 + 1 x $1\frac{1}{2}$ = $19\frac{1}{2}$, then $26 - 19\frac{1}{2} = 6\frac{1}{2}$]. The stock bottoms at 7 in November 1991. In each case, the revised vertical count forecasted the downside move accurately. Chartists not only received good estimates, but they were apprised of current activity in the stock. Revised vertical counts were particularly appropriate in Cincinnati Milacron, since the stock displayed lower tops and lower bottoms throughout most of an 8-year period.

EXPANDING THE HORIZONTAL COUNT

The horizontal count furnishes an intermediate-term price objective. Over time, these projected moves are usually exceeded if general market trends continue. Consequently, technicians who rely heavily on the horizontal count have no recourse in making further intermediate price forecasts. To combat this problem, it is appropriate to introduce a concept that we will refer to as "expanding the base," or "expanding the horizontal count." Figure 10-4 illustrates this concept with a chart of Salomon, Inc.

Expanding the base should be used at major bottoms or tops as stocks experience changes in their primary trends. Three different walls of O's can be identified as separate base patterns in Salomon's chart. In other words, the one large base (or bottom) may be divided into three smaller base patterns. We are, in effect, "segmenting the base." In turn, each smaller base has the potential for a horizontal count. The individual bases are identified as HC 1, HC 2, and HC 3. As seen in our coverage of the Salomon Chart, the first base from right to left is HC 1.

Figure 10-4

EXPANDING THE VERTICAL COUNT

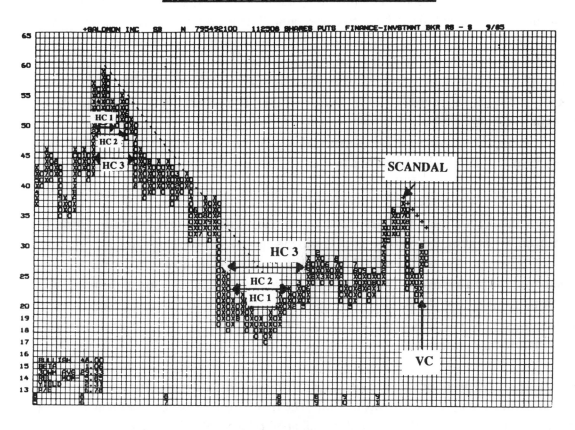

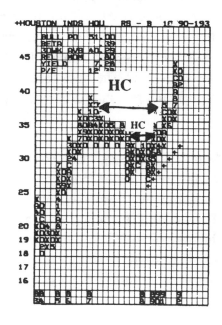

A price breakout is registered at 20 and gives the potential for an initial upmove to 29, which was reached in October 1988 (8 sqs. wide x $1\frac{1}{2}$ pt. reversal rule = 12 + 17 = 29).

When Salomon eventually moves beyond the first count of 29, we can expand the base pattern and thus the potential for the horizontal count. We then refer to HC 2, which suggests that the next leg upward should carry to about 38. To calculate the count from HC 2, we have moved to the left to the next wall of O's and then to the right to locate the breakout which exceeds all tops in the newly formed base. The highest top ("X") is 22. The next upside breakout or buy signal occurs at 23 in January 1988. The second base (HC 2) totals 14 squares and is multiplied by a $1\frac{1}{2}$ point reversal to furnish a product of 21 to be added to the lowest O at 17. The projection for the second segment of the base equals 38. Salomon reaches 37 in July 1991, when news of a trading scandal drives the price back to established support levels.

A full horizontal count may be determined across the entire base (HC 3) by counting 20 squares from the extreme left-hand wall of O's to the breakout at 27. The ultimate horizontal count is 47 (20 x $1\frac{1}{2}$ = 30 + 17 = 47). The highest previous top in the entire base was 26, so the October 1988 price move to 27 achieved an upside breakout and expanded the horizontal count. Interestingly enough, a buy signal at the conclusion of the chart ends the correction downtrend, and a vertical count yields a final price objective of 48. This vertical count confirms HC 3 as an ultimate price target.

The technique of expanding the base also applies in forecasting downside price objectives. Salomon forms a top in April and May of 1986. The first (or top HC) base is six squares wide from the wall of X's on the left to the sell signal at 50 on the right. A product of 18 (6 x 3 = 18) is subtracted from 59 to furnish a first target of 41. In August 1986, Salomon hits 40 and rallies back to 46. The second base measures 8 squares wide and yields a price objective of 35 (8 x 3 = 24, then 59 - 24 = 35). The stock reaches 37 in January 1987. A third base totals 10 squares in width and provides a price target of 29. The stock reaches 31 in May 1987. Three different horizontal counts were accurate in forecasting different segments of the downside price movement.

The Salomon chart also reinforces the principle of using counts conservatively. Price recordings have fluctuated above and below 20, but we chose the more conservative reversal rule from the $1\frac{1}{2}$ point chart. A final point of interest relates to Salomon reaching a bottom in December 1987, after some climatic selling. To reiterate an earlier concept, stocks which make lows in December are downtrend issues which are often driven lower by the pressures of additional tax selling. Stocks that make December lows should be considered for trading purposes because they tend to have post tax-selling "bounces" or rallies. Such stocks are technically oversold and due for an upmove because of investor overreaction to falling prices.

Figure 10-5

MORE ON SEGMENTING THE BASE

FIGURE 10 - 5A

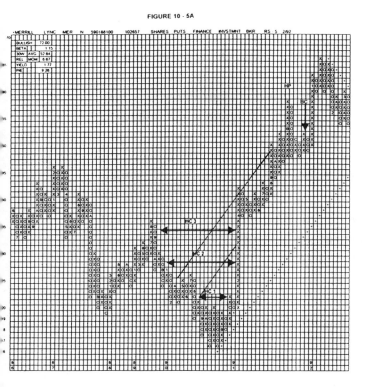

FIGURE 10 - 5B

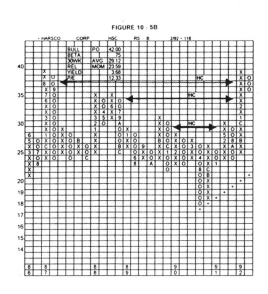

FIGURE 10 - 5C.

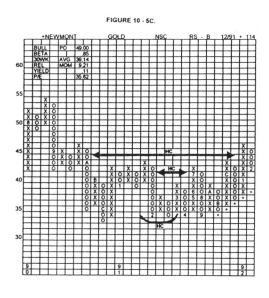

A last point of re-emphasis concerns the long, downside spike or tail in late 1987. Once the bottom is reached, such stocks typically enjoy strong price advances. The Salomon chart in 1987 tells the technician that the extreme selling is overdone. In Wall Street parlance, the stock should be technically "washed out" from the hands of the uninformed public and ready for a strong rally.

A chart for Houston Industries appears at the bottom of Figure 10-4. The first horizontal count (the lowest HC) stems from a base 6 squares wide. When we add 18 to 27 (the lowest O), our first price objective reaches 45. Houston Industries reaches 44 and begins to retrace. For all practical purposes, the stock hit its objective. The count should be expanded by finding the next wall of O's at the higher HC. A move to 37 eliminates all tops in the base and provides a second breakout to accompany the new wall of O's. A 14-square width multiplied times 3 equals 42 plus 25 or 67.

Figure 10-5 provides three more illustrations of expanding the horizontal count by segmenting the larger or overall base pattern at the bottom. As a last point of illustration, let's review the Harasco Corporation chart in Figure 10-5. An 8-square wide base multiplied times 3 yields a product of 24, which is added to 18 for a price estimate of 42. The price breakout occurs in May 1991 at 29, one square above the highest X in the first base. The stock breaks the first resistance point at 35 but fails to penetrate another at 39. The stock has essentially satisfied its first objective. A second objective from the next horizontal count suggests the price could reach 66. Ultimately, a third price objective may be calculated from the top arrow in the chart, although the target would be unrealistic at this point.

A TRADER'S PRICE OBJECTIVE

One objection voiced toward three-square P & F charts concerns their presumed insensitivity toward traders. Critics complain that only intermediate-term and longer-term viewpoints can be addressed. However, Figure 10-6 introduces a concept that we will call a **trader's price objective**.

The bottom in Mylan's P & F chart occurs during the period 1987-1989. The upside breakout develops at $13\frac{1}{2}$ in August 1989, and a line delineates the bottoming process. The letters "TC" represent the trading count which can be derived from the base pattern. The first price estimate can be determined by multiplying the width of the base times 2 of the normal reversal rule [i.e., $12 \times \frac{1}{2} = 6 + 7\frac{1}{2}$ (lowest O) $= 13\frac{1}{2}$]. Traders may choose to sell positions in the 13-14 area. Once the price surpasses the first target, the count can be revised as shown in the bottom portion of Figure 10-6.

Figure 10-6

GETTING A TRADER'S PRICE OBJECTIVE

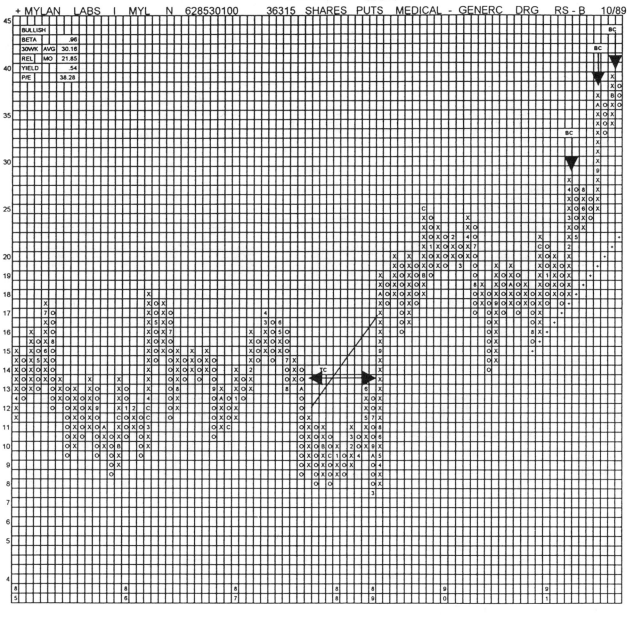

1) 1st TRADING OBJECITVE

    = 12   SQUARE WIDTH   X   1/2 PT   = 6 + 7 1/2 (lowest O)

    = 13   1/2

2) 2nd TRADING OBJECITVE

    = 12   X   1 PT =   12   + 7 1/2   = 19 1/2 to 20

3) 3rd TRADING OBJECITVE

    = 12   X   1 1/2 =   18   + 7 1/2   = 25 1/2 to 26

Figure 10-7

A TRADING COUNT

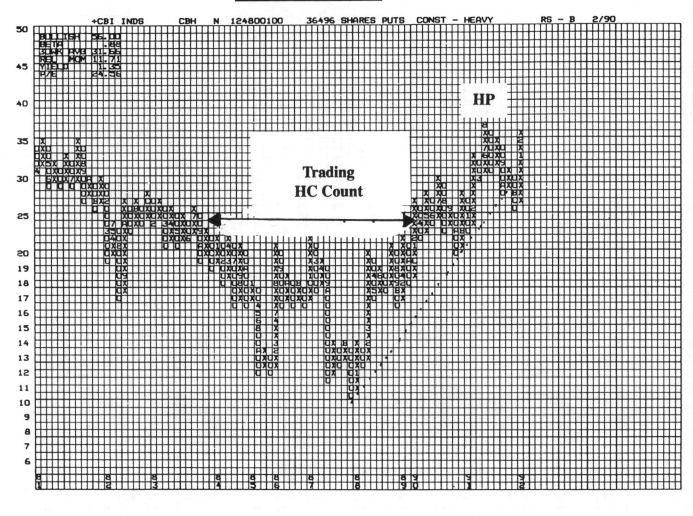

1st TRADING OBJECTIVE
    38 SQUARES WIDE x 1/2 PT = 19 + lowest 0
                    19 + 10 1/2 = 29 1/2 to 30

2nd TRADING OBJECTIVE
    38 SQS.   x   1 PT   =   38   +   10 1/2   =   48 1/2 to 49

3rd TRADING OBJECTIVE
    38 SQS.   x   1 1/2 PTS   =   57   +   10 1/2   =   67 1/2 to 68

Figure 10-8

A FINAL LOOK AT MEASURING TRADING FORECASTS

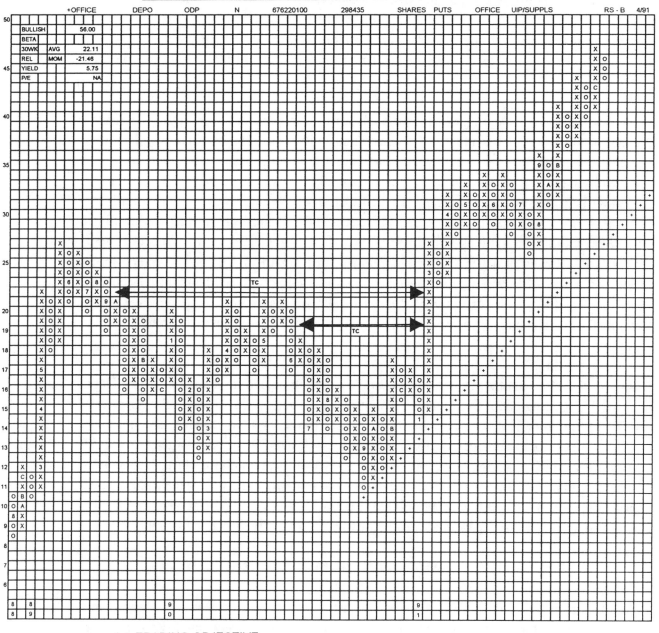

1st TRADING OBJECTIVE

    16 SQUARES WID X   1/2   =   8   +   11 (lowest O)

                                            =   19

2nd TRADING OBJECTIVE

    16 SQS. X   1   =   16   +   11

                                  =   27

3rd TRADING OBJECTIVE

    16   X   1 1/2   =   24   +   11

                                  =   35

To expand the trading target, multiply by $\frac{2}{3}$ of the reversal rule or 1 point between 5 and 20. Mylan reaches the second trading objective at 20 in October 1989 and then consolidates. Once the stock surpasses 20, a third trading count uses a full reversal rule to yield a final trading objective of $25\frac{1}{2}$ to 26. Traders are thus afforded the luxury of three different targets to sell positions on the basis of investment horizon. Shorter-term traders may liquidate at one of the first two targets, while those with more patience will likely hold for the third target.

The trading count may be viewed from a slightly different perspective in Figure 10-7. Let's examine the chart of CBI Industries, where an unusually wide base pattern develops. Rather than segmenting the base or taking piecemeal counts, we elect to run a projection based on the entire base pattern. To calculate a full horizontal count would be premature early in the upmove because any price estimate from such a large base would not likely be realized soon. You may calculate three different trading objectives at the bottom of Figure 10-7. Multiply 38 squares (width of base) times $\frac{1}{2}$ ($\frac{1}{3}$ of reversal rule on $1\frac{1}{2}$ point chart) for a product of 19 to be added to the lowest O at $10\frac{1}{2}$. Our first target measures $29\frac{1}{2}$ to 30. CBI hits 30 and promptly retraces back to 20 where old resistance becomes new support. Second and third targets are $48\frac{1}{2}$ to 49 and $67\frac{1}{2}$ to 68, respectively. By making allowances for interim price moves or legs within the overall uptrend, traders can sell quicker without increased risks from longer holding periods.

Figure 10-8 gives another example of expanding trading objectives using the Office Depot chart. The trading count technique yields price objectives of 19, 27, and 35 respectively. Office Depot hits 27 and corrects briefly to satisfy the second target, while another move carries to 34 prior to a retracement to 26. Once the stock satisfies the third target, two options remain available for chartists. First, original and revised vertical counts may be used. Secondly, you may go to the next wall of O's indicated by the top arrow and repeat the trading count principle over the larger base containing 36 squares. Investors should realize that trading counts may also be used to estimate downside moves in exactly the same fashion.

USING THE MEASURED MOVE FOR TRADING COUNTS

An often overlooked tool in P & F price forecasting is the **measured move.** During well-defined trends, stocks display price movements of approximately equal length known as **legs.** Let's examine the Illinois Tool chart in Figure 10-9. After the October 1987 bottom, the stock enjoys a consistently bullish trend through 1991. To illustrate the measured move, each leg is depicted with numbers included at the bottom of Figure 10-9. Points 1 to 2 form the first major leg upward, while points 2 to 3 indicate a retracement of the primary trend. Then, the

Figure 10-9

THE MEASURED MOVE

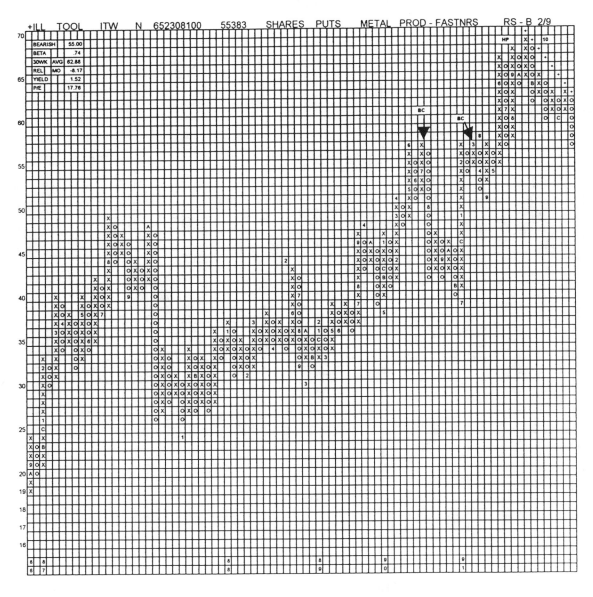

1st LEG = POINTS   to   17 PTS   (26 to 43)
2nd LEG = POINTS   to   15 PTS   (32 to 47)
3rd LEG = POINTS   to   18 PTS   (39 to 57)
4th LEG = POINTS   to   18 PTS   (40 to 57)
5th LEG = POINTS   to 10 17 PTS   (52 to 69)

Figure 10-10

THE MEASURED MOVE DOWN

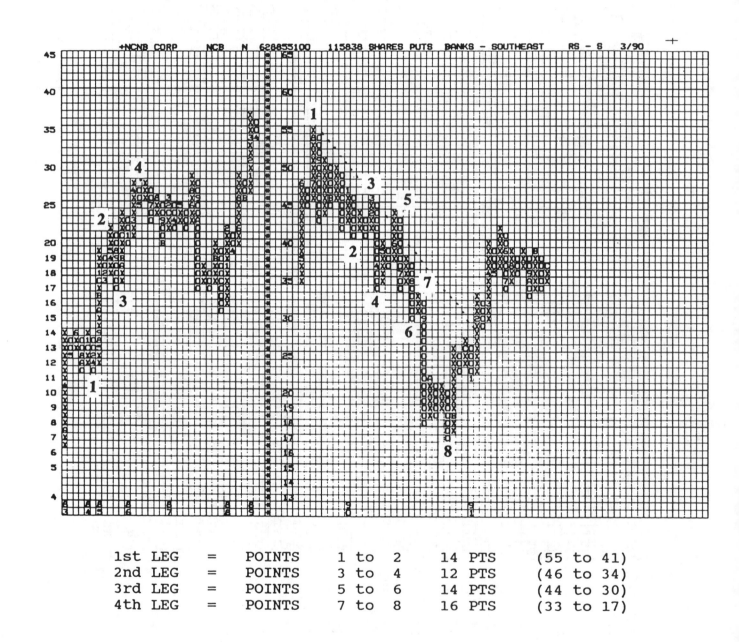

1st LEG	=	POINTS	1 to 2	14 PTS	(55 to 41)
2nd LEG	=	POINTS	3 to 4	12 PTS	(46 to 34)
3rd LEG	=	POINTS	5 to 6	14 PTS	(44 to 30)
4th LEG	=	POINTS	7 to 8	16 PTS	(33 to 17)

192

Figure 10-11

MEASURED MOVES: THE BIG PICTURE

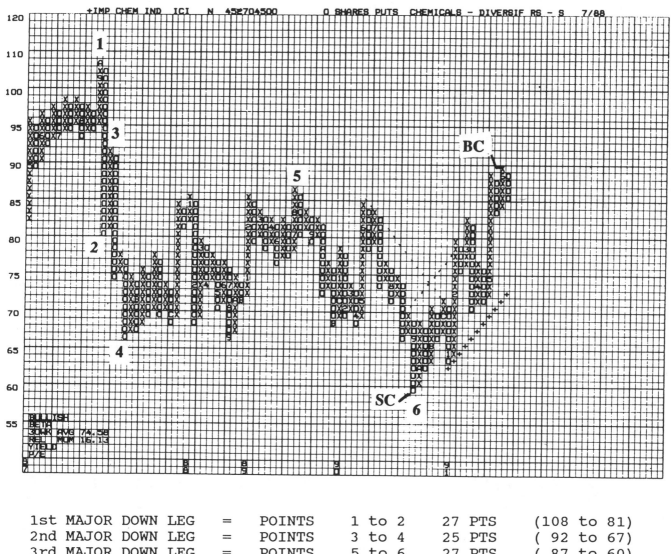

1st MAJOR DOWN LEG	=	POINTS	1 to 2	27 PTS	(108 to 81)
2nd MAJOR DOWN LEG	=	POINTS	3 to 4	25 PTS	(92 to 67)
3rd MAJOR DOWN LEG	=	POINTS	5 to 6	27 PTS	(87 to 60)

Figure 10-12

SUPPORT AND RESISTANCE

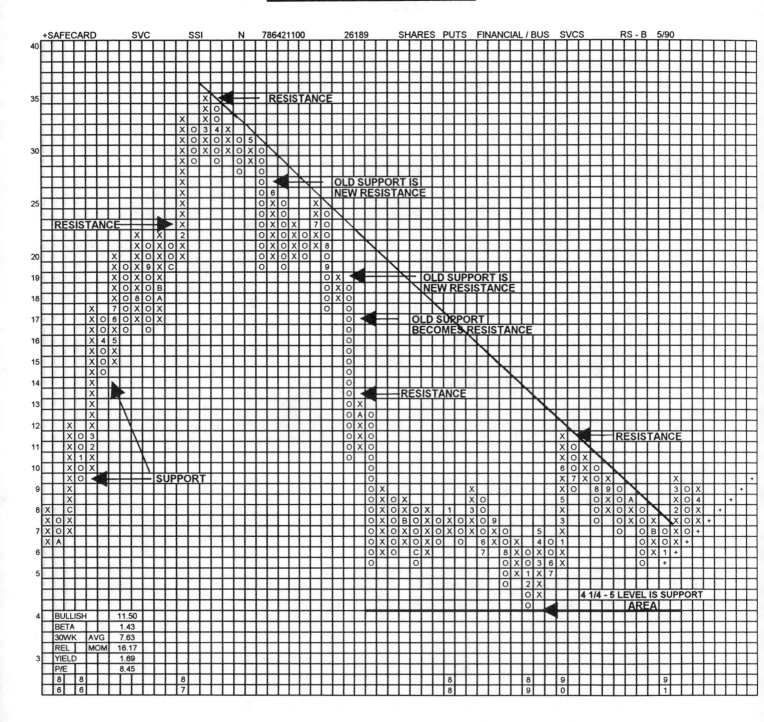

uptrend resumes with another leg from points 3 to 4 followed by a retracement from 4 to 5. To date, Illinois Tool has experienced five well-defined price moves of similar length.

The first leg of 17 points moved from 26 to 43, with the correction retracing about $\frac{2}{3}$ of the primary move. Leg 2 went from 32 to 47 for a 15 point advance, while the 8-point correction accounted for slightly more than a 50% retracement. Corrections may be estimated by recalling Dow's thesis that stocks retrace from $\frac{1}{3}$ to $\frac{2}{3}$ of the primary price move. The third leg totaled 18 points from 39 to 57, while legs 4 and 5 were 18 and 17 points, respectively. Price moves can be estimated by adding the estimated length of the next leg to the low point of the previous correction.

We may find another example in Figure 10-10 in the NCNB chart. The stock reveals four major down legs as indicated below the example. Legs 1 through 4 were 14, 12, 14, and 16 points, respectively. Traders who sell short or buy put options can utilize these cyclical swings to capitalize on downside price swings.

When long-term charts are available, some technicians prefer to utilize the measured move from the vantage point of longer-term price movements. Their preference rests with the overall or "big picture" rather than primarily the near-term. In Figure 10-11, the Imperial Chemical chart discloses three major down legs over a five-year period. The downmoves were 27, 25, and 27 points respectively and are indicated by numbers on the chart. Calculations of the "legs down" appear at the bottom of the chart. Although this long-term view misses some trading moves, it is highly satisfactory for long-term investors.

Support and Resistance

Support and resistance have been topics of conversation throughout the book. The concepts of old support and new resistance along with old resistance and new support are developed within the context of illustrations throughout the book. However, support and resistance play a vital role in forecasting price targets, so it seems appropriate to illustrate them individually.

The Safecard Services chart in Figure 10-12 shows a strong downtrend from 1987 into early 1991. At the right of the example, key areas have been identified. The March 1987 top at 35 now serves as a resistance area. Sell signals at 28 and 27 broke previous support and now constitute resistance for future price advances. Another major downside price breakout at 19 indicates a major point of overhead supply for later uptrends, while lesser resistance points appear from continuation sell signals at $16\frac{1}{2}$ and 10. The $4\frac{1}{2}$ to 5 area offers a key area of support. In each instance where a major sell signal evolves, old support becomes new resistance. When previous bottoms are penetrated, they serve as an obstacle to later rallies.

Figure 10-13
SUPPORT AND RESISTANCE LEVELS ARE ALSO PRICE OBJECTIVES

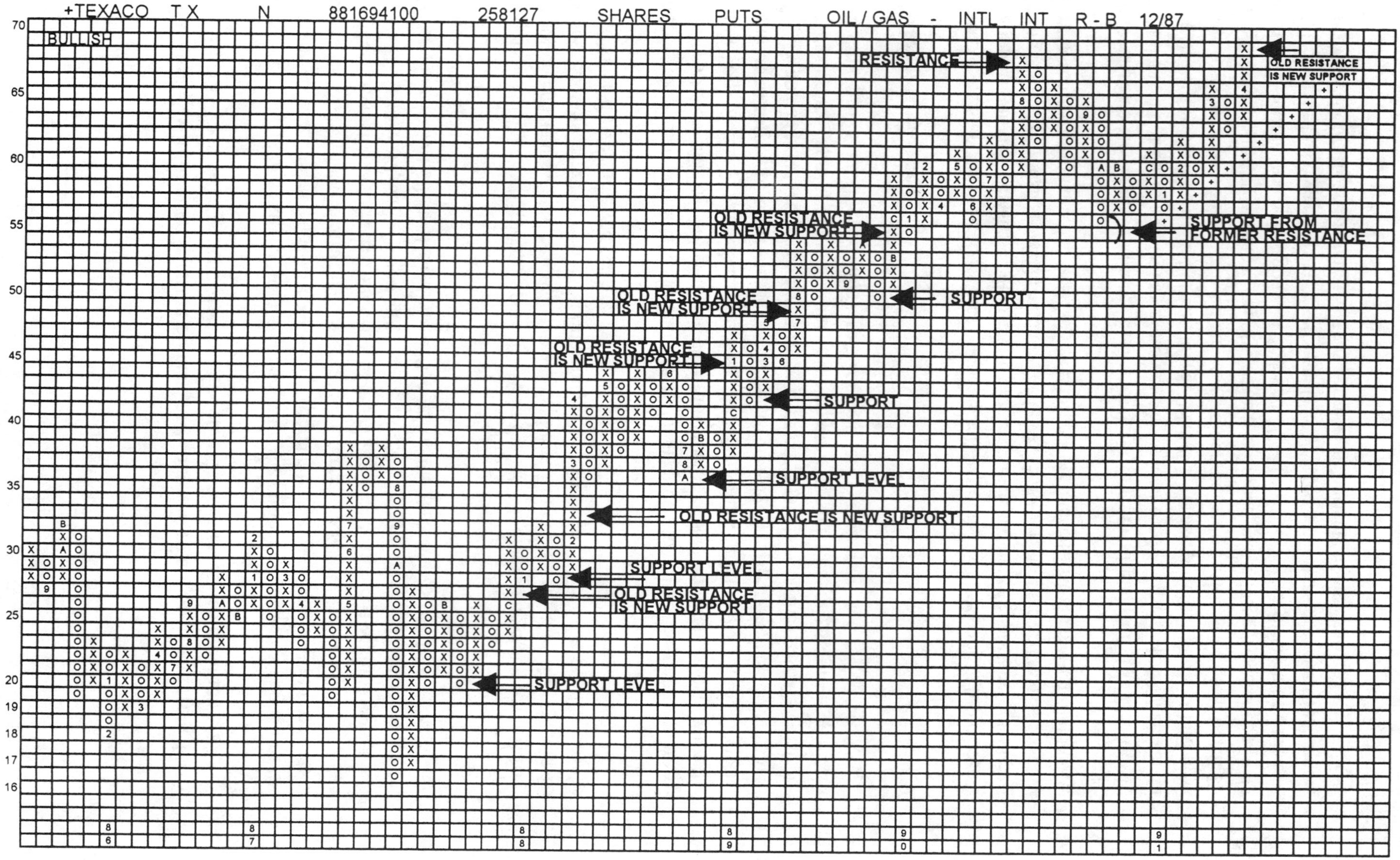

196

In Figure 10-13, the Texaco chart demonstrates a strong uptrend from 1987 into 1991. Major upside breakouts occur at 27, 33, 45, 49, 55, and 62, among others. In cases where a buy signal evolves, old resistance areas become new support for future price declines. The lowest O's in each retracement also serve as support levels. In forecasting moves in either direction, price estimates must consider support and resistance in arriving at targets.

Section 2 has thus far strengthened the overall approach to Point and Figure charting with better price objectives, more sensitive trendlines, and improved chart patterns. We are ready to explore **relative strength,** perhaps the single most important concept in P & F chart analysis. Relative strength serves to eliminate more analytical and timing errors than any other technical tool. Once relative strength has been treated, we will examine Point and Figure charts on industry groups and technical indicators that pertain to the aggregate market. Each segment of additional analysis is instrumental in eliminating strategy errors, improving targets and pattern recognition, and enhancing investment performance.

SUMMARY

Given the volatility in today's markets, price forecasts play an important role in timing the sale of stocks. Investors have been limited by traditional thought in terms of projecting price moves with the horizontal count. By learning to "expand the base" or "expand the horizontal count," there are alternatives in reaching different intermediate-term price objectives. The use of revised vertical counts also lends accuracy to longer-term prognostications. Updated vertical counts can either confirm previous predictions or alter an investor's earlier forecast based on changes in the chart pattern.

Trading counts and measured moves can also assist the chartist in reaching price objectives and developing trading strategies. Market environments have become complex and require accurate approaches to estimating future buying and selling points. Support and resistance must also be taken into consideration in estimating price targets. Investors can afford the luxury of using every available forecasting tool at their disposal to compete in current market climates. A single approach for estimating prices will no longer suffice.

CHAPTER 11

RELATIVE STRENGTH: THE GREAT COMMON DENOMINATOR

One disparaging remark commonly directed at P & F charting concerns the number of false breakouts or misleading signals yielded by individual charts. However, a technical tool known as **relative strength** can differentiate between stronger and weaker performing stocks. Relative strength compares the performance of individual stocks to that of the general market. Stocks with rising relative strength outperform the market, while those with declining relative strength underperform it. Applications of relative strength appear throughout the chapter.

Given the rationale of relative strength, a solid investment strategy would logically include purchasing or selling stocks with a rising or falling relative strength, respectively. Investors need to buy rising stocks with a bullish relative strength accompanied by an increasing market and strong industry group. Conversely, short positions need declining stocks with a bearish relative strength in a market downtrend within a weak industry group. Our investment criteria for stock selection are not only expanded but improved.

First, we need to understand the concept of relative strength, its underlying theories, calculations, and plotting on a P & F chart. Then, we can analyze some actual charts to evaluate the role of relative strength in the decision-making process.

UNDERSTANDING RELATIVE STRENGTH

Most relative strength calculations are made by dividing the weekly closing price of an individual stock by a similar price for a popular market average. Although more technicians use the S & P 500 or NYSE Composite Index, other measures of the general market are also acceptable. Chartcraft, Inc. of New Rochelle, New York ranks among the leading investment authorities in relative strength. Unlike most others, Chartcraft utilizes the Dow Jones Industrial Average (DJIA) as its gauge of the market.

Figure 11-1 features an explanation of relative strength (RS) by Chartcraft as well as a sample presentation of an individual chart from their monthly P & F chartbook. The RS status for Du Pont may be found at the top right-hand corner of the chart and reads

"RS - B 6/91." This reading indicates a buy or bullish signal occurred on the P & F relative strength chart in June 1991. Any type of buy signal provides a bullish relative strength and means the stock will outperform the market in the months ahead. Any sell signal (i.e., RS - S) on an RS P & F chart suggests a bearish relative strength and warns the stock will underperform the market.

Figure 11-1
The Chartcraft Approach to Relative Strength
EXPLANATION OF RELATIVE STRENGTH

AS AN IMPORTANT FEATURE IN THIS BOOK WE PUT THE P & F RELATIVE STRENGTH SIGNALS ON THE UPPER RIGHT CORNER OF EACH STOCK CHART. (THIS SIGNAL IS BEFORE THE INVESTORS DAILY INDUSTRY GROUP.) WE KEEP RELATIVE STRENGTH CHARTS ON ALL NYSE & ASE ISSUES + ABOUT 2000 OTC STOCKS.

THE USEFULNESS OF RELATIVE STRENGTH CHARTS AS AN AID TO STOCK SELECTION CANNOT BE UNDERESTIMATED. AS A REFRESHER WE'LL REVIEW THIS USE.

SUPPOSE A STOCK IS $80 AND THE DJIA IS 2000. IF WE DIVIDE $80 BY 2000 (AND MOVE THE DECIMAL OVER 3 PLACES) WE GET A RESULT OF 40.0. LET US SUPPOSE THE DJIA DROPS TO 1600 WHILE THIS STOCK FALLS TO $72. NOW IF WE DIVIDE THE STOCK PRICE ($72) BY THE DJIA (1600) WE GET A RESULT OF 45.0, AFTER MOVING THE DECIMAL.

WHAT DOES THIS TELL US? FIRST, A CHART OF THE PRICE OF THE STOCK WOULD SHOW A COLUMN OF "O'S" FROM $80 TO $72. SECOND, A CHART OF THE RELATIVE STRENGTH WOULD SHOW A COLUMN OF "X'S" FROM 40.0 TO 45.0.

THE MARKET ITSELF INFLUENCES INDIVIDUAL STOCKS VERY MUCH IN THAT IF IT RISES IT CARRIES LOTS OF STOCKS WITH IT WHILE IF IT DECLINES MOST STOCKS ALSO DROP. WHAT RELATIVE STRENGTH ATTEMPTS TO DO IS ELIMINATE THE MARKET AS A FACTOR IN THE ACTION OF A STOCK. IN THE EXAMPLE SHOWN ABOVE WE SURMISE THAT THE ONLY REASON THE PRICE OF THE STOCK IS DROPPING IS THE DECLINING MARKET. IF THE MARKET WERE TO MOVE SIDEWAYS OR RISE THIS STOCK WOULD LIKELY BE A LEADER ON THE UPSIDE. STOCKS LIKE THIS ALSO TEND TO BOTTOM OUT LONG BEFORE THE DJIA IN BEAR MARKETS.

WE USE SIMPLE POINT & FIGURE BUY AND SELL SIGNALS ON RELATIVE STRENGTH CHARTS TO TRY TO FIND THE STOCKS THAT WILL LEAD THE WAY UP IN BULL MARKETS OR LEAD THE MARKET ON THE DOWNSIDE IN BEAR MARKETS.

SOME STOCKS HAVE R.S. SIGNALS THAT LAST FOR YEARS. GENERAL MOTORS, FOR INSTANCE, HAS GIVEN FOUR RELATIVE STRENGTH SIGNALS IN THE PAST 11 YEARS. "GM" RS GAVE A BUY IN JUNE '82, BEFORE THE GREAT BULL MARKET LIFT OFF, WITH THE STOCK ABOUT $23. THE RS REMAINED BULLISH UNTIL MAY '85 WHEN A SELL WAS GIVEN WITH THE STOCK AT $35. SINCE THEN THE RS HAS REMAINED NEGATIVE, EXCEPT FOR THE BRIEF NOV '88- MAY '89 PERIOD, AND GM IS STILL TRADING ABOUT THE $35 LEVEL. ON THE OTHER HAND THE DOW JONES INDUSTRIAL AVERAGE HAS RISEN FROM 1300 IN MAY '85 TO OVER 3200.

INVESTORS USING RELATIVE STRENGTH WOULD HAVE SIMPLY NOT CONSIDERED "GM" FOR LONG TERM PURCHASE DURING MOST OF THIS PERIOD OF TIME. IF THEY FOLLOWED THE R.S. SIGNALS THEY WOULD HAVE SEEN EARLY GAINS AS AUTO'S RECOVERED FROM 1982 LOWS BUT WOULD AVOIDED YEARS OF SIDEWAYS ACTION IN "GM" WHILE THE MARKETS EXPLODED.

Example of the Presentation of Relative Strength Signals

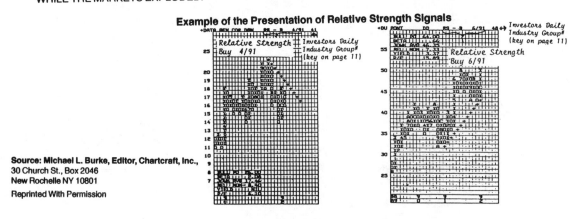

Source: Michael L. Burke, Editor, Chartcraft, Inc.,
30 Church St., Box 2046
New Rochelle NY 10801

Reprinted With Permission

Figure 11-1 describes how a P & F chart can be devised from RS calculations. Once the weekly closing price of the stock is divided by the weekly close of a popular market average (DJIA in this case), we move the decimal place over three places (or however many necessary to convert the calculation to a whole number). The conversion of RS figures to whole numbers makes it possible to construct a regular P & F chart.

Let's review Figure 11-1 for purposes of illustration. ABC stock currently sells for $80, while the DJIA is 2000. An RS calculation may be made by dividing 80 by 2000 and moving the decimal to the right. Our answer is 40. If the DJIA drops to 1600 and ABC declines to 72, the RS calculation reads 45. The most significant feature of this example lies in the disparate movements of ABC's stock price and its RS chart. While ABC stock declines in a column of O's from 80 to 72, ABC's RS advances in a column of X's from 40 to 45. The rising RS means ABC shows strength because the stock has declined less than the aggregate market.

Du Pont contains several other analytical tools furnished by Chartcraft. On each of their P & F graphs, Chartcraft gives a **price objective** (in this case, Bull PO) based on the vertical count. However, readers should calculate their own targets as outlined earlier in the book because our coverage provides more options for price forecasts. **Beta factors** measure the volatility of individual stocks from market movements. For example, ABC stock has a beta factor of 2.0. If the general market increases 10 percent, we expect ABC to rise by 20 percent because the stock is twice as volatile as the market. Beta factors greater than 1.0 suggest aggressive, more volatile issues, while beta factors less than 1.0 suggest conservative stocks with less volatility. Stocks with betas of 1.0 should keep pace with the general market and are classified as neutral. **Thirty-week moving averages** appear on each chart and represent potential support and resistance areas. **Relative momentum** figures indicate the percentage that stock prices are above or below the 30-week moving averages. Obviously, stocks with higher momentum are further removed from the average line, while passive issues with lower momentum numbers stay close to the thirty-week moving average. **Dividend yields** are the current annual dividend divided by the market price. A frequent generalization maintains that overvalued stocks have lower dividend yields while underpriced issues show higher returns. However, investors need to be mindful of a caveat -- growth issues pay little or no dividend, while utilities have attractive payouts.

Price-earnings (PE) ratios divulge what "multiple of earnings" the stocks sell for in the market. A PE ratio of 40 means that investors are willing to pay $40 for each $1 of earnings. Lower PE ratios generally identify with undervalued stocks, while higher PEs ordinarily associate with overvalued issues.

Applying Relative Strength

Perhaps the most important aspect of the buy or sell decision concerns relative strength. The surest approach places both the individual stock and its relative strength on separate P & F charts. When both charts record breakouts in the same direction, the stock's price move is confirmed. However, the easiest way to apply RS may be found in Chartcraft's monthly P&F book which gives updated signals each month. Figure 11-2 furnishes a classic example of relative strength application as provided by Chartcraft. Price charts for both Quanex and Ralston Purina appear on the left-hand side of the illustration. Graphs on the right-hand side contain RS charts for both issues.

A buy signal and upside price reversal surfaced on the Ralston Purina chart in mid-1982 as the general market started to advance. Ralston had been a slow-moving, non-responsive stock during most of the 1970's. However, the RS chart registered a buy signal in February 1982. The RS breakout means Ralston should outperform the aggregate market for the next few years because buy and sell signals on RS charts remain in effect for long periods of time. Ralston's RS buy signal lasted from February 1982 until July 1987. During this time, the stock advanced from $10 to $89. The sell signal proved timely for Ralston as its price was in the 84-85 range when the RS reversed its course.

A contrasting example of relative strength appears in Quanex Corporation. The downside price breakout on the P & F price chart (72) was confirmed by a sell signal on the RS chart in January 1982. During roughly the same five-year period of Ralston's price advance, Quanex lost 90 percent of its value. The stock price declined from $30 to $3, despite an unparalleled advance in the general market

From a technician's point of view, the critical difference in the two stocks was the sharp contrast in their relative strength charts. RS buy and sell signals need to be acknowledged because of their permanence and duration. The RS chart for Quanex did not have a buy signal until July 1987 -- more than five years after the sell signal. Quanex became a buying opportunity in the $7 price range because its stock price breakout was confirmed by a similar buy signal on its RS chart. During the first half of 1989, Quanex reached 19, almost three times its price at the confirmed purchase level.

Always concentrate investment decisions on P & F price breakouts confirmed by breakouts on RS charts. Purchasing a stock on a buy signal without a corresponding buy signal on the relative strength chart suggests a trading opportunity only. Upside price breakouts with bearish RS charts are suspect and warn that the advance usually lacks intensity or conviction. Similarly, selling and/or selling short should be implemented only on downside price breakouts confirmed

Figure 11-2

CHARTCRAFT'S CLASSIC EXAMPLE OF RELATIVE STRENGTH

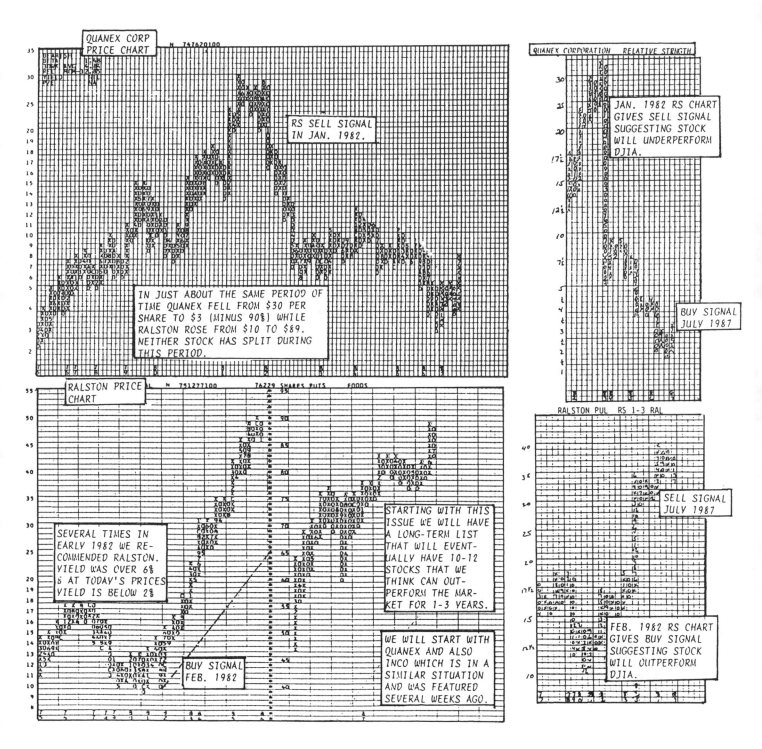

QUANEX CORP PRICE CHART

RS SELL SIGNAL IN JAN. 1982.

IN JUST ABOUT THE SAME PERIOD OF TIME QUANEX FELL FROM $30 PER SHARE TO $3 (MINUS 90%) WHILE RALSTON ROSE FROM $10 TO $69. NEITHER STOCK HAS SPLIT DURING THIS PERIOD.

QUANEX CORPORATION RELATIVE STRENGTH

JAN. 1982 RS CHART GIVES SELL SIGNAL SUGGESTING STOCK WILL UNDERPERFORM DJIA.

BUY SIGNAL JULY 1987

RALSTON PRICE CHART

SEVERAL TIMES IN EARLY 1982 WE RE-COMMENDED RALSTON. YIELD WAS OVER 6% & AT TODAY'S PRICES YIELD IS BELOW 2%.

STARTING WITH THIS ISSUE WE WILL HAVE A LONG-TERM LIST THAT WILL EVENT-UALLY HAVE 10-12 STOCKS THAT WE THINK CAN OUT-PERFORM THE MAR-KET FOR 1-3 YEARS.

WE WILL START WITH QUANEX AND ALSO INCO WHICH IS IN A SIMILAR SITUATION AND WAS FEATURED SEVERAL WEEKS AGO.

BUY SIGNAL FEB. 1982

RALSTON PUL RS 1-3 RAL

SELL SIGNAL JULY 1987

FEB. 1982 RS CHART GIVES BUY SIGNAL SUGGESTING STOCK WILL OUTPERFORM DJIA.

by sell signals on RS charts. Sell signals on price charts while buy signals continue on RS graphs should ordinarily be regarded as temporary in nature. Corrections usually result from such scenarios. Long-lasting price moves in either direction require the same buy or sell signal on both charts.

The Ralston and Quanex examples reveal another basic technical concept. Bear market declines enable investors to select the best prospective stocks for purchase in the next upmove. Conversely, the weakest stocks are manifested in bull markets. For example, Ralston performed well in the bear market which culminated in July 1982. It did not suffer catastrophic price declines, although the general market was notably weak. Therefore, we would expect a strong performance from Ralston when the market turned upward. However, Quanex performed poorly and declined during an unusually powerful bullish trend. Even a good market could not boost the price of Quanex. The strong overall market made the weakness in Quanex highly visible.

EMPIRICAL EVIDENCE OF RS AND BULLISH TRENDS

Let's examine some additional charts to apply relative strength to price trends. Figure 11-3 provides three examples of uptrend stocks with bullish relative strengths. Commodore has an RS buy signal in December 1990 (as shown at the top of the price chart). Commodore reveals a price breakout in October 1990 at 6. The RS buy signal in December of 1990 confirms the move and hints of a strong price advance. The stock reached 21 by April 1991.

Dun and Bradstreet (D & B) performed poorly for several years with lateral price movements and minimal participation in market rallies. However, a buy signal develops on the RS chart in December 1991. D & B shows a price breakout at 50 in October and November of 1991, but chartists won't act on that signal with RS still negative. However, another buy signal occurs in December 1991 with positive relative strength. Once RS confirms the price breakout, we acknowledge the bullish trend and expect it to last for some time.

An excellent example concerning the influence of a positive RS may be seen in the Morgan Keegan chart at the bottom of Figure 11-3. The stock bottoms with a low pole in November 1990. However, Morgan Keegan's RS chart turns bullish in May of 1991 while the price chart gives a second buy signal at $9\frac{1}{2}$. We would not accept the earlier price breakout at $8\frac{1}{2}$ because the relative strength was still bearish in September 1989. By refusing a buy signal with negative RS, one avoided entry into a stock two years too soon. Funds could have been invested elsewhere more productively and reinvested in Morgan Keegan in May 1991. The stock nearly tripled before showing signs of weakness in early 1992.

Figure 11-3

RELATIVE STRENGTH AND BULL MARKET BEGINNINGS

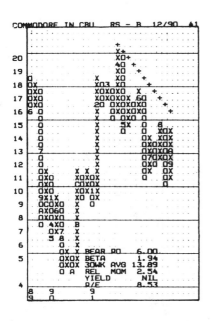

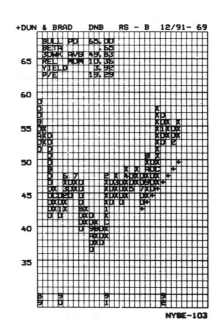

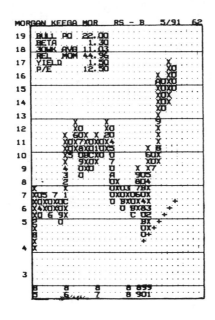

Figure 11-4

UPTRENDS CONFIRMED BY RELATIVE STRENGTH BREAKOUTS

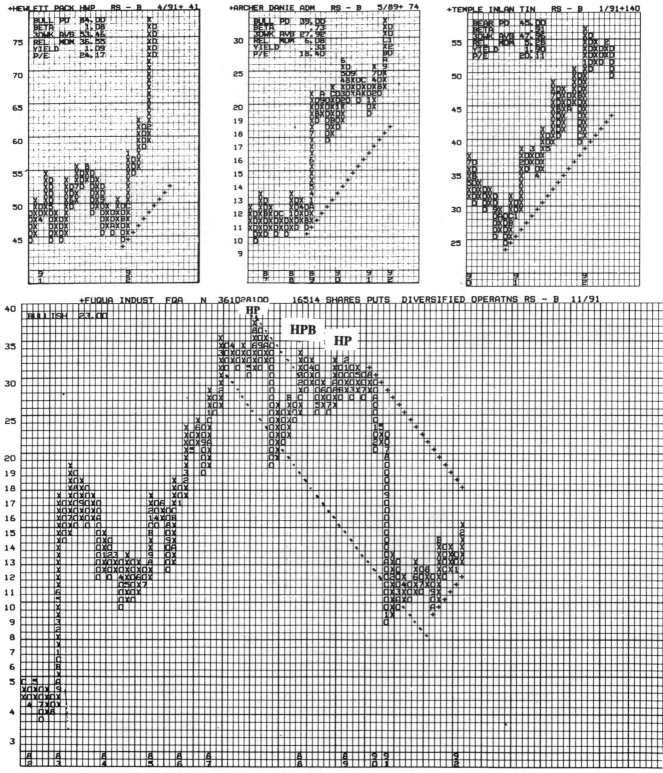

Hewlett Packard (HP) in Figure 11-4 provides an interesting illustration of how RS moves often precede price signals. HP moves laterally during 1991 and does not achieve a buy signal until December 1991 and January 1992, when the price reaches 57. An RS breakout seven months earlier forewarned of increasing technical strength in HP. The stock advanced from 45 to 79 during January and February.

Archer Daniel Midland (ADM) has a buy signal at 14 in May 1989. A breakout on the RS chart in May 1989 confirms the bullish price action which has remained in effect for three years. ADM displays a gradual move and has a lower beta factor than HP. However, conservative stocks often exhibit longer-lasting trends than do their more volatile counterparts.

The Temple Inland chart reveals an upside price breakout at 31 in December 1990 with a bearish RS. However, the RS turns bullish in January 1991, while Temple shows a corresponding buy signal at 33. Temple undergoes an advance from $25 to $57 over a one-year period. The correction in the last quarter of 1991 would ordinarily be tolerated by most investors because it occurred during a period of bullish RS. If Temple's downside breakout at 44 in November 1991 had been achieved with a bearish RS, investors would liquidate holdings because of the potential for a bear market beginning. Since Temple's RS is still bullish, positions are maintained because an orderly correction should take place unless the general market collapses. Relative strength can frequently be utilized by chartists to differentiate between corrections and major price reversals. Downside moves with positive relative strength in the stock usually suggest corrections, while lower prices combined with a bearish RS often forewarn of major downside price reversals.

Recurring high pole formations occur on the Fuqua chart and precede a major downside move. Although not available from the Chart, Fuqua's RS gave a sell signal in April 1989. The stock declined from the low 30's to the 10 area in early 1991 and remained depressed. Fuqua received an RS buy signal in November 1991 and confirmed a price breakout one month earlier. The pullback effect in late 1991 and early 1992 developed under the influence of a bullish RS, so the decline should be short-lived.

Examples in Figure 11-5 illustrate the potency often linked to price trends confirmed by RS signals. Schwab has an upside price breakout at $9\frac{1}{2}$ in February 1991, while its RS chart continues bearish. Since previous tops exist at 11 and 12, we would not enter into a long position at this point. However, the RS chart turned bullish in April 1991 and confirmed the upward trend in price. Schwab's price reached 36 in January 1992.

Figure 11-5

MORE ON STOCKS WITH RISING PRICES AND BULLISH RELATIVE STRENGTH

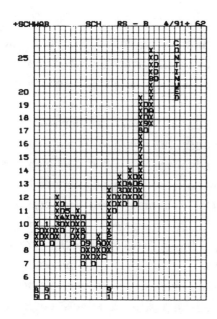

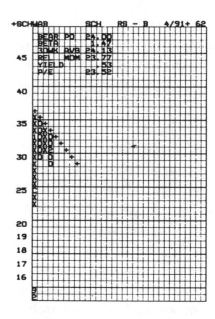

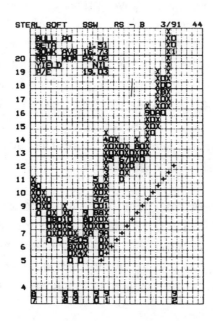

Figure 11-6

DOWNTRENDS AND NEGATIVE RELATIVE STRENGTH

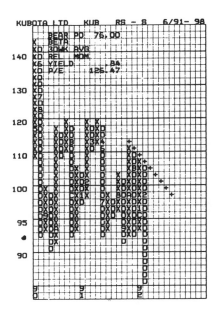

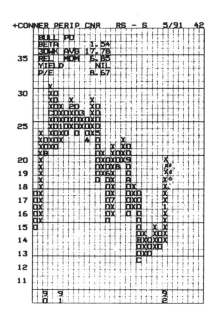

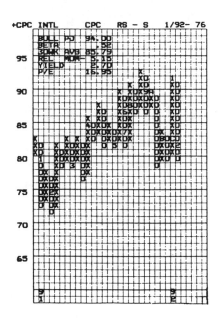

Figure 11-7

MORE BEARISH RELATIVE STRENGTH SIGNALS

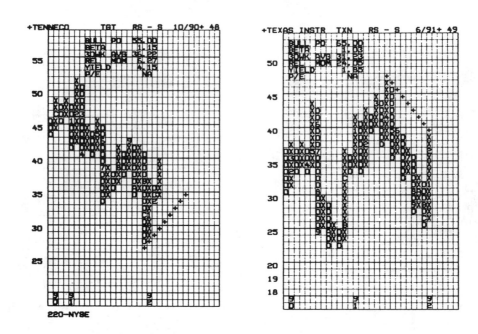

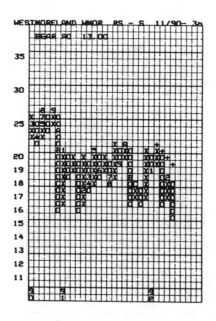

Sterling Software achieved an upside price breakout at $11\frac{1}{2}$ in March 1991. Sterling's RS also turned bullish at the same time and forecasts a major price advance. An interesting point concerning support and resistance evolves in Figure 11-5. Resistance levels from past tops were considered to be a problem on the Schwab chart because the RS was bearish. Sterling shows resistance from earlier tops at 10 and 11, but we don't view these points as a major problem because of a bullish RS. Resistance levels are more easily penetrated with positive relative strengths, while support levels may prove less helpful when stocks show negative relative strength. Both Schwab and Sterling have aggressive beta factors (1.47 and 1.51, respectively) and demonstrate swift price advances.

SOME EXAMPLES OF RS AND BEARISH PRICE TRENDS

Figure 11-6 provides three examples of stocks in pronounced downtrends accompanied by negative relative strength. Kubota serves as an interesting illustration because a first glance indicates the stock is ready to bottom following an extended "wall of O's" on the left hand side of the chart. However, we determine from the top of the graph that Kubota's RS gives a sell signal in June 1991. There is also a downside price breakout at 110 in June. The RS sell signal confirms the downside price breakout and serves notice that Kubota is set for lower prices. A bearish RS would enable you to anticipate a breakdown in the chart below multiple bottoms in the 90 - 95 area.

Some general rules of thumb for anticipating breakouts from base patterns relate to relative strength. If a stock's RS is bullish, you can generally expect upside price breakouts during strong aggregate markets. Conversely, when a stock's RS is bearish, you may usually anticipate downside price breakouts, particularly during weak general markets. In addition, RS signals often precede price signals, but they may also occur coincidentally during the same month. However, an RS signal taking place after a signal on the price chart still confirms the price trend.

Conner Peripheral in Figure 11-6 serves as an excellent example of why investors should buy stocks with bullish relative strengths. Conner shows a pattern of consistently lower tops during the strong bull market of 1991. The stock gave a major sell signal on a downside breakout to 22 during May of 1991. Conner's RS chart flashed a sell signal during the same time period to confirm a bearish trend. Despite some strong performances by technology issues and the overall market, Conner launched a downside move which erased approximately 50% of its value. Two key points should be reiterated. First, stocks which display both bearish chart and RS patterns should be sold and/or sold short but not purchased. Secondly, beware of stocks that reveal consistently lower tops, particularly during bullish markets.

Figure 11-8

BEARISH RELATIVE STRENGTH AND NON-PERFORMING STOCKS

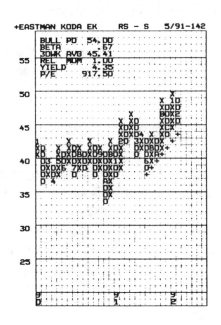

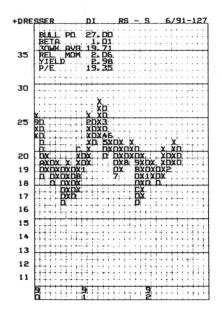

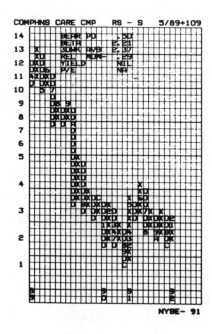

CPC International enjoyed a steady upmove and positive RS during the market advance of 1991. We expect the sell signal in October 1991 to result in a correction because the RS was positive. After retracement, the stock challenged previous highs in the low 90's. However, CPC encountered a sell signal on the RS chart in January 1992 and a high pole formed.

It is appropriate to interject some new thoughts concerning high poles. High pole formations that form in combination with a bearish RS are usually bearish, particularly if the aggregate market appears to be in a state of deterioration. If the general market is strong, high poles forming on stocks with a negative RS may experience only a correction. However, such stocks are technically weak at best.

High pole formations on charts with positive relative strength are different, however. With a strong general market and a bullish RS, sell signals and downside moves from high poles usually mean a correction. If the market appears to be topping out or sluggish, then high-pole stocks with bullish relative strength are vulnerable despite their ability to outperform the general market. It is best for all concerned not to fight the trend of the market.

In the case of CPC, relative strength served as a precursor of the stock's impending weakness and allowed chartists an opportunity to liquidate positions prior to the slide. In this illustration, a downside price breakout will simply confirm what a negative RS has already indicated. For more on the significance of RS as a leading indicator, let's refer to the Tenneco chart in Figure 11-7.

From the upper right-hand corner of the P & F chart, we learn that Tenneco received a particularly helpful sell signal on its RS chart in October 1990. The RS sell signal occurs prior to Tenneco reaching 52 and achieving a new high for the move in February 1991. Once again, a high pole formation occurs with a negative RS. The combination of a high pole and negative RS previews Tenneco's 50% loss of value en route to the trough of a major downmove. Tenneco bottoms in late 1991 and a low pole forms in early 1992. Although the stock appears to have reached a low point, do not become too bullish on Tenneco yet, despite the occurrence of a low pole formation. Our reasoning is based on a continuing negative RS. It would be premature to get overly aggressive with Tenneco at this point in time.

In the Texas Instruments (TI) chart, an RS sell signal develops in June 1991. The relative strength breakout on the downside merely confirms the earlier price breakout in May. We expect weakness in the stock for some time. You need to approach the January 1992 upside price breakout with caution because TI still has a negative RS. Furthermore, do not expect the rally to move above the bearish resistance line with a negative RS. Valid upside trend reversals need to be accomplished with positive RS readings.

Figure 11-9

HIGH POLE FORMATIONS WITH BULLISH RELATIVE STRENGTH

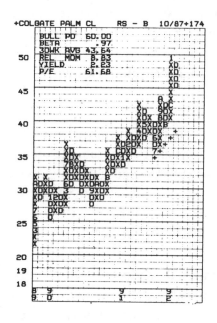

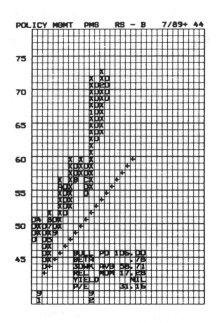

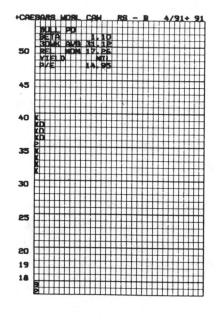

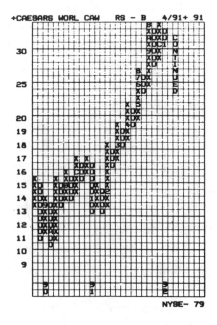

The Westmoreland illustration provides another interesting observation connecting relative strength and price trends. Westmoreland receives a sell signal on its RS chart in November 1990. The negative RS confirms a sell signal on the price chart during the same month. Despite the bull market from late 1990 into 1992, Westmoreland remains dormant. The stock fails to participate and actually gave a sell signal during the early phases of the bull market. Westmoreland serves as a perfect example of why investors need to buy stocks with a positive RS and sell those with a negative RS. Relative strength is perhaps the single most important concept in P & F chart analysis. RS chart signals help investors buy and sell stocks for more permanent moves with a greater degree of accuracy and timing.

Figure 11-8 includes some examples of other stocks which fail to perform during favorable market climates. Eastman Kodak's RS chart gives a sell signal in May 1991, but the stock edges slightly higher from the influence of the general market. Stocks with negative RS can still show price increases because the aggregate market drives prices higher. However, such price increases are less than spectacular because bearish RS stocks fail to keep pace with the market.

Dresser Industries displays a sell signal at 22 in May 1991. The downside breakout is confirmed when the stock's RS chart flashes a sell signal in June. The remainder of 1991 unveils a sloppy performance from Dresser, despite the strong uptrend in the overall market. All upside price breakouts continue to be suspect until the relative strength turns bullish.

Comprehensive Care's RS chart yielded a sell signal in May 1989 and served notice that the stock should be avoided. Even though the stock market as a whole performed well, Comprehensive Care dropped to $1 in late 1990. Upside breakouts in May and June 1991 proved false because of the negative RS chart.

High Pole Formations and Relative Strength

Earlier in this chapter, we introduced the idea that downside moves from high pole formations were greatly influenced by relative strength. In Figure 11-9, the Colgate Palmolive chart has a high pole formation develop from an upside breakout in June 1990. Colgate's RS chart turned bullish in October 1987. The high pole resulted in a very gradual correction followed by a resumption of the uptrend. Colgate follows with another high pole formation in January 1992. If you were making a decision on Colgate, the stock remains bullish because the relative strength continues impressively on the positive side.

Figure 11-10

HIGH POLE FORMATIONS WITH BEARISH RELATIVE STRENGTH

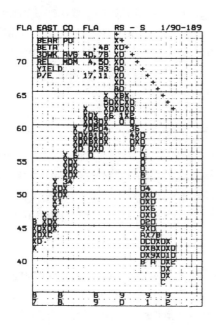

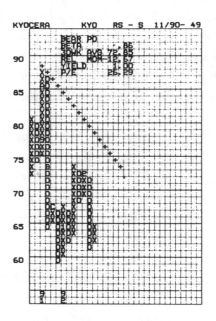

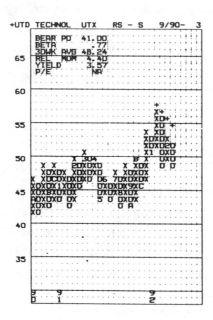

Figure 11-11

LOW POLES AND BULLISH RELATIVE STRENGTH

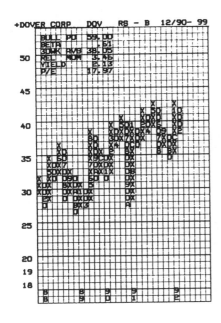

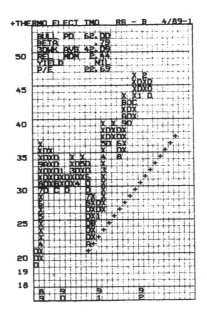

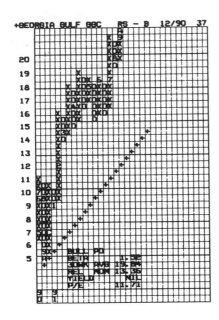

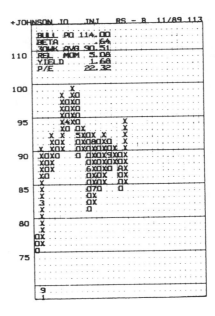

Figure 11-12

LOW POLES AND BEARISH RELATIVE STRENGTH

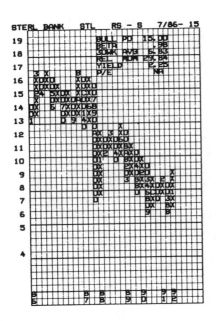

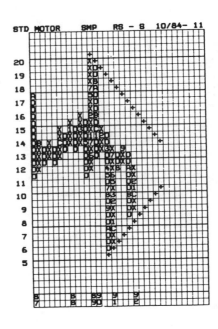

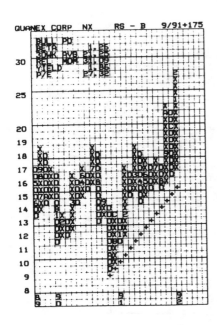

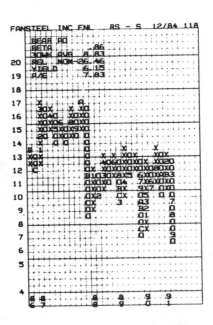

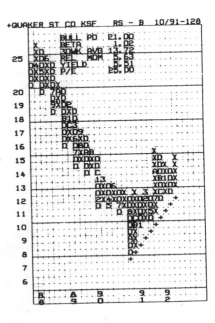

Policy Management reveals an upside breakout at 61 in December 1991 followed by a high pole in January of 1992. However, the stock quickly reverses to the upside and the advance continues. The stock's RS turned bullish in July 1989 and influences the stock's persistent advance. Caesars World forms a high pole from August to November 1991. However, the Caesars RS chart gave a buy signal in April 1991. With the price uptrend confirmed by a bullish RS, Caesars consolidates after the high pole in a triple top continuation pattern which concludes with a breakout at 35 in February 1992. As chartists, we logically anticipate an upside breakout because the stock's RS remains positive in a bullish market. Sell signals from stocks with positive RS charts usually result in a correction during bullish stock market environments. Retracements may be more severe when the overall market trend is bearish.

Relative strength exerts an overriding influence on the severity of downside moves, both from high poles and other patterns. Let's examine Figure 11-10 which includes some high pole formations with negative RS charts. Florida East Coast Industries shows an advance to 73. A high pole formation forms at the end of the move and results in a sell signal at 61 in January 1990. An RS sell signal simultaneously appears on the chart. Florida East plunges rapidly in an almost uninterrupted, bear market fashion.

Kyocera displays a similar chart with the advance culminating in a high pole formations. Sell signals appear on both the price and RS charts in November 1991 and precede rapid downside price moves. United Technologies reveals a high pole formation in January 1992 with a sell signal at 50. The RS chart gave a sell signal in September 1990 and warns us to question the strength of the advance. Aggressive, timing-oriented investors should avoid United Technologies because its upside potential appears limited as an underperformer.

In conclusion, relative strength dictates investment strategy and timing decisions, but it also impacts the duration of price moves. Further, relative strength P & F charts as utilized by Chartcraft are invaluable in discriminating between valid and false price breakouts in either direction. Let's turn our attention to relative strength and low pole formations.

Relative Strength and Low Pole Formations

Figure 11-11 contains four examples of low pole formations accompanied by bullish RS charts. Dover Corporation displays a low pole in October and November 1991 in conjunction with a positive relative strength from December 1991. Dover begins an advance which continues into 1992 with little difficulty. Thermo Electron has a low pole formation in the last quarter of 1990 with a bullish RS from April 1989. The stock exhibits a strong upward move in price with no visible sign of weakness.

Georgia Gulf manifests a low pole formation in the last quarter of 1990, while the RS chart flashes a buy signal in December. A swift advance follows. Johnson and Johnson concludes a correction bottom with a low pole formation in June, July, and August of 1991. After a period of consolidation, the stock resumes its upside advance on the strength of an RS buy signal from November 1989.

Low pole formations that develop with positive RS signals often result in strong advances. However, let's examine some low pole patterns with bearish RS charts and draw a comparison. A review of P & F charts may give the surface impression that low pole formations provide mixed results when compared to high pole formations. However, the use of relative strength as a supplemental tool should enable us to distinguish between strong-performing and non-responsive charts.

Figure 11-12 includes five illustrations of low pole formations. In the last quarter of 1987 and January 1988, Sterling Bancorp builds a low pole pattern which seems to end the slide and prepare for the stock better things to the upside. However, Sterling's RS chart turned bearish in July 1986 and warned of the weakness that followed. Sterling failed to follow through with an advance, and the stock has meandered lackadaisically in a lateral fashion for the last four years. Since the stock was underperforming the market, the low pole formation failed to provide much impetus for a rally.

Standard Motor registered sell signals in March and May of 1990 and a low pole ensued during the first half of 1991. Reference to the upper right hand corner of the graph, however, indicates that Standard's RS chart turned bearish in October 1984. Standard was unable to sustain the rally effort as it underperformed the market during the entire period.

Quanex endured a sharp sell-off to $9\frac{1}{2}$ during the fall of 1990, but a low pole followed during the last two calendar months. Quanex rallied back toward near-term highs at $18\frac{1}{2}$ in 1991. However, the RS chart turned bullish in September 1991, and Quanex achieved an upside price breakout at 19 during the same month. The bullish RS combined with the price breakout spawned a rally that originated with the earlier low pole formation. The Quanex illustration provides a critical insight into the relationship between relative strength and low poles. Until the RS turned positive, Quanex showed a pattern of meaningless consolidation following the low pole with little or no direction. When the relative strength turned bullish, the rally turned into an uptrend. The bull market in Quanex became untracked once the positive RS confirmation appeared.

Fansteel formed a low pole in the last quarter of 1989 and the first half of 1990. However, rally attempts failed and another downside move eliminated previous bottoms in September 1991. Fansteel's low pole formation did not lead to an uptrend because the RS chart remained bearish from a sell signal in December 1984.

The stock did not respond to bullish conditions in the general market during late 1990 and 1991. In contrast, Quaker State formed a low pole in the last quarter of 1990. A price breakout at 14 in October 1991 was confirmed by an RS that turned positive in the same month. Quaker State responded with bullish price action that could be traced to the low pole formation supplemented by a positive RS chart.

In conclusion, low pole formations seem to lead to bullish stock trends when price action is reinforced by an upside breakout on the RS chart. Low poles not supported by RS breakouts tend to result in a drifting, wandering sideways move or in lower prices. Investors are vulnerable to low poles with negative relative strength because abortive rally attempts precede lower prices.

Using relative strength greatly enhances individual stock timing and selection. It is time to turn our attention toward improving decisions and strategies related to analyzing industry groups and the aggregate market. Section 3 includes some up-to-date thoughts on an overall approach to decision-making as it pertains to total security analysis.

SUMMARY

Relative strength probably does more to help investors eliminate false and misleading chart signals than any other single tool. By using relative strength, chartists can determine whether stocks will outperform or underperform the market. In the case of long positions, investors should buy positive stocks with bullish relative strength. The industry group and general market should also be in uptrends. Conversely, short sellers and/or sellers of existing stock positions should focus their attention on declining stocks with bearish relative strength. The general market and related industry group should also be deteriorating.

Buy and sell signals on relative strength (RS) charts typically last for long periods of time. Act on price breakouts that are confirmed by similar breakouts on the stock's RS chart. Buy signals should be reinforced by RS breakouts to the upside. Sell signals should be accepted if a downside breakout occurs on a stock's RS chart. Trends confirmed by both price and RS charts endure for long periods of time.

High pole formations in conjunction with a bullish RS suggest the stock is entering a corrective phase. However, high poles with a negative RS may turn into a bear market decline. Low pole formations often result in a bottoming process and the beginning of a bull market when accompanied by a bullish RS for the stock. However, low poles with a bearish RS frequently result in a corrective bounce which precedes lower downside prices.

SECTION 3

Individual stocks have been analyzed throughout the text. For a perspective on total security analysis, however, we must evaluate the industry group of which the stock is a member. Once industry analysis is complete, attention shifts to the aggregate market.

The old adages "go with the flow" and "the trend is your friend" pertain to the influence of the broad stock market on individual issues. Section 3 includes a chapter on market analysis and its role in individual stock selection. The idea of buying a rising stock with a positive relative strength in a strong market assumes added importance.

Once group and market analysis are examined, we conclude with several illustrations that integrate important principles from the book. You should then be ready to enter the trenches and engage in stock market combat through the medium of point and figure charting.

CHAPTER 12

INDUSTRY GROUP ANALYSIS

Industry group performance exerts a strong influence on expected returns from individual stocks. If a void exists in security analysis, it falls in the area of industry evaluation. Many analysts study individual stocks by devoting countless hours to earnings, dividends, growth rates, sales, payout ratios, and management. Others are armed with a battery of analytical tools to forecast market trends. Much less emphasis is given to analyzing industry trends. An effective technique in forecasting group movements is the bullish percentage approach utilized by Chartcraft.[1]

THE INDUSTRY GROUP BULLISH PERCENTAGE

The industry group bullish percentage measures the percentage of stocks in a group with bullish signals on their P & F charts.[2] The bullish percentage for an industry is plotted on a P & F chart to evaluate the strength and expected trend of the group. Bullish and bearish price movements persist until reversals develop from sell and buy signals.[3]

Near the bottom of a downmove, investor sentiment for an industry group becomes highly negative. Logically, the number of stocks with buy signals on P & F charts is small. We learned earlier that bull markets originate in the depths of pessimism, despair, and disbelief. A dearth of buy signals in an industry group or the market as a whole (treated in the next chapter) serves as a logical confirmation of extreme investor pessimism. Therefore, uptrends begin when the percentage of group stocks with buy signals reaches unusually depressed levels. Readings below 30% indicate the industry group has reached oversold levels. The severity of a decline greatly impacts readings on the bullish percentage indicator. Conversely, readings above 70% warn that the group is extended and trading in overbought territory. Readings above 70%, 80%, or 90% also confirm extreme investor optimism. Bear markets have their beginning in an environment of optimistic forecasts, euphoric reasoning, and a consensus view that "the market can only go higher."

THE CHARTCRAFT APPROACH TO CATEGORIZING MARKETS

When the bullish percentage indicator from an industry group turns upward in a column of X's on its P & F chart from below 10%, 20%, or 30%, we place the group in a **bull alert market**.[4] Less-than-30% readings warn that short positions and put options on stocks in that particular group should be closed out. Also, investors can begin to accumulate some long positions in the group for at least a trading move. Select only stocks with bullish chart patterns and positive relative strength. Do not take chances on weaker issues yet. However, market rallies linked to bullish percentage readings below the 10% and 20% extremes generally are stronger and more enduring.[5]

If a buy signal or move above a previous top occurs on the industry P & F chart, we place the group in a **bull confirmed market.** The group is in an established bull market, and you should have no reservations about accumulating shares in attractive issues. Maintain long positions in stocks and call options and go with the flow of the market. Reject thoughts of selling short or buying puts.

Once an industry group enters a bull confirmed market, that trend should continue with a few intervening downturns. These minor downmoves occur without producing a sell signal and place the trend in a **bull correction market**. Declines occurring in a bull confirmed market from below 70% (covered later in the chapter) with no sell signal indicate a corrective phase in the overall trend.

Let's assume a bull alert market where the group bullish percentage turns upward from below 10%, 20%, or 30% in a column of X's. If the indicator turns back downward below 30% in another column of O's, this is a **bear market bottom.** If two or more columns of O's dip below 30% after rallies from less than 10%, 20%, or 30%, the bottoming process simply requires more time to complete.

Multiple downturns below 30% following a bull alert market advance provide reassurance that little downside risk remains and suggest that investors accumulate long positions and call options. Consider buying longer call options during a bear market bottom when the industry bullish percentage shows multiple columns of O's moving from above to below 30%. Bear market bottom patterns suggest that additional time may be needed before a sustained advance materializes.

As the percentages move above 70%, 80%, or 90%, investors are greedy and overly optimistic. The higher the percentage, the more extreme investor optimism becomes and the greater the downside vulnerability. When the industry group bullish percentage declines from above 70%, 80%, or 90% to below 70%, this is a **bear alert market**. The group now has less than

70% of its stocks with bullish chart patterns. Investors should recognize group deterioration from increasing sell signals. Some short-term traders view any downturn from above 70% as a bear alert market and liquidate long positions in anticipation of more weakness to follow. Other action taken in bear alert markets should be in the form of short sales and put options concentrated on stocks with bearish chart patterns and negative relative strength. Market declines related to bullish percentage readings above 80% and 90% extremes typically are precipitous and longer lasting.

When an industry bullish percentage P & F chart shows a sell signal, this means a **bear confirmed market.** Sell long positions, while short sales and puts for the group are appropriate. In the event that one or more columns of X's follow downturns from above 70%, 80%, or 90%, we call this a **bull market top.** Multiple columns of X's that move back above 70% indicate feeble rally efforts. Such topping formations simply require more time to complete and provide you with additional opportunities to sell short or buy puts.

Once a bear confirmed market appears, we expect recurring downmoves with minor interruptions from short-lived rally attempts. These abortive rallies occur from above 30% and do not give a buy signal. Without a buy signal, the downtrend continues and upside price moves represent only a correction. We call this a **bear correction market.**

An important distinction needs to be made concerning bull and bear correction markets. We emphasized that bull correction markets began their downturns from below 70% with a buy signal intact. If declines start from above 70%, we are in a bear alert market. The whole complexion of the group outlook changes. Once percentage readings exceed 70%, most lay investors realize an uptrend is in progress. The strength of the group becomes obvious, and informed participants recognize a juncture is forthcoming.

Bull correction markets suggest an advance has more to go on the upside because well-defined extremes do not occur until percentage readings exceed 70%. Therefore, downturns from less-than-extreme levels suggest interruptions rather than more permanent trend reversals. Similarly, a bear correction market needs to begin upturns from above 30%. Well-defined extremes on the downside originate below 30%. Rallies from above 30% usually signal a temporary upside reversal but warn of further weakness before the decline concludes.

SOME BASIC ILLUSTRATIONS OF MARKET CATEGORIES

Figure 12-1 includes several examples of bull confirmed patterns in different industry groups. Each group chart has a recent buy signal to place the group in a bull market, so investors can accumulate shares. The banking group also reveals a bear market bottom pattern. After the bullish percentage reaches 10% (i.e., only 10% of bank stocks are showing bullish chart patterns), the group begins a 1990 bullish trend from the depths of extreme pessimism. In

225

Figure 12-1

SOME BULL CONFIRMED PATTERNS ON INDUSTRY GROUP BULLISH PERCENTAGE CHARTS

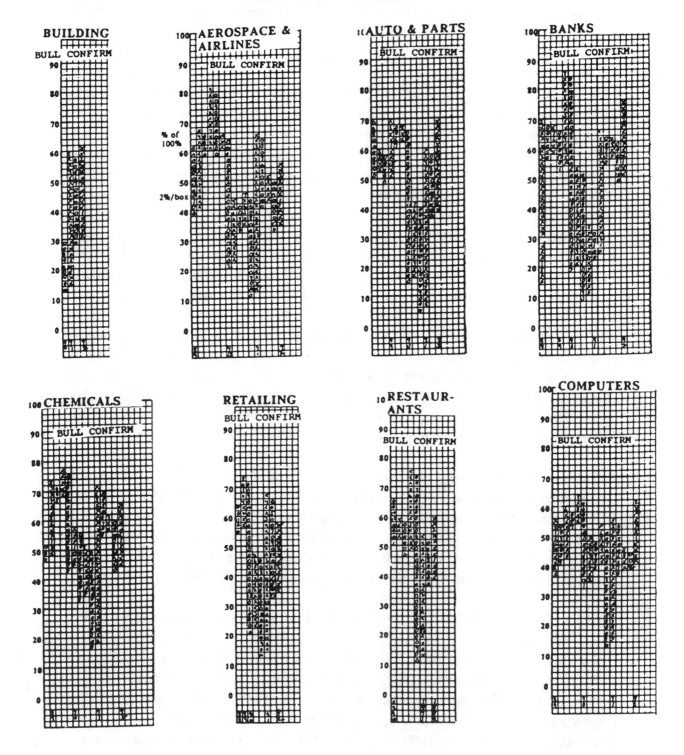

226

Figure 12-2

SOME BULL ALERT PATTERNS ON INDUSTRY
GROUP BULLISH PERCENTAGE CHARTS

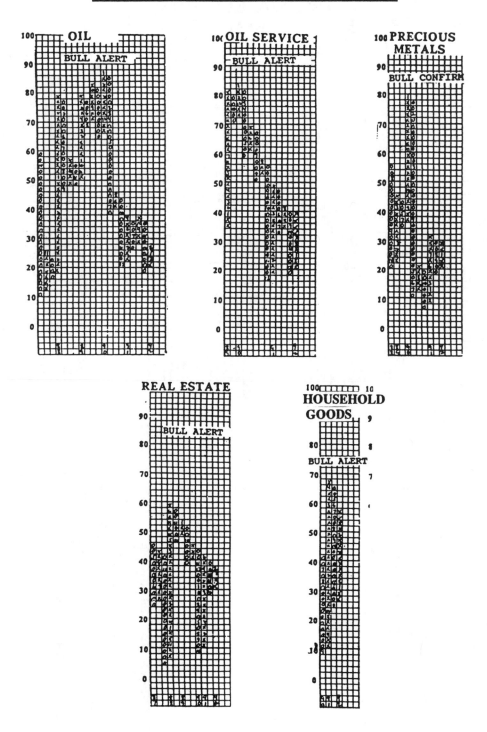

Figure 12-3

SOME BULL CORRECTION PATTERNS ON INDUSTRY GROUP BULLISH PERCENTAGE CHARTS

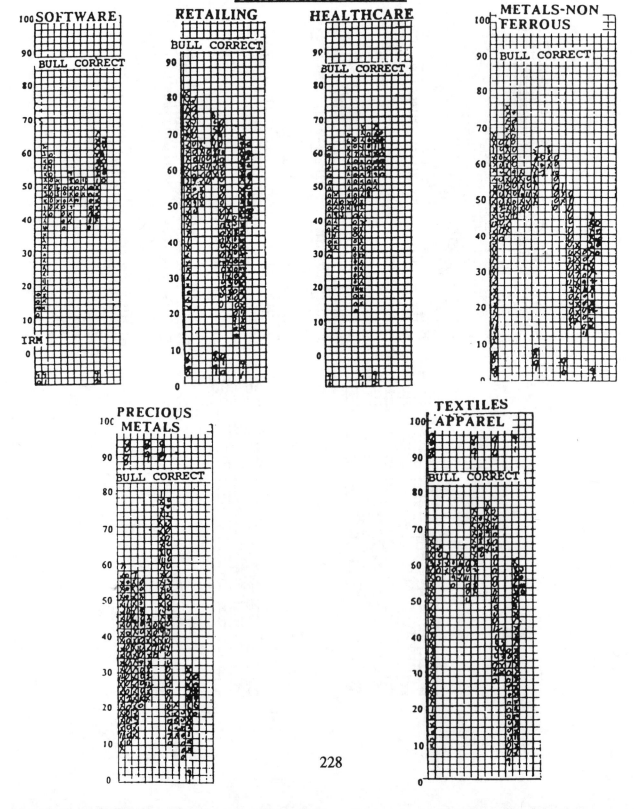

228

Figure-12-4

SOME BEAR CONFIRMED PATTERNS ON INDUSTRY GROUP BULLISH PERCENTAGE CHARTS

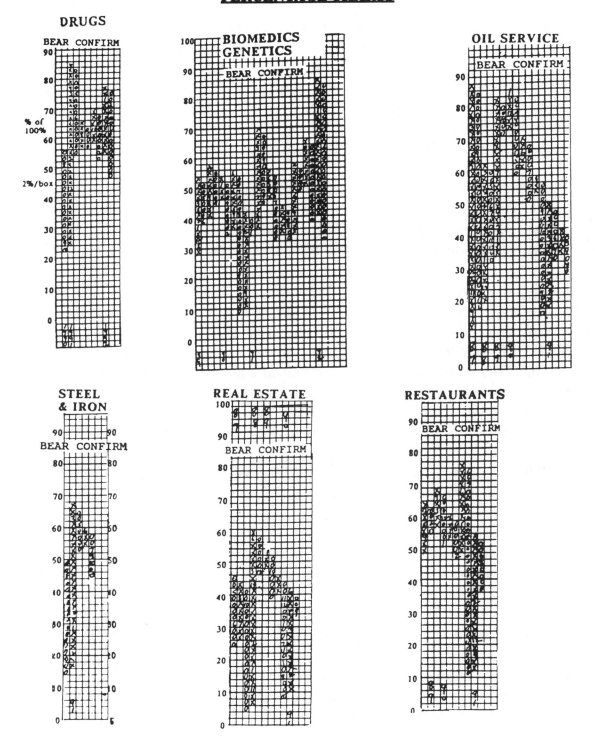

229

1991, the banking bullish percentage dips back below 30% (to 24%) and places the group in a bear market bottom. Since bear market bottoms generally confirm the bottoming process, we do not include these patterns as a separate market category. Both bear market bottoms and bull market tops reinforce chart patterns already in place.

Figure 12-2 illustrates bull alert markets with upturns from less than 30%. A distinguishing feature of bull alert markets is that a buy signal has not yet been received. However, rallies from depressed readings warn the worst is over and offer an early buying opportunity. Initial purchases can be made after the first three-box reversal to the upside. Bull correction markets are shown in Figure 12-3. Each of these groups has previously reached bull confirmed market status. Downturns from below 70% follow. However, these downmoves do not yield a sell signal and indicate the reversal is a short-lived correction.

Bear confirmed patterns appear in Figure 12-4. Sell signals reverse previous uptrends and warn of a more lengthy downturn. When downside breakouts appear at high percentage levels, earlier bear market warnings are registered. However, when sell signals develop at lower percentage readings, the importance of acknowledging bear alert markets is manifested.

Figure 12-5 illustrates bear alert patterns where industry bullish percentages turn down from above to below 70% on the P & F chart. Traders may liquidate long positions and call options at the first sign of a downmove, even though no sell signal results. When readings exceed 80% and 90%, short-term investors must be cautious because investor sentiment is too optimistic. Acting on bear alert patterns at high bullish percentage levels circumvents the criticism of late sell signals leading to bear confirmed markets. Bear alert patterns serve as a reminder that no sell signal has been received. However, bear alert markets advise that the easy money has been made and much of the advance is over. Some traders may elect to sell short or buy put options at the first sign of a three-box reversal to the downside, even though the bullish percentage readings remains above 70%. However, such positions need to be closed out on rallies and resumed when the downside recordings resurface.

Examples of bear correction patterns appear in Figure 12-6. Upmoves take place above 30% after a sell signal places the group in a bear confirmed market. The rallies follow obvious technical deterioration from the downside breakout. However, such advances fail to provide a trend reversal.

INDUSTRY BULLISH PERCENTAGES AND PRICE TRENDS

Thus far, we have learned to anticipate group strength and weakness from bullish percentage charts. Logically, the next step compares group price trends with bullish percentage charts. Figures 12-7 and 12-8 include the group bullish percentage and price trends, respectively, for

Figure 12-5

SOME BEAR ALERT PATTERNS ON INDUSTRY GROUP BULLISH PERCENTAGE CHARTS

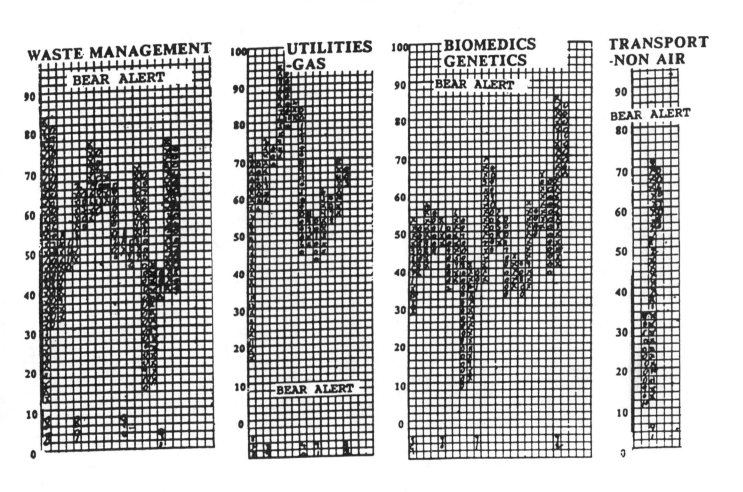

Figure 12-6

SOME BEAR CORRECTION PATTERNS ON INDUSTRY GROUP BULLISH PERCENTAGE CHARTS

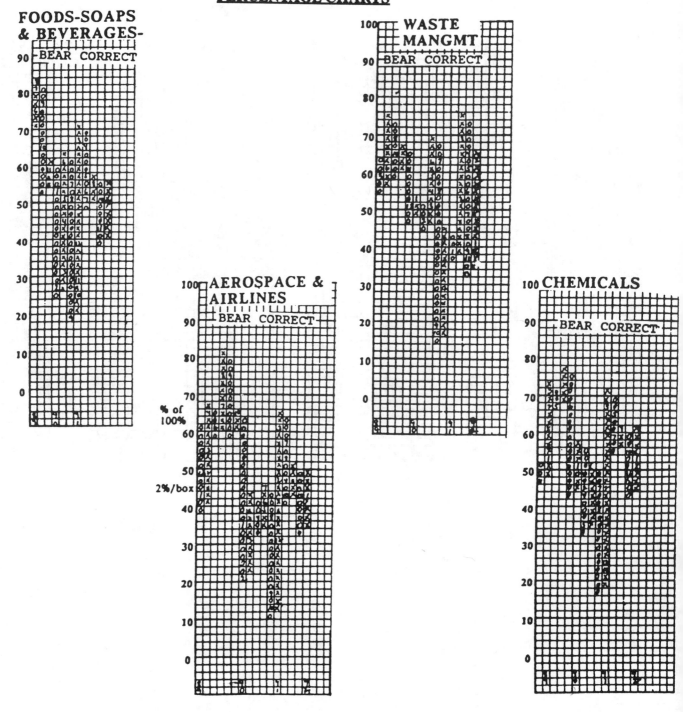

Figure 12-7

THE BULLISH % CHART FOR INVESTMENT FIRMS

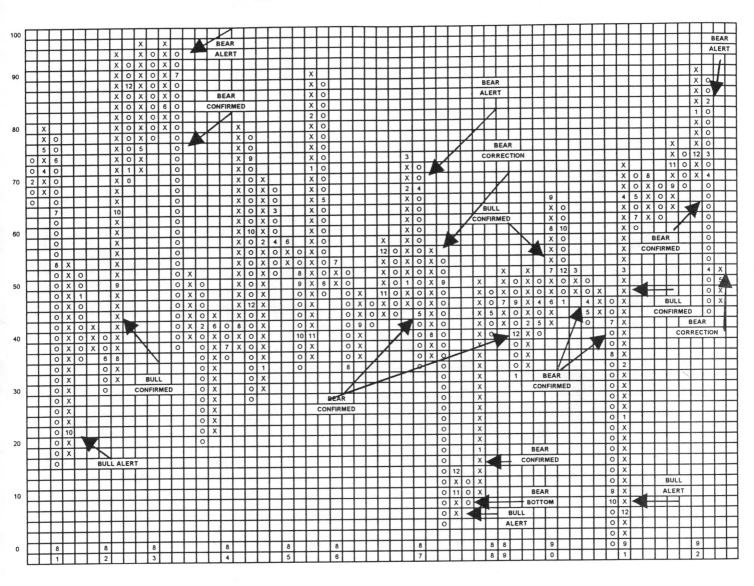

Figure 12-8

GROUP TREND CHART FOR INVESTMENT FIRMS

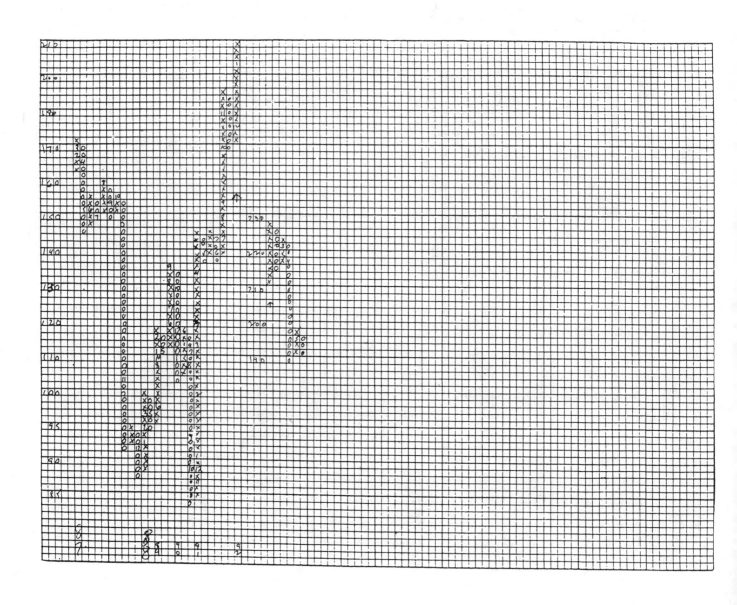

investment firms. Since group prices are available from 1987 into 1992, analysis focuses on that period.

Figure 12-7 has different market categories identified on the bullish percentage chart. A bear alert market forms in April 1987 on the bullish percentage chart for the investment sector. Prices also trended lower during the same time frame as shown in Figure 12-8. A bear confirmed market appeared in May 1987 on the bullish percentage chart. A rally attempt in the form of a bear correction followed. However, the bear confirmed market presaged a steep October 1987 decline in the investment group.

The bullish percentage P & F chart revealed a bull alert market with a 3-box reversal from 8% in November 1987. A bear market bottom surfaced in December 1987 followed by a bull confirmed market on the bullish percentage chart in January 1988. In February 1988, a major price advance occurred in the industry group. Had investors and traders begun purchases at the first sign of a 3-box reversal in a bull alert market, they would have positioned themselves perfectly.

The group bullish percentage shows a bear confirmed market in December 1988 and January 1989. Corresponding weakness appears in the industry group during the same months. However, a major downtrend ensued in the industry price index and lasted through October 1990. A bull confirmed market emerged from an upside breakout in July 1989, but a bear confirmed market resulted from two successive sell signals in May and July 1990. A bull alert market developed in December 1990 from a 2% reading on the bullish percentage chart. Remember, the most potent advances emerge from unusually depressed readings reflecting inordinate amounts of pessimism. Further, pessimistic investment extremes remind us that bull markets are born in a sea of dismay, doubt, and despair. Stock prices went up almost concurrently and in dramatic fashion. A bull confirmed market took place in March 1991. The index price moved from 84 to 228 in January 1992. A sell signal placed the bullish percentage in a bear confirmed market in April 1992, as a downside price reversal transpired in the index.

The bullish percentage technique accurately predicted trend changes in investment firm prices. By reading bullish percentage P & F charts and properly classifying markets, investors can seemingly evaluate group strength. Group performance and market strength strongly impact returns from individual stocks and require precise analysis.

To reinforce key concepts, let's review the bullish percentage and index price trend charts, respectively, for the bio tech group in Figures 12-9 and 12-10. In late 1986 and early 1987, the bio tech bullish percentage displayed a bull alert pattern, so investors and traders could begin buying into the group. A bull confirmed market ensued in January 1987. The bullish

Figure 12-9

THE BIO TECH BULLISH %

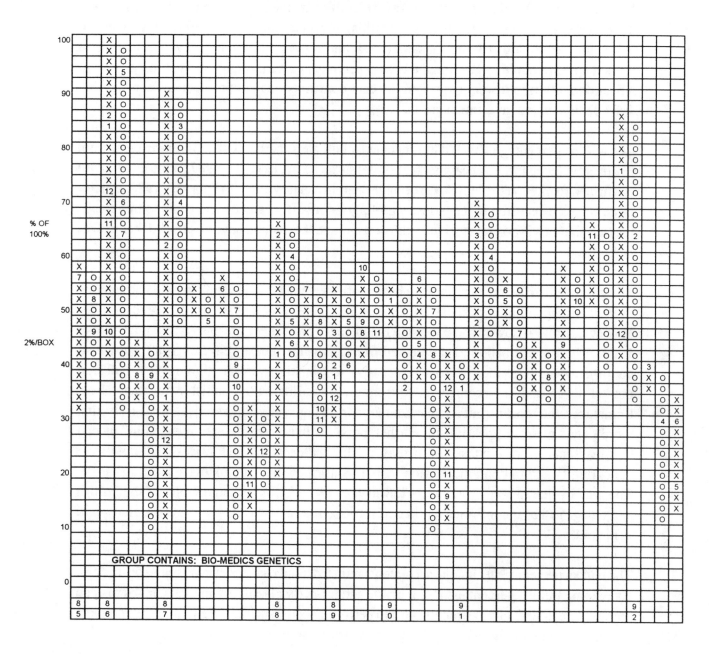

GROUP CONTAINS: BIO-MEDICS GENETICS

236

Figure 12-10

THE BIO-TECH INDUSTRY CHART

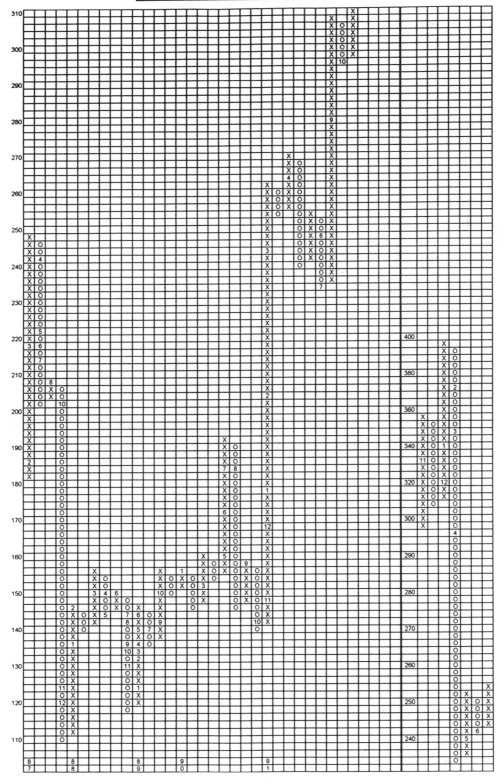

237

percentage chart warned of an approaching bottom and the advance that followed. A bear alert market in March 1987 meant that investors should begin taking profits and become cautious. The group trend turned down a month later. A bear confirmed market in the bullish percentage evolved in July and preceded a major industry downtrend in October. The bio tech group demonstrates exceptional volatility and illustrates the incremental value from using the bullish percentage to forecast prices for the group.

A three-box reversal gave a bull alert signal in November 1987 and previewed a bear market bottom in December. An upside breakout in December 1987 at the 34% level placed the bio tech group in a bull confirmed market. The index uptrend began in December and continued until August of 1988. An August sell signal in the group price chart coincided with a bear confirmed market in the bullish percentage. Afterwards, a bull alert market began from 28% in December 1989. The early stages of a group price advance corresponded to the rise in the bullish percentage. A July 1990 bear confirmed market suggested lower group prices which finally bottomed in October. A bull alert market appeared in September 1990. The bull alert preceded by one month a major group price advance from late 1990 until early 1992 when the index increased from 140 to almost 400. A bull confirmed market emerged in January 1991. A bear alert market in January 1992 hinted of a top in the group. Prices entered a deep slide in which the bio tech group lost almost half of its value in a three-month period.

In conclusion, group bullish percentages proved effective as a leading or coincidental indicator of changes in group price trends. Understanding Chartcraft's approach to group analysis is helpful in selecting industries for investment purposes. Figures 12-11 and 12-12 represent the computer and office equipment group bullish percentage which can be reviewed for points covered in earlier illustrations. Information from Chapter 12 can also be applied to assess the underlying strength in the aggregate market. The same techniques help investors identify both good investments and the optimum timing for decision making.

Figure 12-11

BULLISH % FOR COMPUTERS & OFFICE EQUIUPMENT

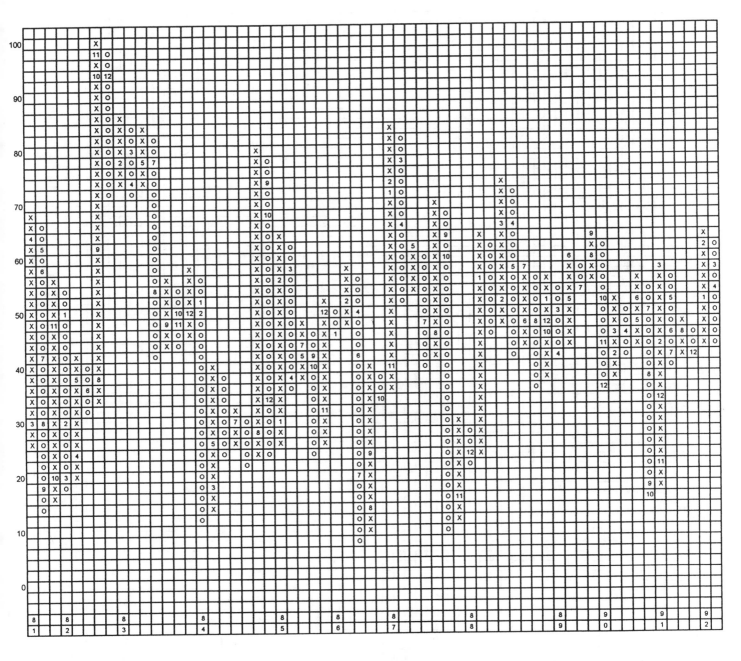

Figure 12-12

INDUSTRY CHART FOR COMPUTERS & OFFICE EQUIPMENT

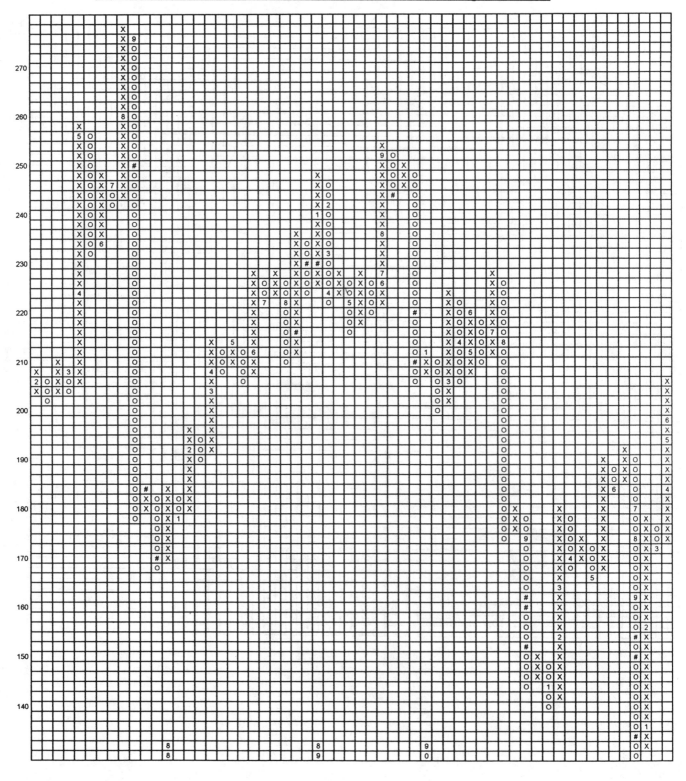

SUMMARY

The bullish percentage indicator shows the percentage of stocks with bullish P & F chart patterns in a particular industry group. Norms or parameters are established on the basis of extremes in investor sentiment. When upturns begin from below 30%, the usual implication is bullish. When less than 30% of all stocks within the group are bullish, investors are pessimistic about the industry. Readings below 20% and 10% represent unusually depressed levels of pessimism. Larger price advances generally result from more depressed readings. Conversely, when 70% or more of all stocks in a group are bullish, most investors recognize that the group is strong and exude optimism. More pronounced declines typically develop in conjunction with more extreme bullish percentage readings above 80% and 90%. The industry bullish percentage ordinarily serves as a leading indicator of price trends for a group.

ENDNOTES

[1]Earl Blumenthal did much of the original work on the bullish percentage under the name of the bullish-bearish index. See Earl Blumenthal, <u>Chart for Profit Point and Figure Trading</u> (Larchmont, NY: Investors Intelligence, Inc., 1975), 65-76.

[2]The author is indebted to Michael Burke and John Gray from Chartcraft for their written and verbal contributions to this chapter. Mike and John also contributed all charts and graphics. For an excellent treatment of many of these ideas, see Michael L. Burke, <u>The All New Guide to the Three-Point Reversal Method of Point & Figure Construction and Formations</u> (New Rochelle, NY: Chartcraft, Inc., 1990).

[3]For additional reading on many of these ideas, see A.W. Cohen, <u>How To Use the Three-Point Reversal Method of Point & Figure Stock Market Trading</u> (New Rochelle, NY: Chartcraft, Inc., 1987).

[4]Initial efforts to categorize markets on the basis of bullish percentage may be found in Earl Blumenthal, <u>Chart for Profit Point and Figure Trading</u> (Larchmont, NY: Investors Intelligence, Inc., 1975).

[5] For the most complete and refined work on classifying markets and industry groups, see Michael L. Burke and John E. Gray, eds. <u>Chartcraft's Options Service</u> (New Rochelle, NY: Chartcraft, Inc., select issues, 1989-1992).

CHAPTER 13

TECHNICAL ANALYSIS OF STOCK MARKET TRENDS

P & F charts provide a clear-cut, objective system for evaluating the aggregate market and its overall trends. By directing our attention toward popular measures of the market and related technical indicators, less time is devoted to news developments and rumors which are clearly not responsible for major trends in the market. Supply, demand, money flows, and investor activities are depicted by technical analysis and underlie market strengths and weaknesses. We have laboriously studied many technical indicators to evaluate parameters for investment strategies.[1] A large number of technical tools have been withdrawn from consideration in favor of those with consistent track records in detecting key market turning points.[2] Let's begin with some blue chip market averages.[3]

SOME DOW JONES AVERAGES

Dow Jones publishes several different averages which have proven effective in evaluating the stock market. Figure 13-1 depicts the **Dow Jones Industrial Average 20 X 60 Chart.** The Chartcraft approach to P & F charting not only applies to individual stocks but works equally well with popular market averages and indexes. Rising columns are denoted by columns of X's, while columns of O's indicate declining prices. Price objectives may be reached in the same manner, while trendlines demand the same respect, interpretation, and construction.

Certainly the Dow Jones Industrial Average (DJIA) receives more attention than all other popular market measures. News commentators and business columnists always cite the DJIA because of its widespread recognition. Market commentators employ the DJIA as "the market" and give quotes to the effect that "the market closed up ten points today", or "the market ended the day 15 points lower in active trading."

In Figure 13-1, each square represents 20 points. A 3-box reversal to establish another column cannot occur without a 60-point price swing. Smaller, potentially misleading price moves are often eliminated, and technicians receive a better defined picture of the long-term price trend. For those who are trading oriented, they will prefer a sensitive chart such as the 10 X 30 or 5 X 15. However, as charts are constructed to be more sensitive, additional recordings must be

Figure 13-1

DOW JONES INDUSTRIAL AVERAGES CHARTS

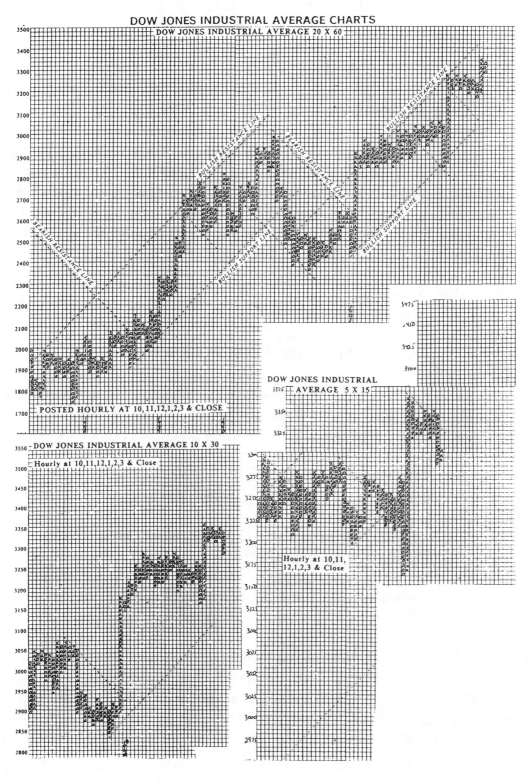

244

posted and the possibility for interpretation error increases. Regardless of the chart utilized, however, the same techniques and evaluation methods apply.

The DJIA should not be regarded as a leading indicator. The DJIA 20 X 60 chart generally displays a buy signal at major tops and shows a sell signal at bear market bottoms. Technicians voice concern over divergences when other market measures do not post new highs or lows along with the DJIA. The DJIA often lags the broad market and essentially confirms what has taken place earlier in other indexes.

Assume the New York Stock Exchange Composite Index, the American Exchange Market Value Index, S & P 500, or NASDAQ OTC Composite Index show lower tops and bottoms while the DJIA is bullish. The broad market diverges from the DJIA and means the general market reveals more weakness than do high quality issues. Conversely, when the indexes comprised of a broad spectrum of stocks (e.g., S & P 500, NYSE Composite, or NASDAQ OTC Composite) show higher tops and bottoms, strength exists in the general market. If the DJIA continues bearish, the broad market converges on the falling blue chip stocks. Strength appears in the general market, while blue chip issues continue their sluggishness.

Technicians should use the DJIA as a measure of high quality stocks only. Reversals occur too late to be a timing tool for most stocks. However, timing on DJIA issues may be improved by using high poles, low poles, triple top failures, triple bottom failures, bear traps, and bull traps. Low poles occurring near market bottoms have proven helpful in identifying turning points. High poles that form near the highs for the move or near all-time peaks generally warn of sustained downmoves.

The DJIA Bullish Percentage

The DJIA bullish % reveals the percentage of DJIA stocks with buy signals, as illustrated in Figure 13-2. Interpretation for the DJIA bullish percentage is consistent with the guidelines for industry group bullish percentages discussed in Chapter 12. The principal weakness of this bullish percentage is that only 30 stocks comprise the DJIA. Upmoves from less than 30% indicate a bull alert market, while a buy signal places the DJIA in a bull confirmed market. A sell signal provides a bear confirmed market. Downmoves from above 70% to below 70% without a sell signal indicate a bear alert market. These different market classifications will be reviewed again later in the chapter when we introduce the NYSE bullish percentage. However, the basic rules from industry analysis will suffice at this point. The underlying significance of the DJIA bullish percentage relates to investors following blue chip stocks. Those in more speculative stocks on the OTC and American Exchange can often ignore the DJIA.

Figure 13-2

D.IIA BULLISH PERCENTAGE

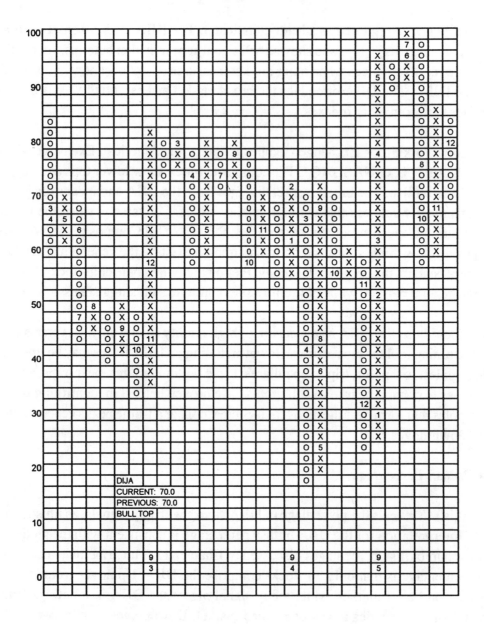

Figure 13-3

DOW JONES UTILITY AVERAGE

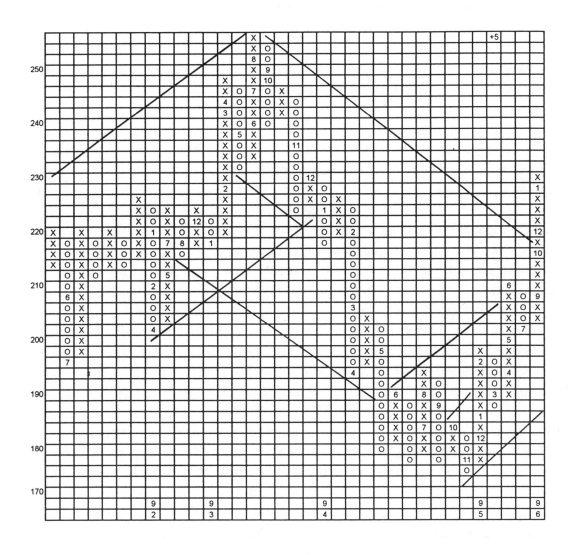

247

The Dow Jones Utility Average

The Dow Jones Utility Average (DJUA) is an often overlooked technical tool which serves as a leading indicator at both market bottoms and tops. Figure 13-3 illustrates the DJUA for a 12-year period. Most investors fail to understand the importance of following utility stocks. However, the rationale is quite simple. The stock market remains highly sensitive to interest rates. When interest rates are high, investors become attracted to lower-risk investment options such as CDs, bonds, and other fixed-income vehicles. They opt for guaranteed returns. As money flows into more conservative alternatives, demand for stocks declines and prices fall. Such scenarios often occur during economic prosperity when strong need exists for borrowed funds.

Low rates force investors into more risk to gain an acceptable return. Fixed-income rates usually hover at low levels during slow economic periods such as a recession. Money then gravitates toward the stock market and added demand drives stock prices higher.

To extend the logic of interest rate sensitivity, utility stocks attract investors with income orientations. They serve as a principal investment competitor to bonds since both appeal to conservative investors. Bond prices bear an inverse relationship with interest rates. Existing bond prices increase with falling interest rates and decline as rates increase. Utility stocks must offer dividend yields that compete favorably with bond yields. Higher interest rates force utility stock prices lower and dividend yields higher. Declining utility stocks and falling bond prices therefore warn of trouble ahead in the stock market. Similarly, as interest rates fall, both bond prices and utility stocks advance as yields adjust accordingly. Such price strength in both security types bodes well for future prices in the aggregate stock market.

The DJUA generally tops out at least a month or more before the DJIA. Similarly, the same relationship holds at major DJIA bottoms. The utilities usually advance in price before any significant movement occurs in the stock market. At market bottoms, the utilities may occasionally perform as a coincidental indicator and turn up with the market. In reading the DJUA chart, buy and sell signals proved effective in detecting trend reversals. Low poles and high poles developed frequently and served as a valuable timing aid in identifying directional shifts.

We may best use the DJUA as a technical indicator by analyzing its P & F chart with trend lines, price objectives, and chart patterns to anticipate changes in direction. Since the DJUA serves primarily as a leading indicator of the DJIA, investors should review the price action in utilities on a regular basis. By accurately identifying junctures in the DJUA, we may gain a timing advantage by entering the general stock market earlier.

Figure 13-4

DOW JONES TRANSPORT AVERAGE

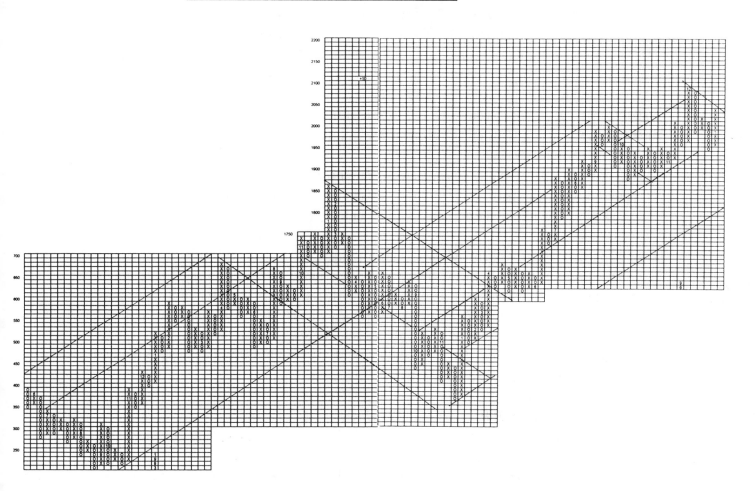

The Dow Jones Transportation Average

Figure 13-4 illustrates the Dow Jones Transportation Average (DJTA), which demonstrates a proven track record of reliability. Many signals received from the DJTA are more reliable than those provided by the DJIA. The DJTA chart is usually maintained in one of two ways. First, a chart can be plotted on a 4 X 12 basis, with each box representing four points. A movement of 12 points opposite to the current price move constitutes a reversal and justifies another column of recordings. For more long-term orientations, investors may elect to construct a 10 X 30 chart, with each box worth 10 points. Thirty-point price moves in a different direction represent a reversal and a new column.

Most P & F chart patterns proved accurate in recognizing key turning points in the DJTA. Low pole formations are particularly helpful in detecting the bottoming process in transportation issues. However, high poles did not possess the accuracy evidenced by its low-pole counterpart.

The DJTA serves as an excellent technical indicator and receives attention from many analysts. A principal reason stems from the highly leveraged nature of the industry. Since most transportation firms rely heavily on debt, they are highly sensitive to interest rate changes and economic vacillations. Technicians cannot only relate interest rate and economic patterns to the DJTA, they may also get an idea of speculative activity. Many transportation issues display erratic earnings patterns and tend to be regarded as highly speculative. Trading in these stocks often suggests increasing or decreasing amounts of speculation.

SOME BROAD-BASED MARKET MEASURES

Most Dow Jones Averages concentrate on a relatively small number of issues ranging from 15 to 30. For this reason, many analysts prefer a more comprehensive market measure consisting of larger numbers of stocks. Figure 13-5 depicts the Value Line Index of 1,700 diverse firms which appeal to individual investors. Different firms with varying degrees of quality are included to make the Value Line measure a better representation of the overall stock market. Figure 13-6 shows the New York Stock Exchange (NYSE) Composite Index, which consists of all issues traded on that exchange. Figure 13-7 illustrates the Standard & Poor's 500 Index comprised of industrial, financial, utilities, and transportation issues. Issues included in the S & P 500 represent a large percentage of the value of all stocks traded on the NYSE.

Following these comprehensive indexes gives chartists a complete view of total stock market activity. Some past markets have been largely restricted to certain segments of the total market

Figure 13-5

VALUE LINE AVERAGE

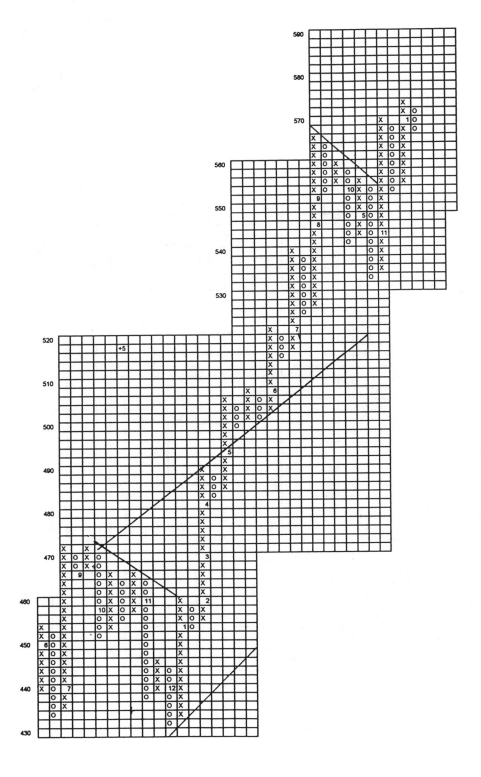

Figure 13-6

THE NYSE COMPOSITE

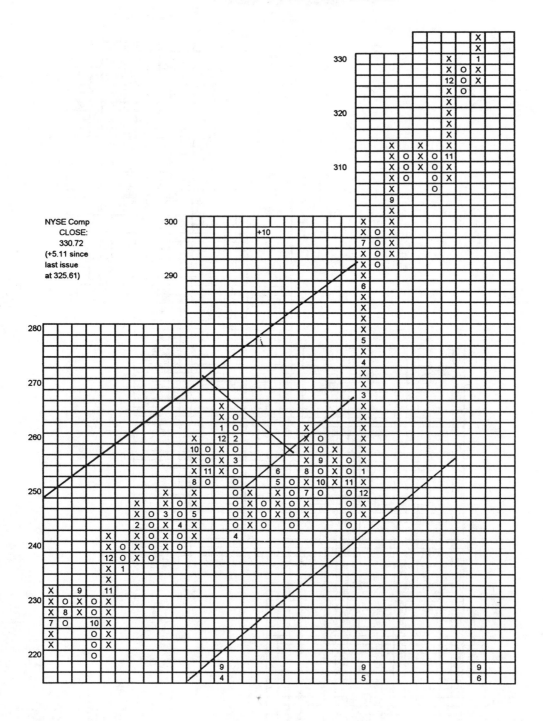

Figure 13-7

THE S&P 500 INDEX

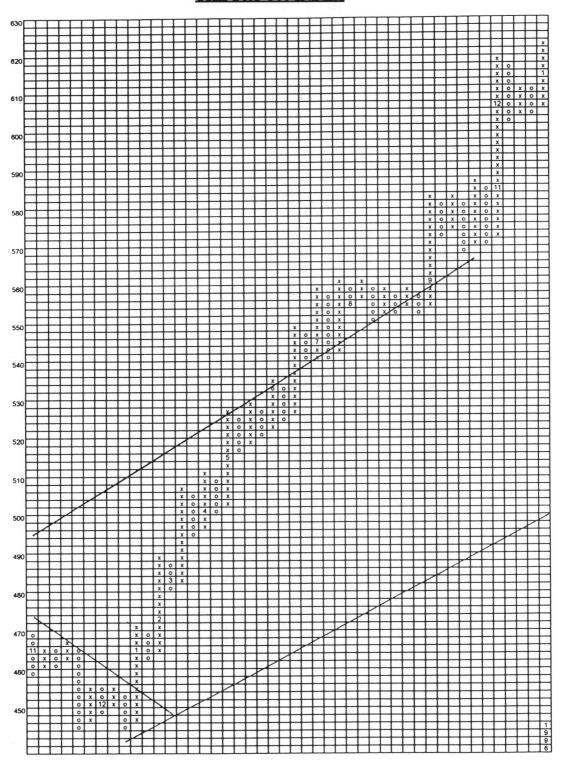

Figure 13-8

THE NYSE BULLISH PERCENTAGE

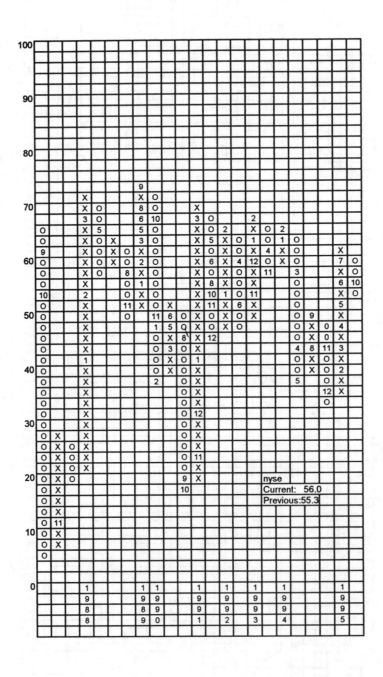

such as OTC issues or blue chip stocks. Chartists must follow all markets much as they do different industry groups. Generally speaking, the market usually possesses attractive opportunities, but they may be confined to a select few industries and/or a particular market. For example, the 1991 market advance focused more on speculative NASDAQ issues, while early 1992 centered on blue chips gauged by the DJIA.

THE NYSE BULLISH PERCENTAGE

The NYSE bullish percentage ranks among the premier technical indicators ever developed for forecasting general market price movements. Chartcraft developed the bullish percentage method in 1955. Although few technicians seem to use it, the technique has withstood the test of time.[4]

The bullish percentage is based on the number of NYSE stocks with bullish chart patterns. Each day the number of bullish stocks is added and divided by the total of all NYSE stocks that are both bullish and bearish. Each box represents 2%, with calculations plotted on a 2 X 6 P & F chart (a 6% reversal move establishes another column).

The NYSE bullish percentage requires some elaboration. Given the importance of this indicator, it needs more emphasis than some other basic technical tools. The NYSE bullish percentage is a **leading indicator;** its signals precede critical junctures or turning points in the market. The long-term P & F chart may be found in Figure 13-8. Although the indicator does not consume many columns nor display much volatility, its effectiveness in providing leading indicators of market turns should be observed. Analysis of the NYSE bullish percentage P & F chart parallels the evaluation methods in evaluating industry groups. Let's review the basic analytical approach developed by Chartcraft.

Upmoves usually conclude as the bullish percentage rises above 70%, 80%, or 90%. The greater the underlying strength in the stock market, the higher the recordings typically carry on the P & F chart. Also, downmoves from higher levels carry bearish connotations. Remember, downmoves from above 70% to below 70% signal a **bear alert market.** If the initial downside move below 70% is followed by one or more attempts to rally above 70% in a column of X's, we regard this as a **bull market top**. Adhere to your original inclination to liquidate long positions and perhaps sell short or buy puts into market strength. Additional rally columns extend the topping process. Downmoves from these high levels imply the market is overextended and vulnerable to lower prices. A sell signal or movement below a previous bottom represents a **bear confirmed market.**

Downmoves ordinarily climax with the percentage below 10%, 20%, or 30%. Normally severe bear markets reach more oversold levels and have lower percentage readings such as 10% or less. Remember that upturns from below 10%, 20%, or 30% on the P & F charts place us in a **bull alert market** where stocks and call options can be purchased. A buy signal means a **bull confirmed market,** which indicates greater certainty about the underlying technical strength in the market. If upturns from below 10%, 20%, or 30% are followed by one or more columns of O's reaching below 30%, we will label this a **bear market bottom.** Your initial recognition of a buying opportunity should not be changed. Regard multiple columns of O's dropping below 30% after the initial upmove as an extension of the bottoming process.

Bull correction markets occur after the formation of a bull confirmed market. Downturns from less than 70% develop without a sell signal. Such downturns are generally short-lived and minor in scope because the market has not yet reached overbought status. Similarly, **bear correction markets** form once a bear confirmed market is underway. Upmoves begin from above the 30% level and indicate a brief rally should follow. Since the market never reached oversold levels, market rallies are typically selective, narrowly defined, and somewhat limited. Trend reversals do not materialize because of the extensive technical damage during the bear market.

When a bear market begins at the conclusion of the distribution process, additional chart patterns for individual stocks move from bullish to bearish and the NYSE bullish percentage declines. Before the bear market concludes, investor sentiment becomes unusually negative. As negativism grows among investors, this accentuates the severity of the decline and the lower percentage readings as sell signals predominate on the charts. Stocks become increasingly oversold across the board and negative thoughts prevail among market gurus and average investors alike.

Bull market beginnings surface as increasing numbers of oversold issues begin to rally and penetrate previous tops on their P & F charts. As the advance strengthens, larger percentages of stock charts are bullish and investor sentiment becomes positive. However, by the time most investors recognize the bull market, the advance has been underway for some time. Investor sentiment quickly reverses, and the bullish percentage rises rapidly on the P & F chart. A cogent advance takes place as the bull market displays reassuring strength. However, stock prices become quickly extended. As the number of overbought issues rises, market players become optimistic. Downside vulnerability at this point increases because the stock market will not accommodate a majority.

Interpreting the NYSE Bullish Percentage

Michael Burke and John Gray have developed the following rules for interpreting the NYSE bullish percentage.[5] First, when 70% or more of all stocks on the NYSE (or any other market) display bullish patterns, most investors are aware of the bull market. Chartists may begin selling into the strength of the market on a selective basis, particularly with issues that have undergone sizable moves and appear extended on the charts.

A second rule applies to bear alert markets when the percentage moves from a column of X's above 70% to a column of O's that carries below 70%. The bull market may endure for several more months, particularly when bull market top patterns appear on the P & F chart for the bullish percentage. However, increasing numbers of stocks are topping out and discriminating profit taking should be accelerated.

Rule 2 serves as an extension of Rule 1 and encourages cashing in unrealized or "paper profits" for the near-term with the intention of re-establishing position as the market's technical strength returns. Market dips will probably be short-lived but frequent, as the market begins a "choppy", sawtooth churning action. Puts and shorts can be utilized for brief trades if other technical indicators confirm overbought condition in the market. The use of protective stops is recommended. The declining percentage reading usually warns of further weakness and the increasing likelihood of stop orders being filled. Liquidity should assume more importance.

A third rule applies when the NYSE bullish percentage drops from above 72% to 68% or less. The indicator ordinarily drops to 50% within a six-month period. Perceive declines to the 68% level as a harbinger of lower prices. Such bear alert markets may result in either a full-fledged downside reversal or a correction. Price corrections are normally associated with rapid drops to 50% in the bullish percentage indicator. Whereas corrections reach 50% within a couple of months, bear markets may require added time and be more long lasting. Readings of less than 50% suggest that over one-half of all NYSE stocks are in bearish patterns. However, corrections in a bull market are healthy because they reduce excesses in investor behavior and thinking. Upmoves with little or no corrective price action tend to exhaust themselves early. Recurring corrections within a persistent, long-term uptrend ensure the general health of the bull market.

Rule 4 advises the use of protective stop orders on puts and short sales when the NYSE bullish percentage reaches 50%. You should ensure that these "stops" trail declining security prices. According to Chartcraft, downmoves from 68% usually reach an average level of 44%. Although alternating columns of X's reflect attempts by the market to rally, investors should be cautious and resist temptations to enter the market too quickly during culminations of the first downmove from 68%. Long positions should be reserved for the "stout of heart" scalpers or short-term traders whose goals are merely several-point profit opportunities.

Rule 5 suggests that consideration be given to taking profits on puts and short positions when the NYSE bullish percentage reaches 44%. Writers or sellers of call options should consider "closing purchase" transactions. However, well-defined downtrend stocks will often move lower. To avoid hasty close-out decisions, you may elect to wait for a reversal in the bullish percentage to a column of X's which warns of some near-term strengthening in the market. However, such interruptions are often temporary and positions may be reestablished as the bullish % returns to another column of O's.

If you are a short seller or holder of puts, there is a more reliable approach to evaluate the first upturn from the 50% level or below. Review the previous column of X's and determine whether it gave a bullish signal by penetrating the top of the X column before it. If so, the overall market trend is judged to be bullish and the first move down is probably a correction. At the first sign of a three-box reversal, stocks and calls should be purchased in preparation for another strong upmove.

We can now review the alternate scenario when an initial downmove occurs from 68%. Once again, determine whether the previous column of X's had moved higher than the top of the X column before it. If the preceding X column failed to turn bullish, we consider the market as still in a downtrend. Upturns suggest only a correction with limited profit potential.

Rule 6 relates to an upturn from below 50% with the trend of the bullish percentage still upward. Trading activities are permissible with protective stops but should be limited to stocks and calls on issues with positive relative strength. However, more uncertainty enters the market picture in this area, so the bullish percentage should be used in conjunction with other technical indicators. If the balance of evidence from other technical indicators emphasizes a move in either direction, go with the overall technical picture as opposed to one indicator.

Rule 7 says that bear market bottoms emerge from oversold extremes below the 10%, 20%, or 30% levels. Very low bullish percentage readings reflect unusual pessimism among investors and a deeply oversold aggregate market. The severity of downside moves becomes obvious at depressed bullish percentage levels. Extreme low readings typically prepare the market for sustained advances. Remember, bullish percentage upturns precede rallies in the market. The most important trait of the bullish percentage centers on its ability to serve as a leading indicator for the overall market.

THE NYSE DAILY ADVANCE - DECLINE LINE

Advance-decline (A-D) lines measure the breadth or plurality of the market, as seen in Figure 13-9. Although the A-D line gauges stock price trends without the use of prices, its construction

Figure 13-9

THE NYSE ADVANCE - DECLINE LINE

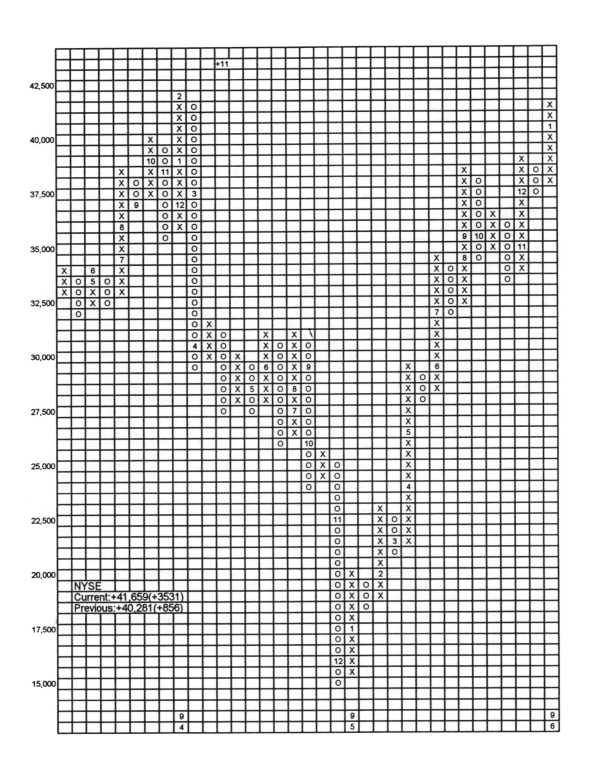

Figure 13-10

DAILY NYSE HIGH LOW INDEX

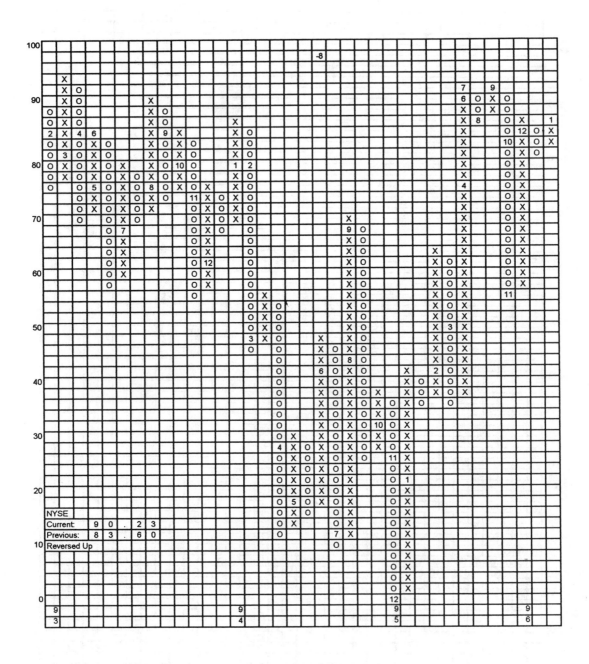

260

depends on all equity issues advancing or declining in price on a daily basis. Each day, stocks in a given market (OTC, ASE, or NYSE) are categorized as having advanced, declined, or remained unchanged in price. The difference between advancing and declining issues is calculated, while unchanged issues are disregarded. If more advances occur than declines, there is said to be positive plurality. When declines exceed advances, negative plurality exists. Each daily subtraction total is assigned to a cumulative total (often called the cumulative differential) which is continually maintained and changed each day. This cumulated total represents the A-D line.

The A-D line ordinarily parallels the stock market. Both move higher in a bull market and lower in a bear market. Their movement together in the same direction confirms uptrends and downtrends. Different market measures may be utilized for comparison with the A-D line. For example, many analysts prefer a broad-based index such as the S & P 500, while Chartcraft opts for the DJIA. Regardless of the market proxy selected, the most significant chart action occurs when the A-D chart shifts and moves in a direction opposite to the stock market. When the A-D chart turns down while the market continues upward, this price action may be termed **divergence**. At market peaks, the A-D chart typically tops out before the stock market, thereby serving as a leading indicator. Lead time may be from several days to several months.

If the A-D chart moves upward in the face of a declining market, such price action is called **convergence.** When the A-D chart moves higher while the market continues to decline, it also represents a leading indicator. However, the A-D chart at market bottoms normally turns upward coincidentally with the market. Before investors attempt "bottom fishing" expeditions, they should always question the validity of a market advance not confirmed by an upturn in the A-D chart. You can improve investment performance by relying on the A-D confirmation to avoid false and misleading signals.

Chartcraft suggests that for an assessment of current market strength, the value of the A-D line should be compared to its level of ten days ago. When current levels are higher, you should view this as a positive because the underlying market breadth has improved. However, if the A-D line declines for two successive days, you should regard such action as near-term weakness and a negative that could only be reversed by advancing back above the level of 10 days ago.

The overall strength of the market should be considered very positive when the A-D charts for the NYSE, ASE, and OTC markets all exceed levels of 10 days ago. However, the market's strength should be viewed suspiciously if all three A-D lines are below levels of 10 days ago.

261

Figure 13-11

% NYSE STOCKS ABOVE THEIR 10-WEEK MOVING AVERAGES

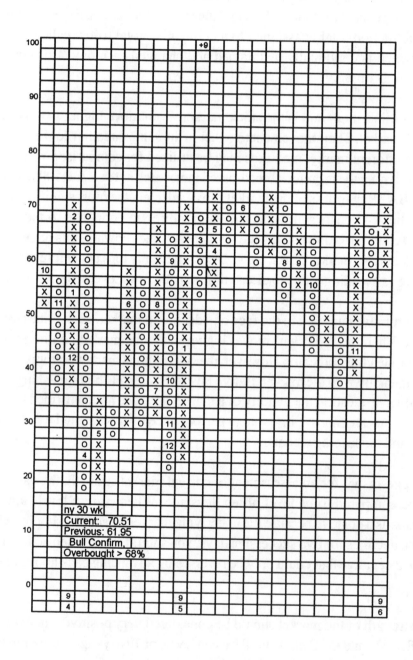

Figure 13-12

<u>UNDERLYING STOCKS BULLISH %</u>

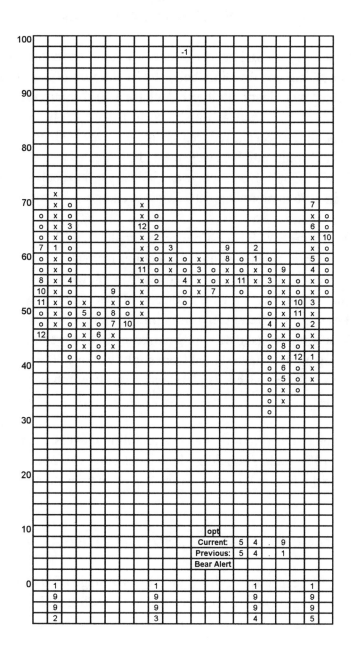

263

One illustration seems particularly helpful at this point. Let's assume that A-D charts on both the ASE and OTC markets surge strongly above recordings from 10 days earlier, while the NYSE chart fails. This should tell chartists that near-term strength and profit opportunities lie in the more speculative stocks traded in the ASE and OTC markets. In effect, investors should be more inclined to speculate with lower quality issues on a short-term basis rather than concentrate their immediate efforts on blue-chip stocks.

THE DAILY NYSE HIGH-LOW INDEX

Chartcraft constructs the daily NYSE High-Low Index by taking the number of stocks making daily new highs on the NYSE and dividing their total by the sum of the stocks making both daily new highs and new lows. Chartcraft then calculates a 10-day moving average and plots the resulting figure on a P & F chart as illustrated in Figure 13-10. The 10-day moving average provides a smoothing effect and reduces the impact of aberrations that might otherwise distort reporting. If only absolute numbers were used, the indicator would prove less efficient. As in the case with the NYSE bullish percentage and industry group analysis, extreme readings vacillate from less than 30% to more than 70%. Market categories remain the same.

Although interpretation for the NYSE High-Low Index parallels bullish percentage and industry group analysis, there are three rules to establish. Declines from above to below 70% usually indicate at least a correction. Typically, downmoves from above 90% to below 70% often warn of an impending bear market or a deep correction. Secondly, downturns from above 90% vary because they require different lengths of time to start their descent. In other words, there is considerable uncertainty as to how long extreme readings remain above the 70% to 90% level. Lastly, recent upturns have started from slightly above 30%, which suggests that oversold parameters should be revised. Traders may assume purchases on rallies from the low to mid-30% readings.

We can inject a remaining perception for traders and option players. On the first upmove of the Index from below 10%, traders should go long stocks and call options with expirations several months out into the future. Since the worst is over, there is no need to wait for a **bull confirmed market.**

PERCENTAGE NYSE STOCKS ABOVE MOVING AVERAGES

Figures 13-11 and 13-17, respectively, illustrate the percentage of NYSE and ASE stocks above their 10-week moving averages. Another commonly used technical indicator concerns the percentage of NYSE and ASE stocks above their 30-week moving averages. Traders

Figure 13-13

OEX AND CBOE PUT CALL RATIOS

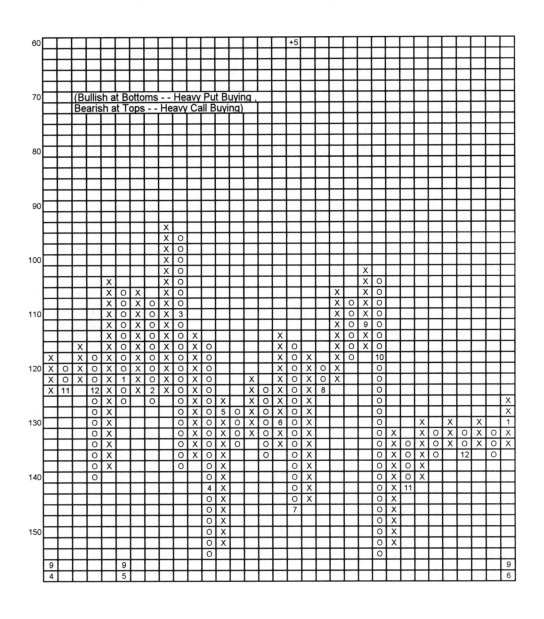

generally prefer the 10-week indicator because of its greater sensitivity. Long-term investors like the 30-week tool because it gives a better picture of the primary market trend.[6]

Relationships between stock prices and their moving averages furnish a valuable investor sentiment reading. As investors become optimistic, they buy more stocks and force prices above their moving averages. Conversely, when investors become pessimistic, they sell heavily and drive stock prices below their molting averages. Pessimistic extremes are reached when readings on the 10-week and 30-week indicators fall below 30%, 20%, or 10%. As the readings reach lower levels, investor sentiment is depressed and the potential exists for larger rallies. When readings exceed 70%, 80%, or 90%, investor sentiment becomes too optimistic and sets the stage for market vulnerability on the downside. Corrections are identified easier by reversals from extremes in the 10-week moving averages. Long-term trend changes can be spotted in the 30-week indicator. Market categories continue to be consistent with other Chartcraft interpretation methods previously discussed in the NYSE bullish percentage and in industry analysis.

UNDERLYING STOCKS BULLISH PERCENTAGE

Figure 13-12 includes the underlying stocks bullish percentage, which parallels the NYSE bullish percentage. Both are proprietary indicators of Chartcraft and have been effective in forecasting market turns. The underlying stocks bullish percentage indicator includes only optionable stocks. Chart patterns for all stocks with put and call options must be analyzed prior to calculating this indicator.

The underlying stocks bullish percentage measures the percent of optionable stocks with bullish chart patterns. Parameters of less than 30% and more than 70% indicate oversold and overbought levels, respectively. Interpretation and market categories continue to be the same as other Chartcraft overbought-oversold indicators.

Remember that bottoms form quicker than tops. Therefore, the underlying stocks bullish indicator will remain above 70% for longer periods than it stays below 30%. However, stock prices decline much faster than they advance. Use this indicator to determine intermediate and long-term price moves. The underlying stocks bullish indicator focuses on movements of longer duration and has minimal value in forecasting day-to-day or short-term moves.

OEX AND CBOE PUT CALL RATIOS

The investment community typically perceives option traders as a relatively uninformed group. In fact, statistics show more than 90% of all options and futures trades lose money. Options players who purchase puts and calls generally magnify sentiment trends in the market. During

Figure 13-14

ASE MARKET VALUE INDEX

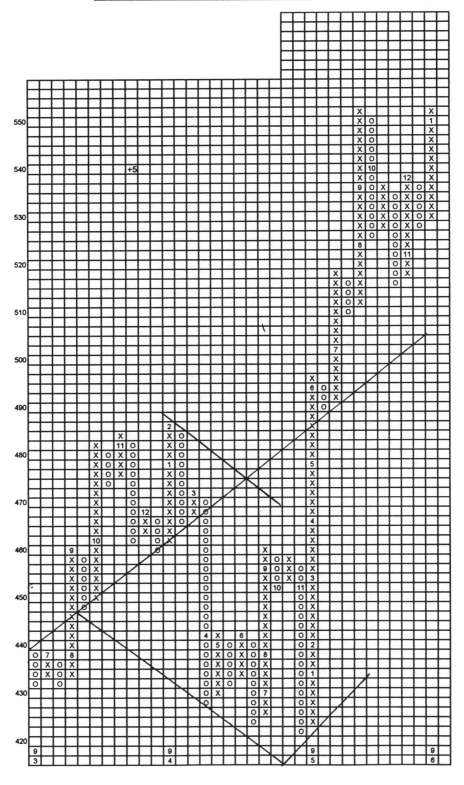

Figure 13-15

ASE BULLISH %

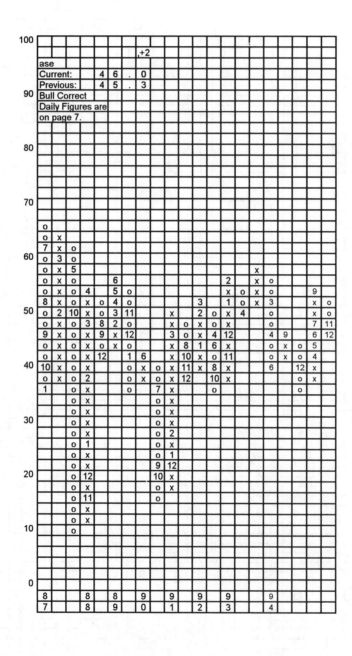

Figure 13-16

ASE DAILY HIGH LOW INDEX

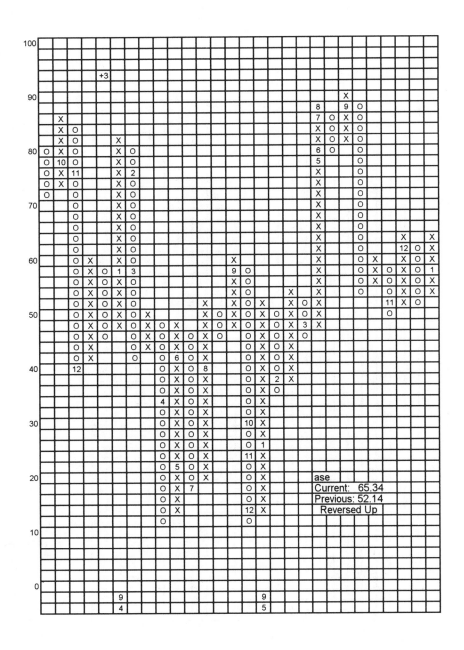

Figure 13-17

% OF ASE STOCKS ABOVE THEIR 10-WEEK MOVING AVERAGE

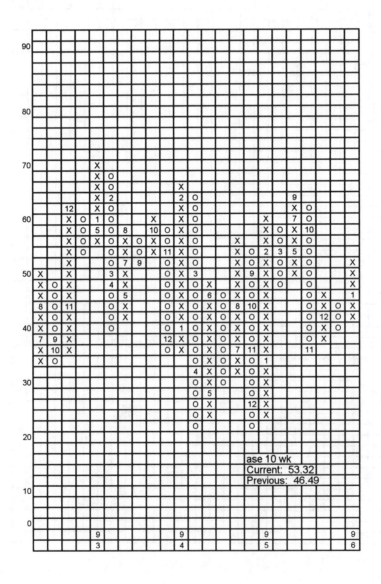

270

Figure 13-18

THE NASDAQ COMPOSITE INDEX AND OTC BULLISH %

FIGURE 13 - 18A

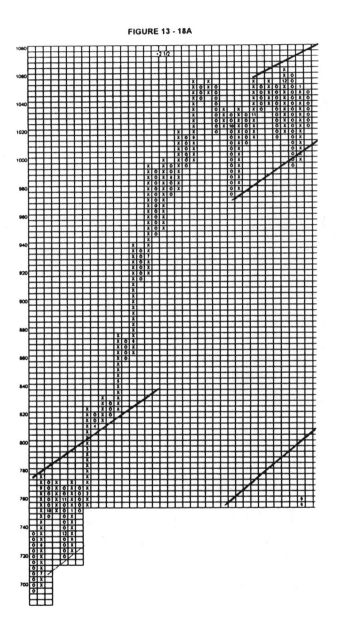

FIGURE 13 - 18 B

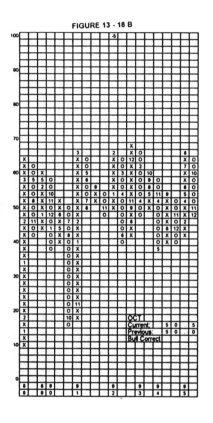

Figure 13-19

OTC DAILY HIGH LOW INDEX

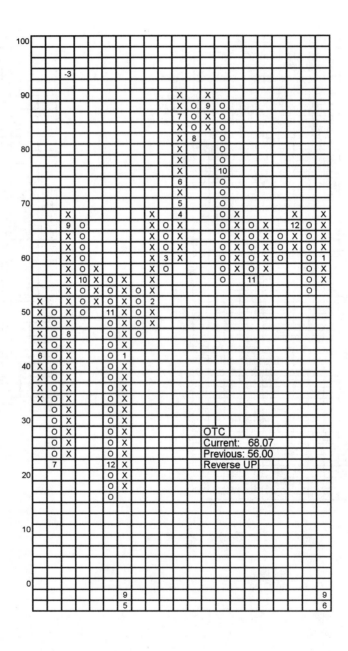

272

Figure 13-20

DOW JONES 20 BOND AVERAGE

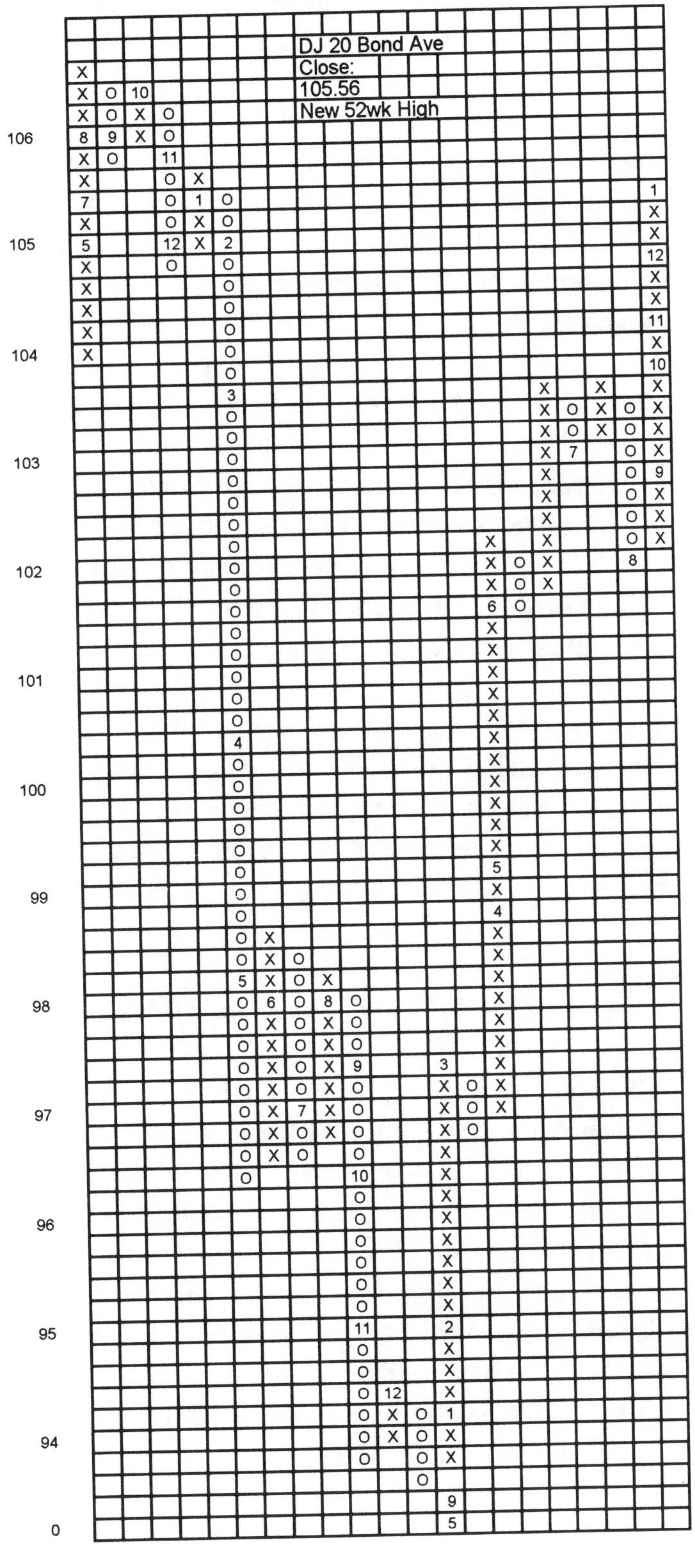

DJ 20 Bond Ave
Close:
105.56
New 52wk High

(Point-and-figure chart with price axis labels: 106, 105, 104, 103, 102, 101, 100, 99, 98, 97, 96, 95, 94, 0)

periods of extreme optimism, speculators heavily purchase call options. Conversely, when investors reach levels of extreme pessimism, they buy puts on a larger scale. Unusual amounts of speculative activity in the option markets identify an opportunity to act in a contrary manner to an uninformed market segment. Tops and bottoms can be recognized from too much or too little speculation as measured by option participation.

Two different option indicators appear in Figure 13-13 -- the OEX put-call ratio and the CBOE put-call ratio. The OEX put-call ratio may be calculated by taking a 10-day moving average of puts purchased on the S & P 100 Index divided by the number of calls bought on the same option. The CBOE put-call ratio is constructed similarly using a 5-day moving average. Aggregate option sentiment on the overall market is reflected by the OEX, while CBOE activity helps gauge speculative participation on individual issues. In other words, we can determine the sentiment or behavior patterns of speculators from their views toward the general market and individual stocks. OEX readings below 80 indicate that speculators are purchasing calls on the market heavily on the basis of their optimism. OEX put-call readings in excess of 100 suggest puts are popular as speculators grow more bearish. Lower readings (< 80) advise you to become more bearish to counteract increasing optimism, while higher readings (> 100) reveal public fear and suggest a bullish mode. We must go contrary to the thoughts of the option segment. Major bull market tops normally form with OEX readings of less than 50, while bear market bottoms await readings in excess of 140.

Readings of less than 40 on the CBOE put-call ratio warn of too much optimism by the public because of their heavy emphasis on individual call buying. Readings greater than 70 represent pessimistic extremes as evidenced by heavy put purchases on individual issues. These put-call ratios provide critical tools in the process of evaluating investor behavior. They are particularly effective in gauging the speculative activity among a relatively uninformed element in the market.

SOME TECHNICAL INDICATORS FOR SPECULATIVE MARKETS

Figures 13-14 through 13-17 provide graphic presentations of the comprehensive ASE Market Value Index, the ASE bullish %, the ASE daily high-low index, and the previously discussed percentage of ASE stocks above their 10-week moving average, respectively. Each of these tools enjoys the same effectiveness and interpretation as do their NYSE counterparts. The principal difference rests with the evaluation of a different, more speculative market for ASE stocks. Serious investors may draw meaningful conclusions concerning investor attitudes and sentiment toward speculative activity. Adequate speculation must be present to sustain enduring bull markets, so the ASE should be monitored regularly. Reading the text material covering these same indicators on the NYSE is helpful, but a review at this juncture would be superfluous.

Figure 13-21

HANDY & HARMON SPOT SILVER PRICES

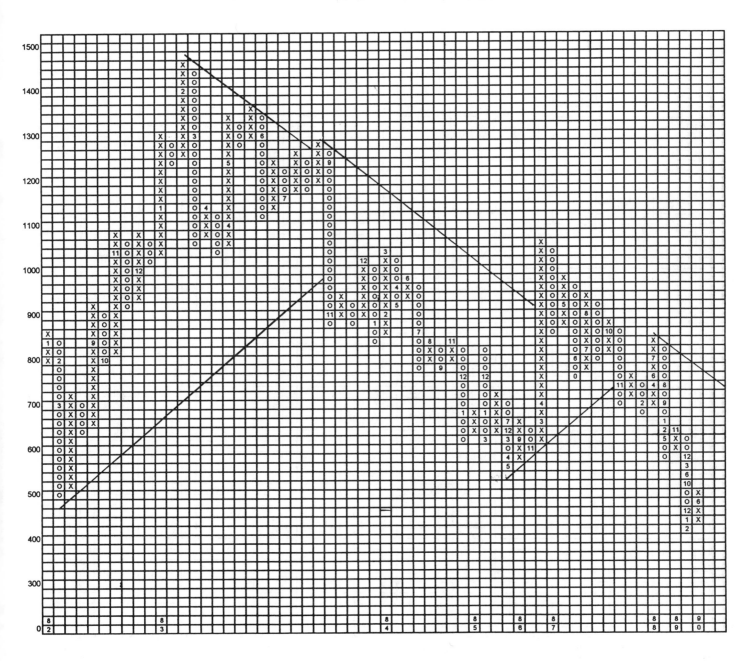

Figure 13-22

LONDON GOLD PRICES

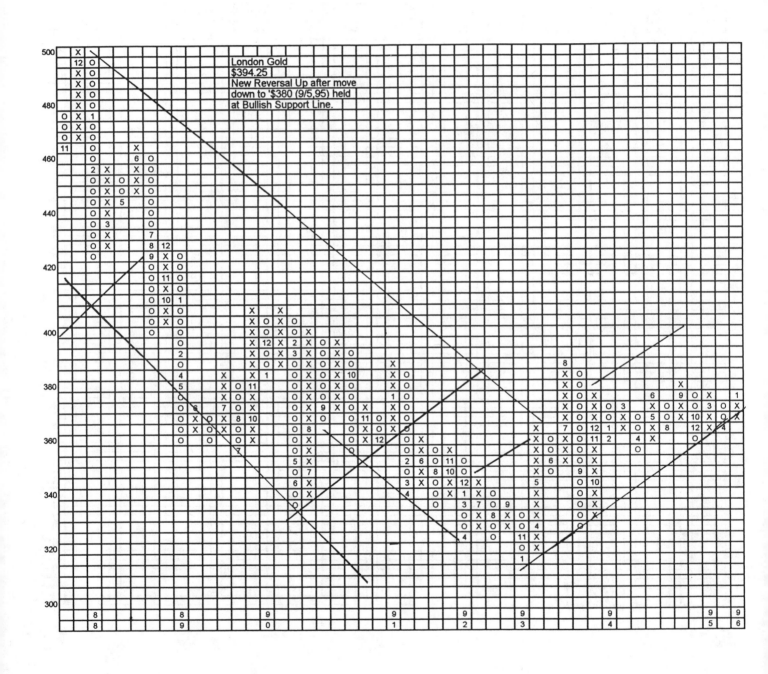

276

Figures 13-18 and 13-19 cover the NASDAQ Composite Index, the OTC bullish percentage, and the OTC daily high-low index, respectively. These indicators also require the same interpretative techniques used on similar indicators for the NYSE. However, OTC activity has replaced the ASE as the premiere measure of market speculation. Parameters and market classifications are the same as those employed by Chartcraft on other technical indicators seeking to identify investor extremes.

BONDS AND METALS

Figure 13-20 illustrates the Dow Jones 20 Bond Average, which helps investors gain some insight into bond prices and market yields. As bond prices rise, yields decline and vice-versa. This bond indicator serves an important function since stocks are interest-rate sensitive. As interest rates rise, money begins to flow away from the stock market toward more conservative, fixed-income investments. When rates decline, investors seek stocks as an alternative because fixed-income rates become unattractive. It should be noted that low-pole formations are particularly effective in detecting bottoms on the DJ 20 Bond Average.

Figure 13-21 contains the Handy and Harmon spot price for silver, while Figure 13-22 illustrates a chart on London gold prices. Precious metal prices should be scrutinized closely because these "hard assets" are perceived to be hedges against inflation. Further, during periods of economic turmoil or uncertainty, investors flock to gold and silver as a haven for safety. As individuals become more uncomfortable with the stock market, money flows from stocks into hard assets. Conversely, increasing confidence normally means investors gravitate toward the stock market and away from investment in metals. Gold and silver should be viewed as counter cyclical to the stock market

SUMMARY

Chapter 13 has focused on technical indicators that have proven effective in forecasting stock market junctures. Although many of these indicators are the exclusive property of Chartcraft and share the same interpretation methods, their track records are well documented. In fact, the consistency in interpretation is an asset in market analysis.

Many of the technical measures incorporated in this chapter center on identifying overbought-oversold levels in the market. Investor sentiment and behavior of different stock market segments constitute a key focus of our technical indicator selection. The inclusive coverage reaffirms that the stock market has two motivating factors -- greed and fear. As extreme feelings evolve in either direction, the market usually incurs an unexpected reversal. The stock market does not accommodate the majority of participants.

ENDNOTES

[1]Most of the indicators in this chapter are included with special permission from Chartcraft, Inc. of New Rochelle, NY. Chartcraft consistently ranks among the top investment advisory firms in the United States because of their pioneering and innovative approaches to stock market analysis. Special thanks are extended to the entire staff for bringing this coverage to fruition.

[2] Michael Burke was instrumental in supplying written and verbal contributions to this chapter. Mike also provided special assistance to the author with his editing of the manuscript.

[3]The author gratefully acknowledges both Michael Burke and John Gray of Chartcraft for their ideas, written portions of the text, charts, and total commitment to the publication of this book. For more treatment of many of these ideas, see Michael L. Burke and John E. Gray, eds. Chartcraft's Options Service (New Rochelle, NY: Chartcraft, Inc., select issues, 1989-1992).

[4]Ibid.

[5]Ibid

[6] For an extensive examination of investor sentiment using the percentage of stocks above their moving averages and investment advisor contributions, see Aby, Carroll D. Jr., J.W. Carland, J.A. Carland, and T.H. Willis, "The Theory of Contrary Opinion: A Tool For Investors." The study was published in its entirety in the Spring 1992 issue of **The Journal of Business & Economic Perspectives**.

CHAPTER 14

THE WRAP UP

There have been many techniques introduced throughout the text. Beginning with generally accepted chart patterns, we continued with traditional views regarding price objectives and trendlines. A second section exposed readers to more contemporary thoughts concerning P & F charts. Section three looks at evaluating industry groups and market conditions.

Total security analysis involves the analysis of individual stocks, industry groups, and the general market. Chapter 14 gives a step-by-step approach to evaluating the total investment decision. The chapter concludes with a revisit of certain key points critical to the decision process.

TOTAL SECURITY ANALYSIS

A beginning step in security analysis is stock selection. Investors need to be comfortable with the stock before looking at industry and market conditions. Figure 14-1 contains a P & F chart of J.P. Morgan, a large commercial bank in New York. One reason to select this stock was its leadership role in the banking group. Its relative strength turned bullish in December 1990 while many banking issues continued weak and unimpressive. An initial buy signal occurred at 36, with a second following at 40 when all tops in the near-term base were penetrated. An examination of the individual stock reveals a bullish chart supported by a positive relative strength pattern.

The Industry Group

Figure 14-2 illustrates a group price trend chart for money center banks. An industry group chart experienced a buy signal at 90 in November 1990. The bullish percentage for the banking group showed a bull alert market with a rally from the 10% level. Bull alert markets from such depressed levels encourage long positions. There is no need to wait for a bull confirmed market.

Figure 14-1

SELECTING THE STOCK

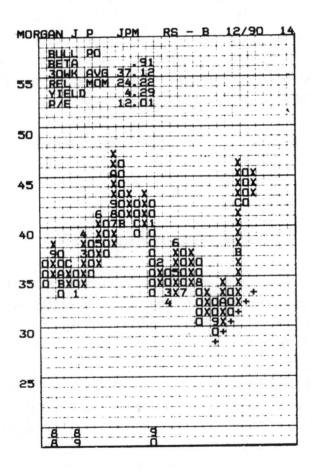

Figure 14-2

EVALUATING THE INDUSTRY GROUP

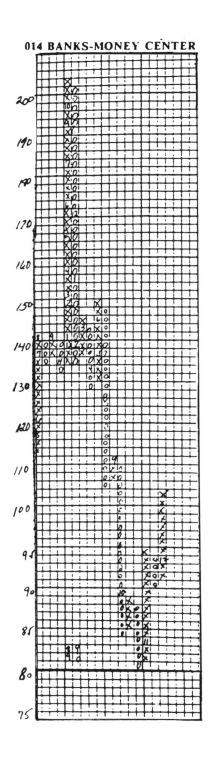

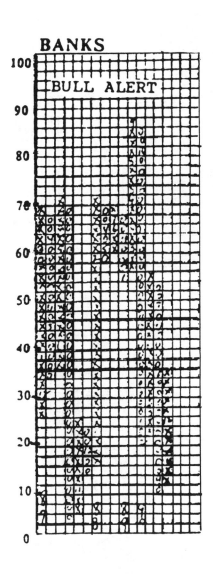

Figure 14-3

CHECKING GENERAL MARKET TRENDS

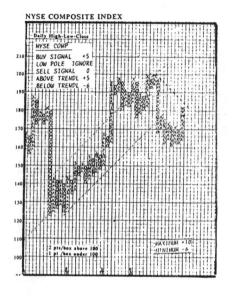

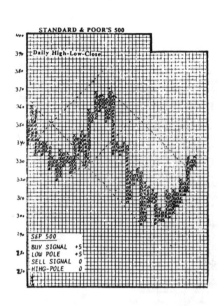

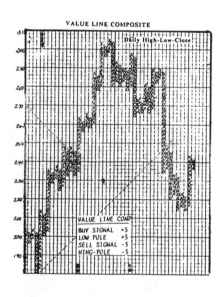

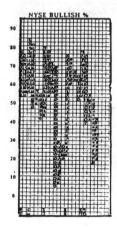

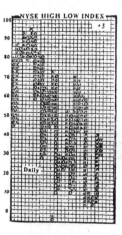

Each of the first two steps strongly supports the purchase of shares in J.P. Morgan. The stock has a bullish chart pattern, positive relative strength, and bullish P & F chart for the industry group. A group bullish % chart also advises the accumulation of bank stocks.

The Aggregate Stock Market

J.P Morgan trades on the NYSE and is perceived by analysts as a quality banking issue. Figure 14-3 illustrates three different market measures which reflect trends on the big board. The NYSE Composite Index seems to have concluded a downmove and resumed its uptrend. Although the NYSE Index is slightly below a bearish resistance line, the likelihood of penetration seems strong.

One reason the NYSE Composite will probably continue to advance can be traced to the S&P 500. This broad market measure has already broken a major downtrend line and reversed to the upside. Similarly, the Value Line Composite has bottomed and penetrated two previous tops. Three broad-based indexes are confirming that stocks are poised for a strong move to the upside.

To support the charting outlook for the market, the NYSE bullish percentage displays a bull alert market with a rally from 18%. In addition, the NYSE High-Low Index reveals a bull confirmed market which began from 4%. Every phase of the decision has bullish implications. Studying individual charts, industry groups, and the overall market constitutes complete security analysis. Chances for success are enhanced because this composite view reduces selection mistakes and eliminates judgmental errors.

SOME INTEGRATIVE EXAMPLES

Figure 14-4 reveals a long-term P&F chart of Merrill Lynch. A bullish support line can be established after buy signals surfaced in January and February of 1991. This long-term uptrend line remained intact until April 1992, when weakness in both Merrill Lynch and the investment group developed. The first bullish resistance line was broken, but a second contained the entire advance and helped identify potential points of resistance.

A trading count (TC) can be calculated across a wide base pattern that formed from 1989 to 1991. At the bottom of Figure 14-4, three potential price objectives have been projected from the "trading count" concept. The base is 22 squares wide with most price recordings appearing on the one-point scale above $20. Although counts should be used conservatively,

283

Figure 14-4

A REVIEW OF MERRILL LYNCH

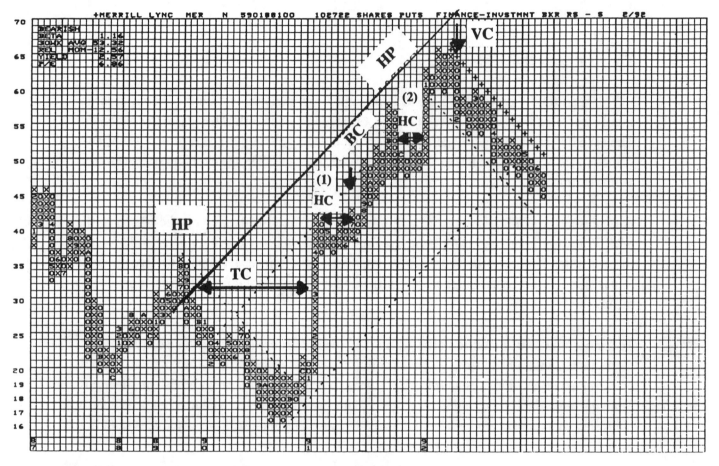

1st PO = 22 * 1 = 22 + 16 1/2 = 38 1/2 - 39
2nd PO = 22 * 2 = 44 + 16 1/2 = 58 1/2 - 59
3rd PO = 22 * 3 = 66 + 16 1/2 = 82 1/2 - 83

Horizontal Counts:

1st (HC 1) = 7 * 3 = 21 + 37 = 58 PO
2nd (HC 2) = 6 * 3 = 18 + 48 = 66 PO

Vertical Counts (VC):

1st PO = 9 * 2 = 18, 66 - 18 = 48
2nd PO = 9 * 3 = 27, 66 - 27 = 39

Merrill Lynch furnishes an example where most of the base formed on the three-point chart. A first price objective may be determined by multiplying 22 times one-third of the reversal rule ($\frac{1}{3}$ x 3 = 1) and adding the product to the lowest O in the base.

A first target counts to the $38\frac{1}{2}$ - 39 area. The firs price objective was satisfied in April 1991 when Merrill reached 42 and then consolidated. The trading count offers a second price estimate in the $58\frac{1}{2}$ - 59 area, which was reached in October 1991 when Merrill hit 58. A final, long-term forecast measured $82\frac{1}{2}$ to 83, but the stock began to decline from 66 in early 1992. Merrill Lynch exceeded the final target in 1993 on the strength of a strong aggregate market and underlying support from a positive group performance.

Two horizontal counts (HC) proved helpful during the advance. The first was calculated from a seven-square base that developed between April and July of 1991. A July breakout at 43 allowed a count to 58 and confirmed our second trading target reached in October. A second horizontal count yielded a target of 66, which marked the stock's top in January 1992. Forecasting techniques were accurate in projecting intermediate and long-term price moves. A vertical count multiplying by both 2 and 3 gave downside counts of 48 and 39, respectively. The longer-term target of 39 seems logical because of the large potential support in the upper 30's to low 40's.

Once the January 1992 sell signal occurs at 59, a bearish resistance line can be drawn at a 45 degree angle. By moving to a wall of X's to the left of the top area of distribution, we establish a bearish support line. This minor channel line encompasses the entire downtrend to date.

Figure 14-5 reveals a long-term P & F chart of NationsBank. A December 1989 sell signal establishes the bearish resistance line which holds until 1991. A first bearish support line embraces much of the decline until the climatic selling in late 1990. A second bearish support line is included primarily for illustration purposes and continues undaunted. The full vertical count suggests a downside move to 19. NationsBank reached 17 in October 1991.

A buy signal ensues at 23 in November 1990 and allows the establishment of the bullish support line. The first vertical count indicates a long-term price objective of 45 which was reached in late 1991. Chartists also had the option of buying the first sell signal in the uptrend in January 1991. This first sell signal permits a second vertical count to 55, which coincides with a prior resistance level from the major top in 1989 at 55.

During the bull market, a large base formed between April and December of 1991. Since charts are to be used conservatively, a trading count is appropriate. When stocks undergo a large price move, the danger exists that chartists will use price forecasts too liberally. We employ a $\frac{1}{3}$ reversal rule for our first target at 44. Once the first objective was achieved in

Figure 14-5

A LONG-TERM LOOK AT NATIONS BANK

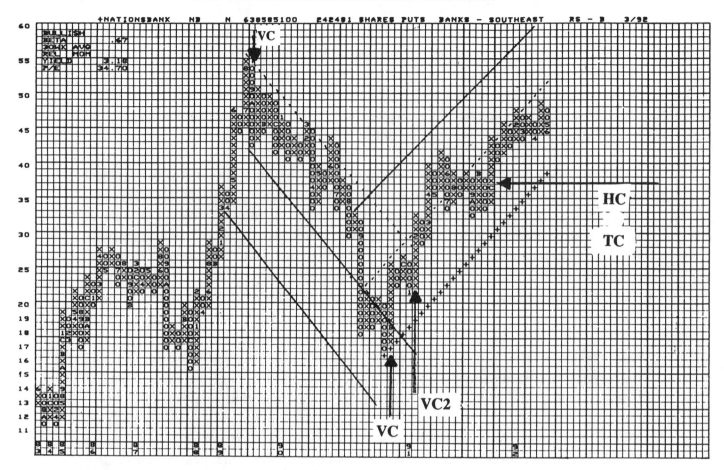

Downside Vertical Count:

PO = 12 * 3 = 36, 55 - 36 = 19

Upside Vertical Counts:

VC 1 = (5 * 1 1/2) + (7 * 3) = 28 1/2 + 17 = 45
VC 2 = 11 * 3 = 33 + 22 = 55

Trading Counts

1st PO = 11 * 1 = 11 + 33 = 44
2nd PO = 11 * 2 = 22 + 33 = 55
3rd PO = 11 * 3 = 33 + 33 = 66 (Note: This is also the full
                                         horizontal count.)

December 1991, we use a $\frac{2}{3}$ reversal rule to calculate a second price forecast at 55. The second estimate confirms our second vertical count to 55. If the uptrend continues, a third price objective from the trading count equals a full horizontal count of 66.

Bullish resistance lines are drawn from a wall of O's to the left of the bottoming process. Once the first line is broken, we draw a second which has remained intact throughout the upmove. To date, the major uptrend line continues unblemished and delineates potential areas of support.

ABSOLUTE TRENDLINES

This book includes detailed coverage concerning trendlines, their interpretation, and construction. Emphasis is also placed on valid trendline breaks which lead to price reversals. However, one additional consideration is necessary to confirm whether the penetration of a downtrend line is actually valid. Michael Burke[1] developed the concept of absolute trendlines. Burke's idea applies to downmoves from above $20 to below $20, or from 3-point to $1\frac{1}{2}$ point charts. Such price recordings involve different scales.

To illustrate, let's refer to Figure 14-6 and the P & F chart of Wallace Computer Service. A February 1991 buy signal at 21 appears to send the chart into a bullish trend. However, a high pole formation develops at the trendline and the stock sells off sharply. Chartists who prematurely acknowledged this buy signal were victimized by their failure to understand the concept of absolute trendlines. Incidentally, another glaring weakness in the Wallace chart was the negative relative strength that has continued since May of 1990.

The top of Figure 14-6 shows the Wallace Computer chart reconstructed with all recordings placed on a 3-point chart with each square worth one dollar. The new 1-point scale displays fewer recordings because three points are still needed for a reversal move to a new column. With all recordings placed on the same scale (3-point chart), the rally in Wallace encountered difficulty at the bearish resistance line. The stock failed to penetrate and resumed its downtrend. By understanding absolute trendlines when charts change scales on the downside, chartists can avoid premature entry into technically weak stocks.

Figure 14-6

BURKE'S ABSOLUTE TRENDLINE

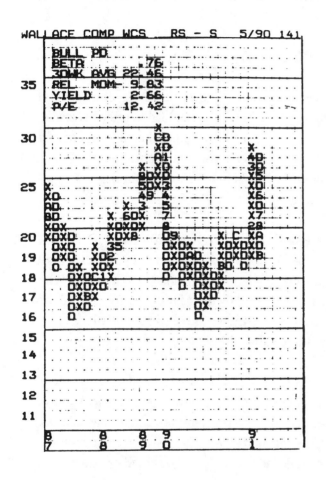

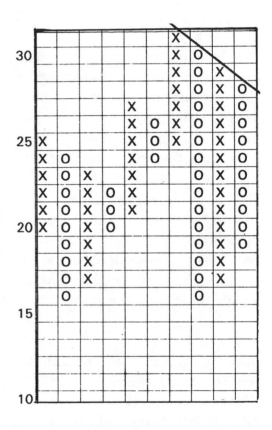

SUMMARY

Chapter 14 attempts to synthesize major ideas on P & F charts. This book does not have to be read sequentially. However, such a reading approach helps place proper emphasis on total security analysis. A complete evaluation consists of studying individual chart patterns, industry groups, and the aggregate market. Trendlines and price objectives represent an integral part of chart analysis. Finally, valid reversals assume a new dimension with the introduction of the absolute trendline concept.

ENDNOTES

[1] Michael L. Burke, <u>The All New Guide to the Three-Point Reversal Method of Point and Figure Construction and Formations</u> (New Rochelle, NY: Chartcraft, Inc.,1990), 64 - 65.

TRADERS PRESS, INC.®

INCORPORATED

P.O. BOX 6206
GREENVILLE, S.C. 29606

Books and Gifts
for Investors and Traders

Publishers of:

Commodity Spreads: A Historical Chart Perspective (Dobson)
The Trading Rule That Can Make You Rich* (Dobson)
Viewpoints of a Commodity Trader (Longstreet)
Commodities: A Chart Anthology (Dobson)
Profitable Grain Trading (Ainsworth)
A Complete Guide to Trading Profits (Paris)
Traders Guide to Technical Analysis (Hardy)
The Professional Commodity Trader (Kroll)
Jesse Livermore: Speculator-King (Sarnoff)
Understanding Fibonacci Numbers (Dobson)
Wall Street Ventures & Adventures through Forty Years (Wyckoff)
Winning Market Systems (Appel)
How to Trade in Stocks (Livermore)
Stock Market Trading Systems (Appel & Hitschler)
Study Helps in Point and Figure Technique (Wheelan)
Commodity Spreads: Analysis, Selection and Trading Techniques (Smith)
Comparison of Twelve Technical Trading Systems (Lukac, Brorsen, & Irwin)
Day Trading with Short Term Price Patterns and Opening Range Breakout (Crabel)
Understanding Bollinger Bands (Dobson)
Chart Reading for Professional Traders (Jenkins)
Geometry of Stock Market Profits (Jenkins)

Please write or call for our current catalog describing these and many other books and gifts of interest to investors and traders.

1-800-927-8222   FAX 864-298-0221
Tradersprs@aol.com

MARKET ART!

The painting pictured on the back cover of this book,
as well as other market-related art, is available through
TRADERS PRESS.

If interested in full details, please contact:

TRADERS PRESS, INC.®
INCORPORATED
P.O. BOX 6206
GREENVILLE, S.C. 29606

Books and Gifts
for Investors and Traders

1-800-927-8222   FAX 864-298-0221
Tradersprs@aol.com

• TECHNICAL ANALYSIS • OPTIONS • TRADING PSYCHOLOGY & DISCIPLINE • SPREAD TRADING • ELLIOTT WAVE • W.D. GANN • INTRADAY TRADING • TRADING STRATEGIES

FREE TRADERS CATALOG

• FIBONACCI • FLOOR TRADING • 31 FREE BOOKS (WITH ADDITIONAL PURCHASE) • MONEY MANAGEMENT • MUTUAL FUNDS • SHORT SELLING / BEAR MARKETS • STOCK INDEX TRADING • SYSTEMS AND METHODS • MANY OTHER TOPICS •

TRADERS PRESS, INC. publishes a 72-page catalog which lists and describes hundreds of books, tapes, courses and gifts of interest to stock, options, and futures traders.
(Regular price $5)

Get your FREE copy by writing, calling or faxing
TRADERS PRESS, INC.

Edward D. Dobson
TRADERS PRESS, INC.®
P.O. BOX 6206
GREENVILLE, SC 29606

Serving traders since 1975

800-927-8222
864-298-0222
FAX: 864-298-0221
Tradersprs@aol.com